❈ ❈ ❈

A Rough Ride
to Albany

Teddy Runs for Governor

❈ ❈ ❈

A Rough

Teddy

New York

Ride
To Albany

Runs For Governor

John A. Corry

Published in 2000 by
John A. Corry
450 Lexington Avenue,
New York, NY 10017

THE TEXT OF THIS EDITION
WAS SET IN MONOTYPE SPECTRUM
PRINTED ON MUNKEN
CREAMY OFFSET PAPER
AND BOUND IN ASAHI CLOTH
BY BY C&C OFFSET PRINTING, INC,
HONG KONG

Distributed to the trade by
Fordham University Press
2546 Belmont Avenue
Bronx, NY 10458

Library of Congress Control Number
00-132969
ISBN: 0-9661570-1-X

Endpapers
Courtesy of the New York Public Library

Design and Production by
Charles Davey *design* LLC
945 West End Avenue Suit 1C
New York, NY 10025

*To the memory
of my father,
from whom I aquired
my interest in history
and politics*

Contents

Illustrations

Prologue

November 7, 1898 – The "Hurricane Windup of a Canvass"

ON JULY 1, 1898, WHICH HE ALWAYS THEREAFTER REFERRED TO AS THE "great day of my life," Colonel Theodore Roosevelt had led his Rough Riders through a rain of artillery shells and bullets to capture the San Juan Heights that commanded the Spanish position at Santiago, Cuba. Now, on this early November day four months later, he was completing an equally challenging campaign: to pull victory from the jaws of defeat and win election as New York State's 36th Governor.

If he had bothered to keep count, Roosevelt might have been impressed by the fact that within a period of 13 days he had already spoken 127 times from the rear of his private railroad car, as well as on numerous other occasions from platforms in cities and towns throughout the state. More likely than not, however, his attention was focused on the arduous schedule of more than fifteen stops that his managers had put together to enable him on this last campaign day to talk to voters in the small towns and villages of the western end of what was known as the Southern Tier. For the most part, this rolling country was solidly Republican, and although its number of registered voters was not large, it was important to convince as many of them as possible to vote and offset the large majority that Tammany Hall and other New York City Democratic organizations were expected to provide his opponent. For, despite official Republican predictions of a Roosevelt landslide and the candidate's strenuous efforts, the most recent betting odds were either even money or only narrowly in his favor. [1]

Nevertheless, throughout the Roosevelt party there was a growing belief that, after coming from behind, they were on the road to victory. Although he had had no contact with New York State politics for 14 years, as the GOP candidate Roosevelt now had to distance himself from scandals relating to the Erie Canal that had tainted the administration of incumbent Governor Frank Black. Moreover, because boss Thomas Collier Platt had supported Roosevelt instead of Black for the Republican nomination, many voters were questioning the candidate's expressions of independence from the unpopular state GOP organization. Although the former Rough Rider drew large crowds wherever he went, this did not necessarily translate into votes, for the New York electorate was more interested in state issues than in Roosevelt's advocacy of an expansionist American foreign policy. Thus, it had been only his exploitation of a miscue by Tammany boss Richard Croker that had enabled him to pull up to and perhaps move ahead of Democratic nominee Judge Augustus Van Wyck.

If Roosevelt needed any evidence to support his growing optimism, it was provided by his reception as his special train crawled westward across the Southern Tier. November 7 dawned bitterly cold, with snow on the ground, but the frigid weather did nothing to limit the size and enthusiasm of the large crowds that greeted him at every station. At one stop, factory whistles blew, and at two others the candidate was serenaded by brass bands. The gathering that greeted him at the village of Little Valley included about 50 mounted Rough Riders.

To these admiring throngs, notwithstanding his thick eyeglasses, Roosevelt was "a splendid specimen of manhood." Only recently turned forty, he was, according to one observer,

"A man of medium height, muscular and erect. He has a muscular lower jaw decorated with a set of shining teeth that have been a boon to every cartoonist in the land . . . He has a trick of jerking down his lower lip which makes the display of ivory complete. He has a good clear complexion which still shows a slight trace of the sunburn placed upon it by the climate of the tropics. His hair is cropped close military fashion and is tossed carelessly away from his forehead. His brown mustache shades a mouth that has firmness and force marked in every line."

At his first stop, Roosevelt introduced the themes he was to stress throughout the day: "civic honesty and national honor." The real issue, he told a crowd of a thousand at the farm trading center of Salamanca, was not the Democratic candidate but whether the state was to be turned over to Croker, "that he might corrupt it, as he had New York City." A local newspaper reporter described his method of delivering these speeches as

"not copied from any method, but . . . distantly his own. He jerks his sentences out in a short snappy way that never fails to impress his hearers with the innate earnestness of the man; he says just what he means . . . in the simplest and shortest manner possible. He shoots his sentences at the people, caring nothing for cheers and applause but only anxious to force his arguments into the brains of his hearers and to show that his premises are perfect and conclusions are logical." [2]

The day's longest stop was in Jamestown, a furniture manufacturing center at the foot of Lake Chautauqua, in the extreme southwestern part of the state. Roosevelt first spoke in a public square to a cheering crowd of 5000 and then to 2000 more enthusiastic supporters in a public meeting hall. His procession through city streets filled with thousands more city residents and farmers was a continuous ovation. Cheering men were joined by a large number of handkerchief-waving

women, whose inability to vote in this pre-Nineteenth Amendment
era did not dim their enthusiasm. When he learned that Jamestown
resident Sergeant E.W. Bucklin was unable to attend either meeting because of wounds suffered in Cuba, Roosevelt immediately ordered his
line of march diverted so that it would pass the former Rough Rider's
house, where it halted while he entered to spend 15 minutes talking
with the veteran. [3]

Between stops, Roosevelt, always a voracious reader, reportedly
rested his voice by dipping into a German translation of the Roman
historian Polybius. However, by 7:30 p.m., when his entourage reached
its final stop at the Lake Erie city of Dunkirk, he had abandoned Polybius, for, according to his close friend, author and municipal reformer
Jacob Riis,

"...this hurricane windup of a canvass . . .[and] the victory in
the air . . . had turned us all, young and old, into so many romping boys. . . . I can still see the venerable ex-Governor and Minister
to Spain Stewart L. Woodford, myself and a third scapegrace,
whose name I have forgotten, going through the streets of
Dunkirk, arm in arm, breasting the crowds and yelling, "Yi! Yi!"
like a bunch of college boys in a lark, again and again falling into
the line that passed Mr. Roosevelt in the hotel lobby to shake
hands, until he peered into our averted faces and drove us out
with laughter. And I can see him holding his sides, while the audience at the Opera House yelled its approval of Sherman Bell's
offer to Dick Croker, who had called Roosevelt a 'wild man':
'Who is this Dick Croker? I don't know him. He don't come from
my state. Let him take thirty of his best men, I don't care how
well they're heeled, and I will take my gang and we'll see who's
boss. I'll shoot him so full of holes he won't know himself from a
honeycomb." [4]

At last, at 10.30, the last meeting ended, the shouting stopped, and Roosevelt's car was attached to a fast mail train that was due to arrive at New York City's Grand Central Station twelve hours later. Over a late supper he and his friends speculated as to the size of what, by now, to them seemed to be a sure victory. In response to their question, Roosevelt was less confident, predicting his election by only a 15,000 to 20,000 vote margin. Above all, he was philosophical:

"I have contributed of my very best. If I am elected, I shall do the best I can to conserve the interests of all our people; if defeated, I shall retire to my home, thankful indeed to those who have supported me, but without any feeling either of antagonism or regret to those who have waged so strong a fight against me."

The next morning his train pulled into Albany, in full view of the Capitol, topped by flags flying. In these first moments of quiet he had enjoyed in some time, one wonders whether Roosevelt's thoughts may have briefly skipped backwards to recall the highlights of the last 18 years that had brought him to the verge of becoming the most important man in the State of New York. For, contrary to the myth that would grow during the next hundred years, his dramatic charge up a Cuban hill was but the most recent part of that history, much of which had been of his own making. [5]

1

"I Rose Like A Rocket"

HIS LIFE IN POLITICS HAD BEGUN INAUSPICIOUSLY ALMOST EIGHTEEN years earlier in a large room over a store on the south side of 59th Street between Fifth and Madison Avenues.* Named Morton Hall after Congressman Levi P. Morton, it was the headquarters of the Republican Association for the 21st Assembly District, which covered the area between Seventh and Lexington Avenues and 40th to 86th Streets. Because this part of Manhattan was the home of the many affluent voters who were moving north from the area to its immediate south and who were reputed to dine nightly on diamond-back terrapin, the district was popularly known as the "Diamond Back" district.

Why did the 22-year-old Theodore Roosevelt begin to visit Morton Hall that autumn of 1880? Only recently graduated from Harvard, he was married to a wife whom he adored, and the socially prominent couple were busy at dinners and soirees with the cream of New York's patrician society. During the day, Roosevelt had begun to attend classes at Columbia Law School, and spent most of his remaining hours busily working on his book *The Naval War of 1812*. Yet, often dressed in evening clothes for the evening's festivities, he was able to find the time to walk the short distance to Morton Hall from the Roosevelt family home at 6 West 57th Street and, in a low-ceilinged chamber redolent with the smell of tobacco, mix with the crowd of mostly Irish ward heelers and saloon keepers who were the district's political operatives. [1]

For a young man of his family background, this participation in

---

* The present site of the General Motors Building.

ward politics was, to put it mildly, unorthodox. To many of his family, it was shocking. Emlen Roosevelt, a cousin, later recalled that they thought that the young man's political activity

"... was, to put it frankly, pretty fresh. We felt that his own father would not have liked it, and would have been fearful of the outcome."

None of this would deter him. Thirty-three years later, he described his reaction to their concern that he might dirty himself by mingling with these low level politicians:

"I answered that if this were so it merely meant that the people I knew did not belong to the governing class, and that the other people did — and that I intended to be one of the governing class, and that if they proved too hard-bit for me I supposed I would have to quit, but that I certainly would not quit until I had made the effort and found out whether I really was too weak to hold my own in the rough and tumble." [2]

There is no reason, however, to believe that in 1880 Roosevelt was doing any more than exposing himself to activities that were conveniently taking place only a couple of blocks from his home. Yet his interest was far from superficial. By now, he must have realized that by nature he was an active participant and not an onlooker, and that although the work on his 1812 book was absorbing, a full-time literary career probably was not for him. The law was the prescribed alternative, but the bewildering complexities of legal pleading and property rights that he was studying at Columbia held little allure. Indeed, as Roosevelt later wrote, "some of the teaching of the law books and of the classroom seemed to me to be against justice." He was also fortunate that he "had been left enough money by my father not to make it necessary for me to think solely of earning bread for myself and my family."

One other personal factor must have motivated his visits to Morton

Hall. Less than three years earlier, while a Harvard sophomore, he had been shattered by the death of his father, Theodore Roosevelt, Senior, at the relatively young age of 46 years. The cause of death was an intestinal obstruction, but the Roosevelts believed that a contributing factor was the Senate's rejection less than two months earlier of his appointment by the reform-minded President Rutherford B. Hayes to the politically important post of Collector of Customs of the Port of New York. Although Theodore Senior was a distinguished New Yorker who had never been involved in politics, the appointment offended Senator Roscoe Conkling, the powerful head of the New York Republican machine, who after weeks of controversy was able to obtain the reappointment of his political lieutenant Chester A. Arthur. It is likely that the young Roosevelt, who idolized his father, believed that by participating in politics he could weaken the influence of the corrupt machines of both parties and thus vindicate him and avenge his defeat.[3]

As the weeks passed, and fall turned into winter and winter into spring, Roosevelt's visits to Morton Hall grew more frequent. As he later put it,

> "I went around often enough to have the men get more accustomed to me and to have me get accustomed to them, so that we began to speak the same language, and so that each could begin to live down what Bret Harte had called 'the defective moral quality of being a stranger.'"

But this young man in evening clothes had not won over "Jake" Hess, the heavy-set professional politician of German extraction who ran the organization with an iron hand. Thus, in April and early May, when Roosevelt moved to have the 21st District Republicans support a Street Cleaning Bill that had been introduced in the legislature by "good government" advocates, he was soundly defeated by a vote of 100 to 3.[4]

From then until October, Roosevelt's mind was largely on other matters, as he and his wife Alice sailed to Europe for a long post-wedding trip which had been deferred so that Theodore could enter law school the previous fall. By the time they returned on October 2, 1881, the American political climate had at least temporarily changed. On July 2, newly elected Republican President James A. Garfield had been shot, and after a long fight for life died on September 19. The assassin was a crazed disappointed office seeker who, referring to Conkling's wing of the GOP, had yelled following his shooting, "I am a Stalwart. Arthur is now President." Since Conkling had just resigned his Senate post following a bitter losing patronage battle with Garfield, there was an immediate public hue and cry against his New York organization.[5]

The next month, the 21st District's Republican incumbent was up for reelection. Although as Hess's hand-picked candidate he seemed sure of renomination, Roosevelt on his return from Europe plunged into an effort to replace him, or, as he colorfully put it, "kill our last year's legislator."

He got into much more than he could have anticipated. One of Hess's chief lieutenants was a burly, red-faced Irishman named Joe Murray. He had worked his way up in the organization by doing his chief's bidding, but was looking for an opening to "make a drive" at him. That autumn of 1881, Murray's political soundings led him to conclude that there was a major risk that the anti-machine tide which had resulted from Garfield's assassination would lead to a Democratic victory in the 21st District if the incumbent was the Republican candidate. But, when he voiced his concern to Hess, the leader brushed him aside, adding, "You don't amount to anything." That did it as far as Murray was concerned. He knew that a number of other organization underlings shared his worries over the November election. All they needed was a viable candidate.[6]

Ever since Roosevelt had made his first appearance at Morton Hall, Murray had been intrigued with the young man's potential as a political "comer." He had been especially impressed by Roosevelt's drive and speaking ability in his unsuccessful effort, which Murray had opposed, on behalf of the Street Cleaning Bill. Roosevelt initially declined when Murray suggested that he seek the seat, but the next evening agreed, and on October 28, much to Hess's surprise, was nominated by a vote of 16 to 9. The candidate had turned 23 only the day before.[7]

On Election Day, Roosevelt's victory margin was nearly double the usual edge in this normally Republican district. His emphasis on good government and the voters' memories of his father as a public-spirited citizen combined to elicit endorsements from prominent citizens who ordinarily would not have lent their names to support a political candidate. He enjoyed the campaigning, but, on a vote-getting stop at a Sixth Avenue saloon, learned that, at least in politics, forthright honesty is not always the best policy:

"I was introduced with proper solemnity to the saloon-keeper – a very important personage, for this was before the days when saloon-keepers became merely the mortgaged chattels of the brewers – and he began to cross-examine me, a little too much in the tone of one who was dealing with a suppliant for his favor. He said that he expected that I would of course treat the liquor business fairly, to which I answered, none too cordially, that I should treat all interests fairly. He then said that he regarded the licenses as too high to which I responded that I believed that they were really not high enough, and that I should try to have them made higher. The conversation threatened to become stormy. Messrs. Murray and Hess, on some hastily improvised plan, took me into the street, and then Joe explained to me that it was not worth my while staying on Sixth Avenue any longer, that I had better go right back to Fifth Avenue and attend to my friends there, and that he would look after my interests on Sixth Avenue.[8]

❀ ❀ ❀

Despite his impressive victory, Roosevelt at least outwardly treated his venture into politics as a temporary fling. Shortly after his election, after describing himself to a college classmate as a "political hack," he cautioned "don't think I am going into politics after this year, for I am not." Thus, although Roosevelt would take his Sixth Avenue experience to heart, his initial appearance in Albany at a Republican caucus on January 2, 1882, confirmed the impression that his future political career was likely to be confined to his "silk stocking" constituency. With his eyeglass at the end of a black silk chain, tight fitting trousers that were bell-bottomed to cover his shoes, and a gold headed cane, he was immediately dubbed "Oscar Wilde" because of his supposed resemblance to the British effete who had just commenced an American lecture tour. Isaac Hunt, a delegate from upstate Jefferson County who later became a political ally, remembered him as "a joke . . . a dude [in] the way he combed his hair [parted in the center], the way he talked – the whole thing." Roosevelt's initial opinion of his fellow legislators was equally negative – "a stupid, sodden, vicious lot, most of them being equally deficient in brains and virtue."

As the weeks passed, however, Roosevelt became known for more than his appearance. In his support of various pieces of reform legislation and with his high-pitched falsetto voice yelling "Mister Spee-kar! Mister Spee-kar!" until he was recognized, he was developing the reputation of a troublesome gadfly to leadership of both parties. But he also quickly became the leader of a few other reform-minded Republicans, and caught the eye of the *New York Times* legislative correspondent, who provided the young assemblyman with extensive and generally favorable coverage. [9]

In late March, Roosevelt's efforts struck paydirt. Hunt, now an admiring friend, had been looking into a surprisingly large number of insurance company insolvencies. He discovered that their receivers had pocketed large sums of money for alleged fees and expenses, and that the payments had been approved by State Supreme Court Justice T.R. Westbrook, whose son and cousin were employed by one of these companies.*

When Hunt described the situation to Roosevelt, the young assemblyman recollected that the same judge had presided the prior fall over matters relating to financier Jay Gould's acquisition of the Manhattan Elevated Railway, and that an article in *The New York Times* had suggested that Gould had taken steps to reduce the price of the company's stock by as much as 95 percent to enable him to acquire it more cheaply. The documents that the *Times* had assembled to support its case against Westbrook included a letter from the judge to Gould stating, "I am willing to go to the very verge of political discretion to protect your vast interests." By the time he had concluded his investigation, Roosevelt had concluded that not only Westbrook, but also the Attorney General, who had also been involved in the matter, should be investigated by the legislature for aiding Gould in acquiring the railway company. On March 29, he rose in the Assembly and offered a resolution that its Judiciary Committee should commence an inquiry.

His action created an uproar. Jay Gould was one of the most powerful financiers of his day, with connections to many leading politicians of both parties. Efforts were made to persuade Roosevelt to back off. His uncle, James Roosevelt, suggested that it was time for him "to leave politics and identify . . . with the right kind of people." Roosevelt later wrote that these pressures were "the first glimpse I had of that combination between business and politics which I was in years after so often to oppose." [10]

Anyone who really knew the idealistic young Roosevelt would have realized that these efforts to dissuade him would be counterproductive.

---

* In the 1880's as well as today, despite its name the Supreme Court was New York's primary trial court.

Late in the afternoon of April 5, 1882, when many of the leading machine politicians had left for nearby watering spots, he seized the floor
to speak in support of his resolution and ask for an immediate vote. In
his speech, which was printed in full in the *Times*, he pointed out that
one of the judicial hearings in the railway company case had taken
place in a "private bedroom" in Gould's office, and that four days after
Judge Westbrook had publicly declared "that the corporation was a
swindle," he "emphatically without any reserve . . . does not write but
telegraphs down an order allowing the road to go . . . back into the
hands of the Manhattan Company, which by that time has become
synonymous with getting into the hands of Jay Gould, Cyrus W. Field
and Russell Sage." * When Roosevelt had concluded his remarks, old
Tom Alvord, the Republican Assembly leader, quickly grabbed the
floor and held it long enough to prevent a vote, which under the circumstances might have supported the motion. In the succeeding days,
with the machines of both parties in control, Roosevelt twice failed to
garner the two-thirds majority required to refer the matter to the Judiciary Committee. During the Easter recess, however, the legislators
heard from their constituents, who had become aroused by the ensuing state-wide press coverage. On April 12, Roosevelt's motion passed
by a lopsided vote of 104 to 6. [11]

After seven weeks of hearings, study and deliberations, the Judiciary
Committee voted 8 to 3 not to recommend impeachment. There were
apparently well-founded rumors that, until the last minute, a majority
was prepared to vote to remove the judge. Hunt later contended that
several members received $2500 to change their position. Although the
New York press, except for the Gould-controlled *World*, urged the Assembly to reject the committee's conclusions, political orthodoxy prevailed, and on May 31 the Assembly supported the committee by a 77

---

* The three men effectively controlled New York City's elevated railroad system.

to 35 vote. Two days later, what the *Times* referred to as "the most corrupt Assembly since the days of Boss Tweed" adjourned for the last time. [12]

Although Roosevelt had not prevailed on the impeachment issue, the publicity he had obtained was remarkable for a freshman legislator. His actions in seeking to expose and punish corrupt behavior won praise from newspapers throughout the State. Cornell University President Andrew D. White and others spoke of him as Presidential timber. Through diligent study and the rough and tumble of legislative combat he had acquired an invaluable knowledge of how the state government operated. His development was extraordinary. As Isaac Hunt recollected:

> "He would leave Albany Friday afternoon and he would come back Monday night and you could see changes that had taken place in him. New ideas had taken possession of him. He would run up against somebody and he got a new perspective in regard to matters. . . . He took on strength just like that."

As his influence grew both in Albany and elsewhere, so also did his zest for politics and his belief that this was an area in which he could make a difference. [13]

❋ ❋ ❋

That November, Roosevelt was reelected by a stunning two-to-one majority. His margin was especially significant in view of a Democratic statewide sweep, with the 300-pound reform-minded Buffalo Mayor Grover Cleveland taking the governorship and his party winning the Senate as well as sharply increasing its Assembly majority.

On January 1, 1883, at the initial Republican caucus of the new legislative session, Hunt took the floor to propose Roosevelt as the party nominee for Speaker. He was nominated by a two-to-one vote, an incredible achievement for a second term 24-year-old who in his first session had been conspicuously at odds with the party leadership.

Although the minority Republicans had no chance to elect their candidate, this did not detract from the fact, that following Roosevelt's defeat for the Speakership, he would be the Minority Leader. [14] In the early weeks of the legislative session, however, there was a growing feeling in Albany that he was acting too big for his breeches, and that he was using his position to secure favorable personal publicity at the expense of the interest of the party. Cleveland, who shared much of Roosevelt's interest in reform, privately echoed these concerns: "There is a great sense in a lot that he says, but there is such a cocksureness about him that he stirs up doubt in me all the time." [15]

By early March, Roosevelt's meteoric rise had apparently been checked by his position on a bill aimed at the unpopular Jay Gould. It would have reduced the fare on an elevated Manhattan railroad owned by Gould from ten cents to five. The proposal was politically irresistible, and Roosevelt enthusiastically joined the strong Assembly majority which passed it. Cleveland, however, took a different position. When the bill had been approved by the Senate and arrived on his desk, he concluded that the legislation breached a contract that the State had made with Gould and was clearly unconstitutional. Although he told an aide that by doing so he would be "the most unpopular man in the State of New York," he sent the Assembly a strong veto message that concluded by stressing that government "should not only be strictly just but scrupulously fair" and that this "can only be done by legislating without vindictiveness." The Governor was surprised to find that the ethical tone of his message struck a responsive chord with the press and much of the public, with the result that the bill's supporters did not have the votes to override his veto. [16]

To an older and more seasoned minority leader, this would have been the end of the matter. After studying Cleveland's message, however, Roosevelt not only concluded that he should not have supported the legislation when it was first before the Assembly but that he should publicly concede his mistake. Against the advice of his closest associates, who argued that Cleveland's veto was sure to be sustained without any help from Roosevelt, he took the floor to confess to his astounded colleagues that in initially supporting the bill he had "weakly yielded partly to a vindictive spirit toward the infernal thieves who have the Elevated Railroad in charge, and partly in answer to the popular voice of New York." Although he "would willingly pass a bill of attainder on Jay Gould and all of his associates, if it were possible . . . I would rather go out of politics having the feeling that I had done what was right than stay in with the approval of all men, knowing in my heart that I have acted as I ought not to."

To newspaper writers and politicians who had been offended by Roosevelt's often blatant self-righteousness, his turnabout was a rare opportunity to attack him as a "weakling" and a "bogus reformer." Most of their scorn could be viewed, at least in retrospect, as fair political comment, some of which was probably deserved. Not so, however, the low blow struck by Jay Gould's World: "The friends who have so long deplored the untimely death of Theodore Roosevelt (Senior) cannot but be thankful that he has been spared the pain of a spectacle which would have wounded to the quick his gracious and honorable nature." [17]

One politician who undoubtedly understood and probably sympathized with Roosevelt's position was Grover Cleveland. Garfield's assassination was widely attributed to the spoils system, and civil service reform headed the action list of most good government advocates. On January 16, 1883, the first Congressional legislation on the subject had become law, requiring at least ten percent of all Federal jobs to be awarded only on the basis of written examination. Only two-and-a-half weeks earlier, Roosevelt had accepted the vice presidency of the New York Civil Service Reform Organization. Cleveland saw in him a necessary ally in pushing through civil service requirements for New York

State. Roosevelt had already introduced such legislation and managed to get it to the floor at a time when the Judiciary Committee chairman and a number of his cohorts were absent. At this point Cleveland risked a break with Tammany Hall's Democratic regulars and summoned Roosevelt and four of his associates to his office to tell them that if they would push for the bill's enactment he would provide enough Democratic votes to ensure its passage. Although several weeks elapsed before he could fully make good on his pledge, the bill passed both the Assembly and the Senate during the session's closing days. [18]

That victory and his position on other issues largely obliterated the memories of Roosevelt's supposed miscue on the five-cent fare legislation. Even before the Civil Service Bill's passage, the *Times* was praising his "rugged independence" and called him a "controlling force on the floor superior to that of any member of his party." His national reputation was spreading as well, with *Harper's Weekly* writing of his "direct plain speech, honesty, wisdom and progressivism." In November, a widening split between Cleveland and Tammany Hall over such issues as civil service as well as the New York Republican organization's newly avowed support for reform on other issues led to GOP victories that gave it control of both houses of the legislature. As the former Minority Leader, Roosevelt seemed to be the logical choice for Speaker when the Assembly convened in January. Thus, years later, he was able to write to his son Ted the following description of his first two years in Albany:

"Immediately after leaving college, I went to the legislature. I was the youngest man there, and I rose like a rocket. I was re-elected next year by an enormous majority at a time when the republican party as a whole met with great disaster, and the republican minority in the house, although I was the youngest member, nominated me for speaker, that is, made me the leader of the minority. I immediately proceeded to lose my perspective.

Unfortunately, I did not recover it as early as you have done in this case, and the result was that I came an awful cropper and had to pick myself up after learning by bitter experience that I was not all important and that I had to take account of many different elements in life."[19]

2

"I Have Been Called A Reformer But I Am A Republican"

As 1884 approached, Roosevelt looked forward to the new year with avid anticipation. Not only was he relishing his impending Speakership, but he and Alice were expecting their first child, due in the February.

1884 instead became the worst year of his life. The first blow came on New Year's Eve. Although he was the obvious candidate for Speaker, he had left nothing to chance. During November and December, he made a number of forays throughout the state to secure commitments, particularly from new Assemblymen who did not know him. Thus, in late November, newly elected Assemblyman Philip Garbutt, a farmer who lived 15 miles from Rochester, was surprised to find Roosevelt looking for him on a country road, peering through his thick spectacles as he asked each passer-by, "Is this Mr. Garbutt." [1]

Sadly, his efforts came to naught. With Conkling and his protégée Thomas Collier Platt in at least temporary eclipse, the new Republican Party leader, Senator Warner ("Wood-Pulp") Miller, had been trying to consolidate his power by securing GOP control of the Assembly. To that end, earlier in 1883 he had told former Assemblyman Titus Sheard, a respected resident of rural upstate Herkimer County, that he would back him for Speaker if Sheard ran for his old seat and was reelected. In addition , 1884 was a Presidential election year, and it was already well known that Roosevelt was opposed to Miller's candidate for the Republican nomination, former U.S. Secretary of State and Senator James G. Blaine. Also, some Assembly members worried that although the 25-year-old Roosevelt was well-suited to lead them as an opposition minority, he was too young and immature to be given the important Speakership post. [2]

Nevertheless, by 5:00 on December 31, with the caucus scheduled to meet only three hours later, Roosevelt apparently had lined up enough commitments for election. At this point, a desperate Miller and his allies mustered a last ditch effort to stop him. The leader called in the New York City delegation and tempted them with promises of "the valuables in the treasury" which would be available if Sheard were elected. He also persuaded another candidate to withdraw and throw his votes to the upstate Assemblyman. Thus, on the first ballot, the caucus picked Sheard by a vote of 42 to 30. [3]

Roosevelt immediately swallowed his sorrow and moved that Sheard's nomination be unanimous. He quickly realized that his strong showing had made him even more powerful than he had been the previous year, especially after Sheard granted his request to chair the powerful Cities Committee and then agreed to his demand to replace a Committee clerk whom he did not know and whom he suspected was a spy for the Party organization. Fulfilling a promise he had made to his constituents the previous fall to attack both the Republican and Democratic New York City machines, on January 31 he introduced bills that would increase liquor license fees, limit municipal borrowing powers and increase the power of New York City's Mayor vis-a-vis the boss-controlled aldermen, thus increasing the influence of the general electorate. His powerful speech in favor of the Aldermanic bill was widely reported and praised, with the *Times* calling it "conclusive." On February 5, by a 61 to 38 vote, the Assembly moved the bill along for final passage. [4]

This flurry of activity would have been more than enough to keep most legislators busy, but not Roosevelt. At his instigation, on January 15 he was appointed to head a committee that had been formed to investigate corruption in the New York City government. Made up of one other Republican and two Democrats, all of whose views were similar to Roosevelt's, it immediately began to hold hearings to investigate waste and graft in the City Department of Public Works. By the second week of February, meeting on Friday, Saturday and Monday at the City's Metropolitan Hotel, it had conducted eleven days of hearings with testimony from mostly evasive witnesses who obviously did not want the public to know the details of a number of questionable transactions. At times Roosevelt could not restrain his anger at their refusal to answer the Committee's questions. When the city sheriff claimed that an inquiry as to transportation costs was "going into a gentleman's private affairs," with his fist pounding the table, he shouted back:

"You are a public servant . . . We have a right to know what the expense of your office is; we don't ask for the expense of your private carriage that you use for your own convenience; we ask what you, a public servant, pay for a van employed in the service of the public."

Faced with these obstructive tactics, the Committee made slow progress but at last was able to secure the arrest of the City's undersheriff for fraudulently diverting $5,000 dollars of public funds. [5]

Thus, by early February Roosevelt had put the disappointment of the lost Speakership behind him and could justly claim credit for a record of outstanding legislative accomplishments. Sadly, bitter personal tragedy was about to strike. Alice was due to give birth at any time, with the doctors predicting Thursday, February 14, as the due date. Her health appeared excellent, and she was staying at the Roosevelt family home with Theodore's older sister Bamie, with her parents at a nearby hotel. Thus, when the Committee's hearings adjourned on February 11 so that its members could return to Albany for their legislative duties, although his mother was in bed with what appeared to be a bad cold, Roosevelt decided to take an express train early the next morning and join them. The Aldermanic Bill was to be voted on the next afternoon and he wanted to be in the Assembly chamber to lead the debate for its passage. He planned to return to New York by Thursday evening to appear at a Cooper Union mass meeting supporting the legislation. [6]

Early Wednesday morning, Roosevelt received a telegram that late the night before Alice had given birth to a baby girl. Although it said that she was "only fairly well," he decided to stay in Albany for the afternoon debate. Later that morning, however, a second telegraph arrived that led a suddenly "worn" Roosevelt to rush from the chamber to catch the next train back to New York. An intense fog that for several days had blanketed the Eastern seaboard delayed the journey, and it was not until 10:30 p.m. that he reached the family home on West 57th Street. There his younger brother Elliott confirmed the news contained in the telegram that, as he told their sister Corinne earlier in the day: "There is a curse on this house. Mother is dying, and Alice is dying too." In his mother's case, the cause was typhoid fever, of which her cold had been the first stage. In Alice's, it was nephritis, then called Bright's disease, a chronic inflammation of the kidneys, which surprisingly had gone undetected until the strain of labor suddenly brought it on in acute form. There was nothing that Roosevelt could do but hold his barely conscious wife in his arms until she died at 2:00. the next afternoon, leaving her room only to join his brother and two sisters at his mother's bedside when she expired an hour later.[7]

Later that year Roosevelt was to write that "when my heart's dearest died, the light went out of my life forever." Fortunately, his Assembly duties permitted him to bury himself in his work. As he wrote to the influential political reformer Carl Schurz from Albany on February 21, "I think I should go mad if I were not employed." Thus, after the joint funeral on Saturday, February 16, and Baby Alice's christening the next day, he left his newborn daughter with Bamie, and was back in his Assembly seat on Tuesday. Upon learning of his loss, his fellow members had already expressed their sympathy by the unprecedented act of adjournment. [8]

Even measured by his past performance, the volume of Roosevelt's efforts during the rest of the legislative session was formidable. His week would begin with New York City hearings of the City Investigating Committee, followed by a late Monday evening or overnight train to Albany for three days of meetings of his Cities Committee and Assembly discussion and debate. Then it was back to New York, usually by overnight train, for day-long Friday and Saturday Investigating Committee hearings. The week of February 25 saw him reporting 11 bills from his Committee, and the following week the number was 19. When he decided that the draft of the Investigating Committee report that he had been furnished was a "whitewashing performance", throughout one night and into the next afternoon he completely rewrote what was printed by the day's close as a 47 page 15,000 word document. By the session's end, the hearings led to the introduction of nine different municipal reform bills, seven of which were passed despite strong opposition from Speaker Sheard and other organization Assemblymen. [9]

❧ ❧ ❧

In addition to this seemingly frantic activity, Roosevelt found the time and energy to involve himself forcefully in the contest for the 1884 Republican Presidential nomination. The leading candidates were President Chester A. Arthur and Blaine. In view of Arthur's background as a loyal organization Republican (or 'Stalwart'), his accidental accession to the Presidency had shocked GOP reformers who had had high hopes for the recently elected Garfield. To their surprise, he had turned out to be his own man, supporting civil service reform and vetoing a major piece of pork barrel legislation. This, however, had made him unacceptable to the Stalwarts, who had turned to Blaine.

James G. Blaine was one of the most controversial figures in 19th century American politics. No one doubted his ability, which had been evidenced during his service as House Speaker, Senator and Secretary of State, or his sophistication and charm. To his many devoted followers, he was their "Plumed Knight." His fatal flaw was an undisguised desire for personal economic gain, which in 1876 had led an investigating committee of the Democratic controlled House to accuse him of using his influence as Speaker in a previous Congress to obtain a land grant for an Arkansas railroad and then secure a liberal commission in selling its bonds. By obtaining the "Mulligan letters," which had formed the basis for the charge, and then reading what later turned out to be only selected parts in defending himself before the full House, Blaine exonerated himself in the eyes of his supporters. Nevertheless, a smell of corruption remained and cost him the 1876 Republican nomination to the irreproachably honest Rutherford B. Hayes. At the 1880 convention, Blaine was defeated by Conkling's Stalwarts, whose leader never forgave him for once calling Conkling a "grandiloquent swell" with a "majestic, super-eminent, overpowering, turkey-gobbler strut." [10]

Now, in 1884, Conkling's power had waned, and Blaine's turn apparently had come. To Roosevelt and other reform-minded Republicans, however, he was anathema. With no enthusiasm for Arthur, their candidate was Vermont's hardworking, honest but dull U.S. Senator George F. Edmunds. In supporting him against Blaine, Roosevelt would also have the chance to beat Boss Warner Miller, and repay him for denying Roosevelt the Assembly Speakership.

The issue was joined at the Republican state convention, which that year convened on April 23 in the Mohawk River manufacturing city of

Utica. With the 128 district and alternate delegates already chosen, the convention's chief business was to elect four delegates-at-large to the national convention. Roosevelt was determined that they should be himself and three other Edmunds supporters. Their election would send a strong signal throughout the country that, with this evidence of its strength in the state with the largest delegation, the reform movement must be seriously reckoned with. [11]

With as many as 70 of the nearly 500 delegates as potential Edmunds backers, and with the remaining delegates divided between Blaine and Arthur, Roosevelt saw a good chance of success. He arrived in Utica two days early and immediately set to work, negotiating between both sides on the basis that the antagonism between them was so great that each would be willing to concede much to the independents rather than allowing the other to prevail. It soon became apparent that, pressured by Miller and by Platt, who had returned to the political wars, the Blaine supporters had an edge over Arthur's backers. By the evening of April 23, the Arthur delegates had concluded that "all was up" with their candidate as far as the convention was concerned and that they would vote for four Edmunds delegates-at-large. As the *Times* reported the next morning:

> "This programme, while it did not accomplish the victory hoped for by Arthur's admirers, would at least be gratifying in that it would help the Arthur stalwarts to strike an effective blow at . . . Warner Miller . . . and the whole company of half-breeds who were determined to commit the convention to Blaine."

The Arthur delegates honored their commitment when the convention held its single session the next day. The state of play became clear when Roosevelt, delaying his entrance until everyone else was seated, marched down the center hall to loud and prolonged applause. After he successfully moved that an Edmunds supporter should be the meeting's chairman, he and three other Edmunds men were selected for the at-large seats. His 472 votes were nearly double those for Miller, whom a New York *Sun* reporter wrote had been "pulverized finer than his own pulp." An observer later recalled that an exuberant Roosevelt crossed the aisle to where a dazed Miller was sitting, and shaking his fist, shouted to him, "There, damn you, we beat you for last winter!" [12]

The Edmunds victory established him for the first time as a viable Presidential candidate. It also burnished Roosevelt's reputation throughout the state and gave him his first nationwide publicity as a young man to watch. It was clear to both his friends and foes that he had been the moving force behind the Edmunds triumph. The editors of the *Evening Post* went so far as to describe him as "the most successful politician of our day." While savoring his victory, however, he must have realized that it was only an initial step in the nomination process, and that a hard uphill fight lay ahead. [13]

❀ ❀ ❀

When Roosevelt arrived in Chicago two days before the 1884 national convention's June 2 opening gavel, he quickly appreciated the magnitude of the task before him. It was clear that Blaine was in the lead, and there was increasing doubt that Arthur had the potential strength on his own to stop him. Although some of Blaine's support was represented by "brass bands and brag," the next day, as "a great Blaine multitude . . . filled the streets and hotels" with "no boasts . . . too great for it to make," a *Times* reporter wrote:

> "The tide has been settling toward Blaine today. The impression among politicians in and around the hotels this afternoon was that he had made some gains and that he would be far in advance of Arthur on the first ballot. Allowance must be made, of course, for the loud talk and the exaggerated claims which have always been the most prominent features of a Blaine canvass, but after making that allowance, there seems to be some ground for the confidence which the Blaine men feel." [14]

Yet, for Roosevelt, the situation was not hopeless, for as the *Times* concluded, "Blaine does not yet control a majority of the convention." He hoped to secure a result similar to that he had reached in Utica, with Edmunds and other lesser candidates combining with the Arthur forces to hold off Blaine long enough for someone else – possibly Edmunds – to emerge as a compromise choice. To that end, he had been active during the five weeks between his Utica triumph and the Chicago Convention. As he wrote the Secretary of the Indiana Republican State Committee on May 5, "I am now in communication with the various delegates from New York and New England who think as we do." On May 23, he reported progress:

"There are between 60 and 70 delegates from New York and New England who are 'independents' or 'Edmunds men.' They are going to meet in conference on Monday afternoon at the headquarters of the Massachusetts delegation at the Leland House; will you not be there with as many of the Indiana men who think as we do, as possible? Please notify any other delegates whom you happen to know; we must get organized as soon as possible." [15]

In his quest for Edmunds votes, Roosevelt's chief ally was a 34-year-old Massachusetts patrician named Henry Cabot Lodge. Lodge was chairman of the Massachusetts Republican Committee and a candidate for Congress that fall. Unlike Roosevelt, he struck all but his closest associates as cold and aloof, but he shared Roosevelt's high-minded approach to politics, as well as a Harvard education and membership in its elite Porcellian club. He also had a deep interest in scholarly matters, especially American history, and, like Roosevelt, had a preference for the Hamiltonian concept of a strong central government and against Jeffersonian democracy. Despite their nine year age difference, he was to be Roosevelt's closest personal friend until they broke over Roosevelt's unsuccessful 1912 fight to replace President William Howard Taft as the Republican candidate. [16]

The reputation gained by Roosevelt's Utica success had preceded him. As he went from hotel to hotel buttonholing delegates he was, according to the *Evening Post*, "more specifically an object of curiosity than any other stranger in Chicago." During the afternoon of Monday, June 2, he and Lodge settled on a strategy that at least might halt the movement toward Blaine. They learned that his forces planned to nominate as the Convention's temporary chairman Powell Clayton, a former Arkansas governor who reportedly had agreed to support Blaine in return for a cabinet position in his administration. This so outraged a number of independent delegates that Roosevelt was able to gain their support for John R. Lynch, an Afro-American Congressman from Mississippi, who agreed to oppose Clayton. Far into the night, Roosevelt and Lodge promoted his candidacy with the Arthur forces as well as backers of possible dark horses in what the *Evening Post* called "a brilliant flank movement executed while the Blaine cohorts were dreaming triumph on the morrow." [17]

What transpired on June 3 was Roosevelt's finest hour at the convention, and the high point of his political career for many years. After Lodge had moved the substitution of Lynch's name for Clayton's, as reported in the *Times*:

"Up from the midst of the Empire State delegation rose a slight, almost boyish figure. It was that of an active, nervous, light-haired, gray-eyed man who had just thrown off a straw hat and scrambled to his perch in the chair . . . Everyone knew the man, for there is not a State head-quarters which he has not visited in his canvass for Edmunds. . . . It was Theodore Roosevelt of New York, the leader of the younger Republicans, and he was greeted with a routine round of applause as he stood waiting to speak. When he spoke it was not the voice of a youth but that of a man and a sensitive, practical man." [18]

For that era of long orations, Roosevelt's speech was brief, but it was interrupted several times by cheers and applause and, as reported in the *Times*, "went home" and "stirred the opponents of Clayton to the uttermost." Its most stirring passage, particularly to the many Civil War veterans who heard it, came at its close:

> "It is now, Mr. Chairman, less than a quarter of a century since, in this city, the great Republican party organized for victory and nominated Abraham Lincoln, of Illinois, who broke the fetters of the slaves and sent them asunder forever. It is a fitting thing for us to choose to preside over this convention one of that race whose right to sit within these walls is due to the blood and the treasure so lavishly spent by the founders of the Republican Party." [19]

After the oratory had stopped, Lynch was elected by a 424 to 384 vote. Following this preliminary victory, however, Roosevelt must have realized that Edmunds' cause was stalled. Meanwhile, even Arthur's strongest backers were privately agreeing with the press headlines that the President was beaten. The only possibility for stopping Blaine was for them and all the other anti-Blaine delegates to agree on another candidate. Unfortunately no name that was suggested mustered even the faintest enthusiasm. On June 4, there was a feeble attempt to launch a boom for Civil War hero General William Tecumseh Sherman, but he quickly defused it with his soon to become historic telegram:

> "I would not accept the nomination if tendered me. I would not serve if I was elected. [20]

The final blow came on June 5 when Blaine's name was placed on nomination by Ohio Judge William H. West. In a scene that was indelibly etched in the memory of anyone who watched it, the speaker, described by the *Herald* as "a long, tall, emaciated old man, thin to haggardness, sightless and awkward," was led to the platform. There, as Roosevelt wrote to his sister, amid a thunderous din, the blind orator

> ". . . stood looking with his sightless eyes towards the vast

throng that filled the huge hall. As he became excited his voice rang like a trumpet, and the audience became worked up to a condition of absolutely uncontrollable excitement and enthusiasm. For a quarter of an hour at a time they cheered and shouted so that the brass bands could not be heard at all, and we were nearly deafened by the noise." [21]

When the voting began the next day, Blaine's 334 first ballot delegates fell 77 short of the 411 required for nomination. His 58 vote lead over Arthur was enough, however, to lead to what the *Times* described as a "prodigious demonstration of applause" both within and outside the hall. Edmunds' 93 votes led the rest of the field. On the second and third ballots, Blaine's total increased to 348 and then to 375 at the expense of both Arthur and Edmunds, whose support faded to 69 delegates. As the delegates "screamed as if they would go mad" and then began to stamp on the floor in "a deep thunder roar that rolled back and forth beneath the wide-spreading roof," in what seemed "the only hope of defeating Blaine's nomination," Ohio's Joseph Foraker moved for a recess. In the bedlam that followed, the chairman first rejected the cries of Roosevelt and other for a roll call on the motion but after the hall erupted with cries of "Fair play! Fair play!" reversed himself. [22]

As the voting proceeded, Roosevelt knew that his side had been defeated. The motion's rejection by 450 to 364 presaged Blaine's victory on the next ballot. When his 541 votes there were announced, Ohio's William McKinley asked Roosevelt to second a motion to make the nomination unanimous, but he was so overwrought that he could answer "no" only by shaking his head. To reporters seeking to find out what he would do next, he was as noncommittal as his emotions permitted. The *Times* recorded him as stating that he was far from "satisfied" with Blaine, that although as a participant in the convention he "would be expected to support the nominee," he believed that many "independents . . . would not give Blaine any support whatever" and that he had "nothing further to say." Whether he would support Blaine, he told a *World* reporter, "is a subject that I do not care to talk about." He was "going cattle-ranching in Dakota for the remainder of the summer and a part of the fall. What I shall do after that I cannot say." [23]

In fact, the cumulative effect of the events and incessant activity of the last four months, beginning with the loss of his wife and ending with this political defeat, was almost too much for him. Thus, later that evening he told an *Evening Post* editor that "any proper Democratic nomination will have our hearty support." Yet, by the time he had changed trains in St. Paul, the anticipation of the weeks ahead on the range had steadied him, and he said to a local reporter:

"I have bolted the nomination of the convention by no means. I have no personal objection to Blaine . . . I have been called a reformer but I am a Republican." [24]

Roosevelt had spent part of the previous September away from his pregnant wife hunting in the Little Missouri Valley in the extreme western part of what is now North Dakota. He instantly developed a strong attachment to the area and the rough outdoor life he could lead there. Before returning to New York, he had purchased a cattle ranch and it was to it that he repaired immediately after the convention. He had already decided that he would not seek a fourth term in Albany. As he wrote in response to a congratulatory letter from the editor of a Utica newspaper following his victory at the state convention:

"I realize very thoroughly the absolutely ephemeral nature of the hold I have upon the people, and a very real and positive hostility I have excited among the politicians. I will not stay in public life unless I can do so on my own terms, and my ideal, whether lived up to or not, is rather a high one." [25]

Even in these dark June days, however, Roosevelt was unable to ignore the challenge of putting that ideal to work. Thus, when he paid a short visit to the East in July, after visiting Lodge and discussing with him the implication of the Democratic nomination of Grover Cleveland on July 11, he announced on July 19, as Lodge already had, that he would definitely vote for Blaine:

> "I am by inheritance and education a Republican; whatever good I have been able to accomplish has been accomplished through the Republican party; I have acted with it in the past, and wish to act with it in the future; I went as a regular delegate to the Chicago convention, and I intend to abide by the outcome of that convention." [26]

Most of Roosevelt's and Lodge's political friends were taking a different course and backing Cleveland. They were derisively given a Narragansett Indian chief's name of "Mugwumps," because of their assumed air of superior character and intellect, and did not hesitate in branding Roosevelt as a traitor to the cause of reform. As he wrote to Lodge on July 28, in response to his announcement: "I received shoals of letters, pathetic and abusive," from these former allies "who seem surprised that I have not developed hoofs and horns." Typical of the press comment was editor E.L. Godkin's attack in the July 21 *Evening Post*:

> "Young men like Mr. Roosevelt owe all their lives in confidence in their absolute integrity. . . . There is no ranch or other hiding place in the world in which a man can wait for Blaine and the Mulligan letters to 'blow over' for they will never blow over until justice is done." [27]

Several days later, after responding to some of these attacks "with vivacity or ferocity, according to the circumstances of the case," Roosevelt returned to his Dakota ranch. Although he had stated in his July 19 announcement of support for Blaine that he did not "expect to take any part in the campaign this fall," the bite of the political bug and a sense that his political future demanded that he actively assert his Republicanism were too strong. By early October, he returned to New

York and, between October 14 and November 3, made seven speeches for the Republican ticket.

On November 8, in one of the closest Presidential elections in history, a Democrat was sent to the White House for the first time in 28 years. Unlike Roosevelt and Lodge, most Mugwumps were so opposed to Blaine that they supported Cleveland and made possible his election. At one point, the bachelor New York Governor's campaign was set back when he admitted that in his younger days he had fathered an illegitimate daughter – whose support he had paid. On reflection, however, most of his backers took the position that, "We should elect Mr. Cleveland to the public office which he is so admittedly qualified to fill, and send Mr. Blaine to the private life which he is so admirably fitted to adorn." Nevertheless, Blaine might have been elected if, at an October 29 meeting of New York clergymen that he attended, a Presbyterian minister had not labeled the Democrats as the party of "Rum, Romanism and Rebellion." Blaine was exhausted after weeks of campaigning and failed to notice and repudiate the statement, which was quickly picked up and widely circulated by the Democrats. The backlash among the Irish Catholics whose support Blaine was cultivating was enough to put New York in Cleveland's column by 1149 votes. Its 36 electoral votes gave him victory by 219 electoral votes to Blaine's 182. [28]

Roosevelt's initial reaction was that, as he wrote Lodge, "I have not believed and do not believe that I shall ever be likely to come back into political life . . ." In the long run, however, he benefitted greatly from Blaine's defeat. If the Republican nominee had won, he likely would have rewarded Roosevelt with a government position. Through a kind of "guilt by association" with Blaine's Old Guard supporters, this would have made it difficult for him to maintain the reformer, pro good government reputation which was to be essential to his future political career. Equally important to a young man who had risen so fast was a pause during which he could reach maturity outside both the political arena and his privileged social milieu. In Roosevelt's case, the experience of men and life he was about to gain in the Dakota Badlands would provide just that. [29]

3

"In All Probability This Campaign Means My Final and Definite Retirement"

LESS THAN TWO WEEKS AFTER THE ELECTION, ROOSEVELT WAS BACK AT his Dakota ranch. During the next two years, he was to spend more time there than in New York. Although ranching was not to be a financial success, he soon gained the respect and friendship of the hard-bitten men who were trying to make a living in this beautiful but desolate country. Some of them would remain lifelong friends and fellow Rough Riders in the war with Spain over Cuba that took place more then ten years later.

His long days in the saddle also benefitted Roosevelt physically. Reporters who had observed him at the 1884 Chicago convention found him so frail that his whole body shook when he tried to make himself heard above the din from the delegates and galleries. During the summer of 1885, however, after participating in a 32-day cattle roundup during which he rode nearly a thousand miles, he returned to New York, in the words of one newspaperman, "rugged, bronzed, and in the prime of health." To another reporter, this previously "pale, slim young man, with a thin, piping voice and a general look of dyspepsia . . . is now brown as a berry and has increased 33 lbs. in weight.

The voice . . . is now hearty and strong enough to drive oxen." [1]

During his Western sojourns, Roosevelt also found time to work on three books: *Hunting Trips of a Ranchman,* and biographies of the earlier 19th century Senator Thomas Hart Benson and the late 18th century statesman Gouverneur Morris. When he was in New York, he became acquainted with his baby daughter and stayed for the first time at the hilltop house at Oyster Bay on Long Island's North Shore that he named Sagamore Hill, after the Indian sagamores, or chieftains, who had held war councils there in bygone days. In early October, 1885, he met for the first time since Alice's death his childhood sweetheart Edith Carow, and the two were immediately attracted to each other. On November 17, they became engaged, but resolved to keep their plans secret for at least a year, since marriage less than two years following Alice's death would violate the strict moral proprieties of the Victorian Age. In March, therefore, Roosevelt returned to Dakota, where he tried to cope with a continuing drought and cattle prices that were less than the expense of raising and shipping the animals. By late summer, he realized that he had no future as a rancher, and increasing rumors that he was engaged to Edith brought him East by early October. His fiancée was traveling with her mother in Europe, and he planned to join her for a December wedding in London. [2]

❋ ❋ ❋

Thus, as he returned to New York, a future political candidacy was far from the forefront of Roosevelt's mind. Although he had participated in the 1885 Republican state convention and had worked for the unsuccessful GOP gubernatorial candidate, his efforts went largely unnoticed and seemed to confirm that he had no political future.

Events immediately disproved that notion. When Roosevelt arrived in New York, the city was engaged in the most heated mayoralty campaign in years. The excitement was created by the formation of a United Labor Party, and its choice of social reformer Henry George as its mayoral candidate. In his 1879 best-seller, *Progress and Poverty*, George had contended that the economic problems of the day were caused by the speculative investment in land of otherwise productive resources, with a resulting failure of wages to increase along with productivity. The answer, he argued, was to assess a single tax on land and abolish all taxes borne by industry and thrift.

In 1886, the American labor movement was asserting itself for the first time. Earlier in the year, 45,000 New York City workers had joined a nationwide general strike for higher wages. In August, their leaders began to consider running their own candidate for mayor. With the City's extremes of poverty and wealth, as manifested by the unbroken ranks of Fifth Avenue palaces that were in the process of construction, George's proposal to tax wealthy New Yorkers made him a natural candidate for these voters. Although not a New York resident, he agreed to run after more than 30,000 electors signed a petition promising their support.

As George charged that the city's workingmen were "toiling perhaps for Mrs. Astor," or "the heirs of some other dead Dutchmen," and proposed to tax land which its owners would be forced to sell to provide homes for tenement dwellers, the city's business and political establishment moved to assure his defeat. They realized that a candidate of ability and impeccable integrity was needed. The concern of the reform-minded, well-heeled Swallowtail Democrats * was shared by Tammany Hall and its leaders, who realized that the George effort was a direct threat to their power base. Tammany's powerful leader "Honest John" Kelly had only recently died, but his right hand man Richard Croker quickly assumed power and, choosing what seemed the lesser of two evils, backed Abram Hewitt, a wealthy iron manufacturer who was not unfriendly to labor and who had managed Samuel

---

* So-called because they purportedly regularly dressed in stylish swallowtail coats.

Tilden's unsuccessful 1876 Presidential campaign. The son-in-law of re-vered philanthropist Peter Cooper, Hewitt won enthusiastic Swallow-tail support, and was easily nominated. [3]

With a strong reform candidate in the field and to prevent George from winning over a divided opposition, the Republicans could have endorsed Hewitt or sat out the election without a nominee. Their lead-ers did neither. Instead, they hoped that George would win enough Democratic votes so that a Republican candidate backed by them might be elected. Accordingly, on Roosevelt's return and only a few hours before the October 15 evening meeting at which the Republican candidate was to be chosen, he was visited by what he described to Lodge two days later as "a succession of the influential Republicans of the city to entreat me to take the nomination for Mayor." As a loyal party man, his only excuse for declining was his upcoming wedding, but that was still a well-kept secret. Thus, with no time to think over the matter, he "did not well see how I could refuse" and "with the most genuine reluctance" agreed to run. [4]

Roosevelt was realistic about his chances, writing to Lodge that it would be "a perfectly hopeless contest." As he saw it, it was a "no win" situation: "If I make a good run it will not hurt me, but it will if I make a bad one, as is very likely." He was not worried about George, "whose canvas is not at all dangerous, being mostly wind." His chief concern was that many "decent Republicans" were already "panicky" and that "if the panic grows thousands of my supporters will go for Hewitt for fear George may be elected – a perfectly groundless emotion." His hope "at the best, is to make a good run and get out the Republican vote." Three days later, he was even more pessimistic, writing to Lodge that "[T]his must not be spoken outside, but in reality not only is there not the slightest chance of my election, but there is at least an even chance of my suffering an unusually heavy and damaging defeat." He con-cluded that although "at least I have a better party standing than ever before," "[in] all probability this campaign means my final and definite retirement as an available candidate." [5]

Yet, true to character, Roosevelt plunged into the campaign with his full energy, giving the impression that he could actually win. After a visit to Oyster Bay, he returned to the city early on October 18 and immediately determined that the series of rooms previously reserved as Republican headquarters was too small. While the candidate met with a steady stream of visitors, his aides took over a much larger suite in the fashionable Fifth Avenue Hotel at the corner of Fifth Avenue and 23rd Street. Volunteer committees were organized and speaking engagements were scheduled in a rush of activity that reflected the imminence of the November 2 election, less than three weeks away. It was a far cry from the late 20th century's protracted periods of campaign organization, both before and after a candidate's nomination. [6]

After a few days, his natural exuberance and the efforts of his supporters had convinced Roosevelt that he could actually win. Their enthusiasm exploded at an October 27 mass meeting at Cooper Union. The unabashedly pro-Roosevelt *Times* reported the rally under the headline "ROOSEVELT SURE TO WIN":

> "Red fire filled the open space outside Cooper Union last night, while rockets and roman candles illuminated the cloudy sky with a brilliant glare. The pavement in front of the building was black with people, who poured in a steady stream through the doors and down the stairs into the hall . . . They were going to one of the biggest and most enthusiastic Republican mass meetings ever held in this city – a meeting that meant business and was full of hope."

When the distinguished lawyer Joseph H. Choate escorted Roosevelt to a platform above which hung his large crayon portrait, the audience rose as one and cheered for several minutes. It applauded at every opportunity, especially when the meeting's chairman asked it to "[m]ake the Cowboy of Dakota the next Mayor." In what for that day of long-winded oratory were brief remarks, the candidate promised to serve all the people of the city without regard to religion, politics or color. When he asserted, "The time for radical reform has come, and if I am elected you will have it.", a man in the crowd yelled, "You will be elected!" As if on cue, Roosevelt responded, to loud applause, "I think so, myself."[7]

A reading of the headlines of the Republican press * would have convinced any but the most skeptical readers that this was a reasonable prediction. Thus a *Times* subscriber was greeted at breakfast by "ROO-SEVELT STILL LEADING," "ROOSEVELT'S STEADY GAIN," "HEWITT'S LEADERS SCARED" and "ROOSEVELT WINNING VOTES AT EVERY TURN." The Democratic press † was equally optimistic over Hewitt's chances, with the *Sun* giving extensive coverage to rallies such as a Steinway Hall mass meeting organized by a Busi-ness-men's Municipal Association, where "Mr. Hewitt's name was greeted with a roar of applause, which broke out with redoubled force when Mr. Hewitt himself, in evening dress and looking fresh and vigorous, stepped upon the platform." [8]

❀ ❀ ❀

Like a sprinter who can see the tape just ahead, Roosevelt was campaigning with even more than his usual energy. Thus, at 8:00. on October 29, he began his evening by being driven from his Fifth Avenue headquarters three blocks west on 23rd Street to address a predominantly black Republican audience at the Grand Opera House. After a five minute speech that stressed party loyalty, he left the hall and with his carriage driver liberally applying the whip, arrived only 15 minutes later at an East Side rally in a building at Avenue A and Third Street.

---

* *Times, Tribune, Commercial Advertiser* and *Daily Express*
† *Herald, Sun*, and *World*

*Theodore Roosevelt as the Republican candidate for Mayor
of New York City*
(Courtesy of the Corbis-Bettman Archives)

This was his second campaign visit to the area, and the large and mainly German American crowd lustily cheered as he promised to "clear out City hall from top to bottom." Then he was off again, this time to the Eighteenth Assembly District headquarters on Third Avenue in the mid-Thirties, where he castigated any Republican who deserted the cause, and predicted that "[w]e shall get from the Democrats enough material support to put us up to 90,000 votes if we keep our ranks solid."

The evening's high point came when his carriage sped him to Grand Central Station where, shortly after 9 o'clock and after clambering over several platforms, he boarded the *Monitor*, William H. Vanderbilt's private locomotive, which had been made available by New York Central President and Republican leader Chauncey M. Depew. There he sat with the railroad's Superintendent and four other men in a compartment in front of the engineer's cab. As the next morning's *Times* described what ensued:

"'We'll have to run a little cautiously in the night,' said the Superintendent, as he jerked a bell, which was the signal for the start. The run was undoubtedly cautiously made, as he suggested, but caution is evidently no bar to speed on this railroad. Red lights, white lights, and green lights appeared along the track, flashed for a moment, and then were lost to sight behind the flying locomotive. It was 9:18 when the *Monitor* pulled out of Grand Central Station; 13 minutes later it hauled up at the Tremont station, just eight miles away. The Superintendent smiled at the astonishment of those tender feet in his party who had never flown over the country before on top of an engine's boiler." *

---

* In 1999, the fastest commuter train time from Grand Central to Tremont, including a stop at 125th Street, was 16 minutes.

The meeting hall was only a hundred feet from this lower Bronx station, and in no time Roosevelt was introduced and cheered as "he spoke of the improvements to which this growing area of the city are entitled, . . . and when he added that the residents could have those improvements if they had an honest and economical city government, the cheers were redoubled." The enthusiasm became even greater when "a sweet little girl toddled up under the weight of a magnificent floral horseshoe and presented it to him" and he "stooped down and shook her stubby little hand."

The candidate's evening was not yet over, however. He quickly returned to the *Monitor*, which flew back to Manhattan and stopped 30 blocks north of Grand Central to deposit him and his party at the end of a tunnel at 73rd Street. There, wrote the *Times* reporter:

> ". . .Superintendent Bissell, with a red lantern in one hand, guided Mr. Roosevelt through numerous passages in the big, brick tunnel and at last brought him to the surface of the ground through an opening which was strongly suggestive of a manhole leading out of a sewer in Paris."

After a "brisk walk," he shortly arrived at the 72nd Street and Third Avenue headquarters of the 22nd Assembly District Republicans, where he delivered his fifth and last speech of the evening. Then, it at last was home and to bed. [9]

❊ ❊ ❊

The next evening, Roosevelt closed his campaign at a vociferous Steinway Hall rally. At the first sight of their candidate, the *Times* reported, the "great crowd" was on its feet,

> " . . . and shouted and yelled until the building shook. Hats, canes, umbrellas, and handkerchiefs were waved while the people gave three cheers, three cheers, and a tiger over and over again."

Before Roosevelt's arrival, the meeting's chairman predicted he would receive 85,000 votes, well ahead of Hewitt's projected 75,000 and George's 60,000. [10]

As he was doing at every stop, in his Steinway Hall speech Roosevelt urged his listeners not to be persuaded to desert him by men "who are trying to scare weak-kneed Republicans by putting Hewitt in the wholly unexpected role of a savior of society." By then, however, he knew that defections in large numbers were already taking place. On November 1, election eve, with his formal campaigning completed, he wrote Lodge the news of his upcoming marriage and then summed up his position:

> "I have but little chance. I have made a rattling canvas with heavy inroads on the Democratic vote, but the 'timid good' are for Hewitt. Godkin, White and various others of the 'better element' here have acted with unscrupulous meanness and a low partisan dishonesty and untruthfulness which would disgrace the veriest machine leaders. May Providence in due course give me a chance to get even with some of them."

The influence of some of these men extended beyond the "better elements," as in the case of the influential German emigré Carl Schurz's appeal to many of the German-Americans that Roosevelt had been so actively courting. [11]

In addition to arguing that a large Roosevelt vote would assure a George election, the Hewitt forces were directly attacking the Republican candidate. As Election Day approached, they were not content to limit themselves to Hewitt's damning with faint praise that Roosevelt "at some future time . . . will receive the reward due to his energy, his ability and his character, but he has made a mistake. He has made himself the tool of designing men." Instead, they sought to prey on the fears of voters who might be concerned over giving a 28-year-old "boy" the power to run American's largest city, and belittled his legislative performance. [12]

Contrary to Roosevelt's prediction, as the election drew closer George's campaign did not fade. Instead, it seemed to gain in strength. On Saturday, October 30, tens of thousands of his backers braved a cold, drenching rain to show their support as they marched from the Bowery to Union Square, all the while shouting "Hi! Ho! The leeches must go!" Due to the efforts of a pro-labor Catholic priest, Edward McGlynn, George was making inroads into Tammany's Irish-American power base. To combat him, Tammany boss Croker persuaded the Catholic vicar general to announce that "[t]he great majority of the Catholic clergy of this city are opposed to the candidacy of Mr. George." Tammany saw to it that the statement was distributed to worshippers as they attended church on October 31. [13]

If this was not enough to assure a Hewitt victory, by 2:00. on Election Day, the large voter turnout in beautiful Indian Summer weather apparently prompted Republican boss Thomas Platt to spread the word that his cohorts should abandon Roosevelt and vote for Hewitt. The cumulative effect of these developments was that the Democratic candidate won handily with 90,552 votes, compared with George's 68,110. Roosevelt finished third, with only 60,415. On its face, it was a stunning defeat. The voter turnout was nearly 20,000 greater than in the preceding gubernatorial election, yet Roosevelt's vote was 20 percent less than that of the losing Republican candidate in that contest. Roosevelt himself estimated the number of Republican deserters at 15,000, and that most of them had gone to Hewitt. They would almost have given him the election if they voted Republican. Hewitt, not surprisingly, estimated the total at a lower 10,000. [14]

To Roosevelt, the political future looked dim. It was not only the size of his defeat, but also the fact that the Republicans were out of power in the nation, state and city. Yet, as with the defeat of his candidate at Chicago two years earlier, the result was probably good for him in the long run. With New York primarily a Democratic city, his occupancy of the mayoral office would have been frustrating and largely unproductive. At least through the end of the 20th century, New York mayors have never gone on to become major players on the national stage, and even Roosevelt, with all his energy, would have found it difficult to buck that trend. As it was, by running at the behest of the Republican hierarchy, he had proved himself a good party man who would be an acceptable candidate at some future time. He had also garnered favorable publicity as a candidate with qualities that would fit him for high public office in future years. As a pro-Hewitt New York *Sun* editor had written in the heat of the campaign:

"To be in his youth the candidate for the first office in the first city of the United States, and to poll a good vote for that office is something more than empty honor. . . . He cannot be Mayor this year, but who knows what may happen in some other year? Congressman, Senator, President?" [15]

At this point Roosevelt had more important things than politics on his mind. On November 6, he and his sister Bamie sailed for London, where on December 2 he and Edith were married. Over the years, she and their five children were to provide him with an especially fulfilling family life, and the important emotional support that was to anchor his future career.

4

Shaking Up The Police

SHORTLY AFTER THE NEWLY MARRIED ROOSEVELTS RETURNED TO New York in late March, 1887, Theodore hurried West to inspect the damage caused by the blizzards, sub-zero cold and floods of the Bad Lands' worst winter in recorded history. The cattle herds had been decimated, and at least for the time being, his ranching business there had been ruined. Roosevelt had lost most of his $80,000 investment. Apart from the birth of their first child, named Theodore and called Ted, the ensuing months were discouraging. The political prospects seemed no better. Cleveland was enjoying a wave of popularity, and there was a good possibility that Blaine again would be the Republican Presidential nominee. After the Democrats prevailed in the 1887 New York State elections, Roosevelt complained to his sister Bamie that his party "seems moribund." Two months later, he wrote to former legislative colleague Jonas Van Duzer that "I shall never be in politics again." [1]

With ranching and politics seemingly dead ends, Roosevelt turned more actively to pursuing a literary career. His *Gouverneur Morris* had received generally unfavorable reviews, yet as he wrote to Van Duzer, "I should like to write some book that would really take rank in the very first class." With his personal interest in the West, he conceived the idea of writing a several-volume history of the expansion of the United States from the Eastern seaboard across the continent to the Pacific. Entitled *The Winning of the West* and taking nine years to complete, it would be the work by which his career as an author would be best remembered. Most of his time during 1888 was spent in researching and composing its opening chapters and in writing and selling a number of articles to different periodicals so as to earn royalties that would help meet his now straitened financial circumstances. [2]

By year end 1888, Roosevelt's prospects had become brighter. To his pleasure, the Republican Presidential nominee was not Blaine but Benjamin Harrison of Indiana, whom he regarded as a "clean, honorable man" with a "sound" position on civil service reform. In early October, accompanied by Edith, he campaigned for Harrison in the upper Midwest, having "immense fun" as he acted "as target and marksman alternatively." When Harrison was elected, he wrote to his good English friend Cecil Spring-Rice that "though my ranch almost burst me, I am happy as a king — to use a Republican simile." [3]

Initially, Roosevelt's hopes for Harrison were dashed. He wrote to a friend in mid-April 1889 that "in the New York appointments . . . [he] has deliberately set to work to build up a Platt machine, he has utterly ignored the progressive wing of the party, and has distinctly lowered the standard of appointments." All the while, with the aid of Lodge, who was now a second-term Congressman, Roosevelt was trying to obtain a position in the new administration. Perhaps because the President shared the opinion of Blaine, who was the new Secretary of State, that Roosevelt was too "brilliant and aggressive a man" to hold a high post, the efforts were rebuffed. Eventually Harrison relented, and agreed to appoint Roosevelt as one of three Civil Service Commissioners. [4]

Few men were better qualified for the position. From his early days in Albany, when he had backed civil service reform in New York, Roosevelt had been an active supporter of merit requirements for government employees. Most possible appointees with political ambition would have turned down the post on the basis that to do any effective job would lead to constant conflict with influential Republican politicians who wished to reward their associates with postmasterships and other government jobs without regard to their qualifications. As he had already demonstrated, however, Roosevelt relished conflict, especially when it would be an opportunity to, as he would boast when he ran for President in 1912, "do battle for the Lord." [5]

Roosevelt was to spend the next six years in Washington. For the most part, he enjoyed his sojourn there. Although he would devote his extraordinary energy to trying to increase the Commission's effectiveness and public reputation, he also had time to work on *The Winning of the West* and other literary efforts. In addition, his impeccable social standing and outgoing personality gave him a unique opportunity to mingle with Cabinet members, ministers of leading foreign governments and members of Congress. He "ate out" nearly every night and entertained frequently at lunch and with Sunday evening suppers, where the food was of the plainest and the company of the best. He also became a member of a diverse group of friends that included Lodge, powerful House Speaker Thomas B. Reed, historians Henry Adams and John Hay, naturalist Clarence King, artist John LaFarge and sculptor Augustus Saint-Gaudens.

Although Roosevelt spent most of his time in Washington, he made occasional investigative forays around the country, seeking to administer "a galvanic shock that will reinforce his [Harrison's] virtue for the future." The Post Office, as the leading source of patronage employment, was his major focus. On occasion, he struck pay dirt, as with the Milwaukee postmaster, who had had civil service examination papers altered so that his own candidates would appear to have passed their tests. His efforts soon brought him into direct conflict with Postmaster General John Wanamaker, whose qualities as an outstanding administrator did not prevent him from emphasizing Republican loyalty in his appointments. Their row eventually led to an investigation by the Democratic-controlled Congressional Committee on Reform in the Civil Service, which was less interested in reform than in casting discredit on the Harrison Administration. [6]

When the President ran for reelection in 1892, Roosevelt made amends for what some party regulars considered previous disloyal behavior by writing a well-circulated article which claimed that no post-Civil War administration had "so excellent a record in its management of our foreign relations." His position on the officially nonpartisan Commission, however, significantly limited his involvement in the election campaign itself. This turned out to be a blessing. With the candidate of the newly formed Populist Party receiving more than a million votes, mostly from disgruntled Republican farmers, Cleveland with strong Mugwump support handily defeated Harrison and returned to the White House for a second time. Roosevelt had been happy in Washington, and he viewed Cleveland as a fellow advocate for civil service reform. With no political prospects in New York, he first persuaded himself and then others that there was no reason why he should not continue to serve on the Commission. By now he had convinced most Mugwumps that despite his continuing support of Republican candidates, he was and would continue to be a vigorous civil service advocate. Among others, leading Mugwump Carl Schurz went to bat for him with Cleveland, who agreed to reappoint him. Not long thereafter, however, Roosevelt was suggesting that Schurz and his friends were "pitching into" Cleveland's Postmaster General "too severely." [7]

Notwithstanding his complaint to Schurz, by late 1893 Roosevelt had concluded that "as regards civil service reform we are getting along just about the same under this administration as we did under the last," and that under Cleveland the Treasury Department, an important patronage dispenser, "is very much worse than it was under Harrison." Thus, although he continued to dominate the three-man Commission, he had an increasing feeling of *déja vu*. Meanwhile, with the country sliding more deeply into its worst economic depression since the Civil War, Republican prospects were brightening for both the fall 1894 elections and the Presidential contest that would follow two years later. It was time for him to move on. [8]

❋ ❋ ❋

Roosevelt's opportunity was waiting for him back home in New York City. Hewitt's City Hall tenure had lasted only one term. Now 65 years old, he was becoming an irascible old man with none of the tact that makes political independence acceptable. An egregious example occurred when he offended his Irish constituents, first by breaking a custom of 39 years and refusing to review the St. Patrick's Day parade, and then by responding to protests by announcing that he would not permit the traditional flying of an Irish flag atop City Hall. Although he initially appointed Croker his Fire Commissioner, they soon were at odds over patronage matters. Meanwhile, with George and his labor supporters no longer a viable threat, Croker was free to devote his time to reorganizing Tammany into a more potent political force.

When Hewitt ran for reelection in 1888, he was successfully attacked as an aristocratic Anglophile. On Election Day, he ran third, behind the second-place Republican candidate, as Tammany's Hugh J. Grant became New York's first Irish-American mayor. Grant, whose immigrant father had been a successful saloon owner, was a respectable Columbia Law School graduate who was happy to let Croker wield the power behind the mayoral throne. He easily won reelection in 1890. [9]

On February 14, 1892, Tammany's rule was challenged from an unexpected source. In his Valentine Day's sermon at the Madison Square Presbyterian Church, its minister, the Reverend Charles Parkhurst, delivered a blistering attack on Mayor Grant and his cohorts, accusing them of "an official and administrative criminality that is filthifying our entire municipal life, making New York a very hotbed of knavery, debauchery and bestiality." When Tammany challenged Parkhurst's charges on the basis that they were grounded entirely on unsubstantiated newspaper reports, he hired a detective and with him made personal expeditions to some of the city's most notorious brothels, opium dens and other dives. To look like a patron, he wore black-and-white checked trousers, a red flannel scarf and a slouch hat. Armed with the evidence that he collected, in his sermon five weeks later Parkhurst delivered a detailed attack on the "disgusting depths of this Tammany-debauched town." [10]

Parkhurst's efforts led to mass meetings and the formation of a City Vigilance League. Nonetheless, he and his allies could not prevent that fall's Democratic sweep from electing county undersheriff Thomas Francis Gilroy as Grant's successor. The crusading clergyman did not give up, however, and with the aid of the Chamber of Commerce, persuaded Republican boss Platt to initiate an investigation of the Police Department. Platt was a regular attendee at Parkhurst's church, where one commentator imagined him

> "...rather shriveled and somewhat dry, sitting up in his pew and exulting at the statements which the servant of the Lord was making in favor of the Republican Party. Dr. Parkhurst's intentions were of the best, but Mr. Platt could calculate, as he carefully held his silk hat between his knees, the number of votes that sermon would produce." [11]

The ensuing investigation took more than 10,000 pages of testimony from 678 witnesses. Its report detailed a shocking story of police lawlessness and corruption. The city's business and good government forces saw in the resulting widespread public outrage a chance at last to bring an end to Tammany's rule. All they needed was a strong candidate in the 1894 mayoral election. Roosevelt seemed a natural choice, and Platt asked his associate Lemuel Ely Quigg to sound him out. The two men had been friends since Quigg had covered the young Assemblyman's activities as an Albany reporter for the *Tribune*. Quigg was aware that Roosevelt was becoming frustrated in his civil service job. He was thus surprised when he received a negative response: Roosevelt couldn't afford the financial expense of running and, having lost once before, a second defeat would be the end of his political career. [12]

In fact, as Roosevelt later wrote to Lodge, he "would literally have given my right arm to have made the race, win or lose. It was the one golden chance, which never returns..." Edith was adamantly opposed, however, and that was that. Perhaps she feared that Platt and his associates would knife her husband as they had done in the campaign's closing days eight years earlier. Whatever may have been her actual motivation, Roosevelt sat on the sidelines as the Republicans nominated William L. Strong, a millionaire businessman with solid party credentials. He was elected by a three-to-two margin over former Mayor Grant, who was the only candidate a desperate Tammany could find to try to stem the good government tidal wave. [13]

Shortly after the new administration took over City Hall, Roosevelt told Quigg that he would be interested in becoming one of four Police Commissioners. He realized that the nonpartisan nature of the post might force him to maintain a low profile in the 1896 Presidential campaign and thus reduce his eligibility for a high position in Washington in the likely event of a Republican victory. Nevertheless, since the job would provide broad publicity that he could use to burnish his reputation, on April 9, 1895, he accepted the post, "subject to honorable conditions." [14]

❧ ❧ ❧

On May 6, Roosevelt and the other new Commissioners were sworn in at City Hall. Reporter Lincoln Steffens, who was waiting with fellow journalist Jacob Riis at police headquarters at 300 Mulberry Street, described the scene as Roosevelt approached, well ahead of his three colleagues:

> "He came ahead down the street, ... and running up the stairs to the front door of police headquarters, he waved us reporters to follow. We did. With the police officials standing around watching,

the new board went up to the second story, where the old commissioners were waiting in their offices. T.R. seized Riis, who introduced me, and still running, he asked questions: 'Where are our offices? Where is the board room? What do we do first?' Out of the half-heard answers he gathered the way to the board room, where the old commissioners waited, like three of the new commissioners, stiff, formal and dignified. Not T.R. He introduced himself, his colleagues with handshakes and then called a meeting of the new board; had himself elected president – this had been prearranged – and then adjourned to pull me and Riis into his office."

"Now, then, what'll we do?" [15]

Roosevelt realized that it was essential that he lose no time in exercising his authority. By the end of May, he had forced the resignation of Police Chief Thomas F. Byrnes, who had reached friendly arrangements with certain leaders of organized crime, including an understanding that they exempt the financial district from their activities. In return for this favored treatment, Byrnes had become wealthy from stock market tips given him by grateful Wall Street tycoons. Roosevelt also fired the notorious Inspector Alexander "Clubber" Williams, who had earned his nickname by bashing heads on Manhattan's Lower East Side, whether or not the reputed criminals were actually engaged in nefarious activities. Williams, who had managed to find money to invest successfully in Japanese real estate, had succinctly expressed the philosophy that guided him and other practitioners of police brutality: "There is more law at the end of a policeman's nightstick than in a decision of the Supreme Court." [16]

Recognizing that favorable publicity was essential if he was to make headway against the Police Department's entrenched interests and their political allies, Roosevelt assiduously cultivated the New York press. Steffens and Riis were his special favorites. The 29-year-old Steffens was a reporter for good government advocate's E.L. Godkin's *Evening Post*, and would go on to become a leading muckraker, whose attacks on political corruption were later collected in his influential book *The Shame of the Cities*. "Clubber" Williams had been his special target, and when Roosevelt was about to fire the notorious inspector, he "threw open his second story window, leaned out, and yelled out his famous cowboy yell, "Hi yi yi . . . Steffens, come up here." As the reporter hurried up to Roosevelt's office,

> ". . . there in the hall stood Williams, who glared as usual at me with eyes that looked like clubs. I passed on in to T.R., who bade me sit down on a certain chair at the back of the room. Then he summoned Williams and fired him; that is to say he forced him to resign." [17]*

Whereas Steffens was an impressionable aspiring young journalist, Riis was an influential widely-read reporter for the *Sun*. A Danish immigrant, his 1890 book *How the Other Half Lives* for the first time brought to the general public's attention the terrible living conditions to which new arrivals to America were subjected in New York's teeming ghettos. As soon as he read the book, Roosevelt visited the *Sun* offices and said that he had "come to help." The two soon became fast friends, for, as Riis later wrote:

> "I loved him from the day I first saw him; nor ever in all the years that have passed has he failed of the promise made then." [18]

Taking a page from Parkhurst's book, the new commissioner soon began making personal inspections of policemen who were supposedly on duty. Believing that he could learn more if he proceeded incognito, he made these tours in the wee hours of the morning. He was accompanied by Riis, who with relish described their initial foray:

---

* Shortly thereafter, Williams entered the insurance business, where he became a multimillionaire.

"I laid out the route, covering ten or a dozen patrol-posts, and we met at 2 a.m. on the steps of the Union League Club, objects of suspicion on the part of two or three attendants and a watchman who shadowed us as night-prowlers till we were out of their baili-wick. I shall never forget the first morning when we traveled for three hours along First and Second and Third Avenues from Forty-second Street to Bellevue, and found of ten patrolmen just one doing his work faithfully. Two or three of them were chat-ting on saloon corners and guyed the President of the Board when he asked them if this was what they were there for. One was sitting asleep on a butter-tub in the middle of the sidewalk, snor-ing so that you could hear him across the street, and was inclined to be 'sassy' when aroused and told to go about his duty." [19]

According to Riis, as a result of these nocturnal prowls, "The whole force woke up. . ." So also, at least temporarily, did the fascinated pub-lic, which had never before encountered a public official with such a combination of verve and ability to use the press for his own purposes. Both newspapers and readers applauded as Roosevelt, at least for the moment, rooted out much of the corruption and sloth that had plagued the force under Tammany's regime. He and his fellow com-missioners also adopted a merit system for appointments and promo-tions and instituted such practical improvements as placing call boxes on strategic street corners and, with automobiles still only a gleam in their inventors' eyes, adding a Bicycle Squad to help patrolman appre-hend lawbreakers more quickly. [20]

In his first two months on the job, Roosevelt was having the time of his life. He even had great fun showing off a letter delivered to police headquarters that bore no other address than a pair of glasses over a double row of clenched teeth, gleefully enthusing, "Few men live to see their own hieroglyph." Despite going without sleep on the nights of his "midnight rambles," he happily wrote Bamie that "I really doubt whether I have ever been in better health." A week later he enthused to her:

> "My whole work brings me in contact with every class of people in New York, as no other work possibly could, and I get a glimpse of the real life of the swarming millions. Finally, I do really feel that I am accomplishing a good deal." [21]

❦ ❦ ❦

Shortly thereafter, however, he was to "run up against an ugly snag." The problem was his decision in June, 1895 to enforce a 38-year-old New York State excise law, which prohibited the Sunday sale of intoxicating beverages. During most of the time it had been on the books, it had been ignored by law enforcement officials. Roosevelt had reason to believe that in many cases the law was being used as an excuse for corrupt police officials to extort payments from saloon-keepers so that they could keep their bars open on the Sabbath. Far from being a Prohibitionist, he believed that if he closed the bars on Sunday, the public outcry would be so intense that the legislature would repeal the law, thus bringing an end to this extortion racket. [22]

Roosevelt's prediction proved only partly correct. His action did create a loud hue and cry, but for the most part the blame fell on him rather than on the law. Especially incensed was the German community, which had continued its pre-immigration Sabbath habit of quaffing a sociable stein or two in comfortable beer gardens while listening to waltzes and other pleasing airs. Since large numbers of German voters had helped Mayor Strong win election only a few months earlier, the political fallout seriously weakened Roosevelt's ability to adopt other reforms. His problems were exacerbated when he tried to meet accusations that his efforts primarily affected only the poorer classes by raiding Sherry's and other favorite spots of the wealthy, a number of whom joined his foes. The last straw came when the legislature amended the law to permit sales of liquor with meals in "hotels," defined to include any establishments with at least ten bedrooms. Saloon-keepers quickly took advantage of this loophole by building cubicles inside their premises, which they would rent out at handsome profits to prostitutes and unmarried couples. [23]

In the meantime, as summer turned into fall, Roosevelt continued to enforce the Sunday law, despite pleas from worried Republican leaders and Strong that he moderate his efforts, at least until after Election Day. The result was a decisive Tammany victory at the polls, with the estranged Germans voting overwhelmingly against the Republicans in favor of Sunday beer.

Elsewhere in the state, however, the Republicans won a resounding victory, so that they now held not only the governorship, but also both houses of the legislature. This set the stage for the first in a series of conflicts between Roosevelt and boss Platt. The two men could not have been more different. Platt, born 62 years earlier in the small south-central New York country town of Owego, was old enough to be Roosevelt's father. Despite occasional setbacks, he had gradually risen to the top of the political pyramid, first in his home Tioga County and then in the state. Following his active involvement in Mayor Strong's 1894 election, he now controlled the New York City GOP as well. [24]

Tall, thin and stooped by a developing arthritis, the parchment skinned and elegantly dressed Platt resembled a New England college professor or a retired clergyman more than a successful practical politician. Quigg, who as his longtime lieutenant probably knew him as well as anyone, said that he appeared listless even when he was shaking hands. Thus, his success did not come from a strong personality but instead from an acute instinct. As Quigg later put it in a letter to Roosevelt years later:

"Now, Platt had mental 'feelers,' antennae . . . those things that bugs and women have . . . and it was one of the secrets of his power that he was able to sense what was bound to happen anyway, to get behind it at the appropriate time, and then to claim the credit for having brought it about, which he unfailingly did and a little lustily."

Unlike Roosevelt, who almost always dealt directly with people and relished a good fight, Platt enjoyed sly maneuvers and was always seeking harmony. In conversation he was invariably conciliatory, and always spoke in pleasant, low tones. For these reasons, he was known as the "Easy Boss." [25]

Platt owed his power to more than his political skills. As Roosevelt recollected in his *Autobiography*:

"Big businessmen contributed to him large sums of money, which enabled him to keep his grip on the machine and secured for them the help of the machine if they were threatened with adverse legislation . . . When the money was contributed there was rarely talk of specific favors in return. It was simply put into Mr. Platt's hands and treated by him as his campaign chest." [26]

Platt's use of these funds furthered his absolute control. According to one observer:

"Suppose you were a candidate for senator up in Oneida County. You would come down to him and say, 'I have a mighty hard fight up here. I have got to have some money for advertising in the newspapers, for placards, bill-boards, for hiring halls, carriages on election day to take the voters to the polls and all that sort of thing.' Platt would say, 'How much do you need?' You would say, '$5,000.' He would give you $5,000 which he had collected from corporations and other sources interested in legislation in Albany."

As far as financial matters were concerned, Platt's reputation was that of an honest man, and none of this money apparently ever "stuck to his fingers." Like most well-connected politicians of the day, however, his business friends provided tips and other opportunities that

Thomas Collier Platt
(Courtesy of the Corbis-Bettman Archives)

The Fifth Avenue Hotel
(Courtesy of the Corbis-Bettman Archives)

permitted him to make money in other ways. Moreover, although Platt himself undoubtedly adopted a "holier than thou" attitude, his lieutenants were not above following the time-honored practice of buying votes by small favors or padding the voting lists. For example, at one time the rolls of one Republican-controlled New York City election district contained the names of 220 Republican voters, even though a house-to-house check found only 81 Republicans living in the district.[27]

Although Platt had an office in lower Manhattan, he conducted most of his political business at the Fifth Avenue Hotel at 23rd Street, which for many years had been the Republican Party's unofficial headquarters. Because upstate GOP leaders were otherwise occupied during the week, most important meetings were held there on Sunday, after Platt had saved his soul at Parkhurst's church on the other side of Madison Square, which for him served as a kind of buffer between church and state. On two sofas at the end of a broad hotel corridor, he would confer with his upstate and New York City lieutenants in what were called Platt's "Sunday School classes." The conferences would invariably close with his associates intoning "Amen" as Platt announced a meeting's decision to the reporters who had been waiting nearby, hence bestowing on the spot the name "Amen Corner." According to Chauncey Depew:

"Here were made governors, state senators, and assemblymen, supreme court judges, judges of the Court of Appeals, and members of Congress. Governors thought the capitol was in Albany, yet really took their inspiration and the suggestions for their policies from the Amen Corner. State conventions would meet at Rochester, Syracuse, or Saratoga, but the eight hundred members would wait before acting to know what had been decided in the Amen Corner."

The result was what the politically attuned lawyer Elihu Root described as "invisible government." [28]

✿ ✿ ✿

When the Republicans swept the 1894 statewide elections, Platt saw an opportunity to bring about his long-standing goal of the unification of New York (then including both Manhattan and the Bronx), Brooklyn, Queens and Staten Island into a single New York City. This would permit him to extend his influence and patronage from Manhattan into these other communities. Also, with middle-class Brooklyn more strongly Republican than Tammany-controlled New York, it would give him greater opportunity to exercise that power. A referendum in November, 1894, had shown voter majorities for unification, but in Brooklyn that vote was so close and the opposition so strong that the plan had been set aside. Platt would go to work, however, and in May, 1896, legislation was enacted that approved the new megacity, which would be born on January 1, 1898. [29]

Among the advantages Platt sought to gain from unification would be control of a single Police Board (which also acted as the Board of Elections), and he saw no reason to wait until 1898 for that to happen. He had not been happy over Mayor Strong's appointment of the independent-minded Roosevelt, and saw in the voter displeasure with his Sunday law enforcement an opportunity to remove him without major opposition. Roosevelt also believed that Platt was annoyed that he was supporting his friend House Speaker Thomas Reed for President instead of Platt's candidate, New York Governor Levi P. Morton. On January 19, 1896, he had what he described to Lodge as "a very interesting conference with Platt," which, as might have been expected with the Easy Boss, was conducted "in an entirely pleasant and cold-blooded manner." Although "[w]e got along very well," the message was clear: "They intend to legislate me out in about 60 days." [30]

True to form, Roosevelt was not about to take this lying down. In a previously scheduled meeting the next morning before a group of Methodist ministers, he warned against "many politicians who . . . will bend every energy to destroy us" and, clearly referring to Platt, the "politician who wishes to use the Police Department for his own base purposes." Later in the week, the *Times* entered the fray with front page articles headlining "The Republican Plot to Oust Roosevelt" and "Political Cowards and Assassins Would Strike Him Down for His Honesty and Courage." Realizing that publicity of this sort would undermine his efforts to have Morton nominated by a Republican convention that would want to avoid even the merest whiff of scandal, Platt backed off. Roosevelt was safe, at least for the present. [31]

Nevertheless, his days of real power and glory as Police Commissioner were now behind him. Unhappily, he wrote to his sister that "I usually get home in the evening between six and seven," and that "If it wasn't wrong I should say that personally I would rather welcome a foreign war." At about the same time, he discovered that fellow Commissioner Andrew D. Parker, whom he regarded as a close ally on departmental matters, had turned against him. Their disagreement soon became a matter of public knowledge. As with his Civil Service Commission post two years earlier, he realized that it was time to seek greener pastures elsewhere. [32]

5

The Road To Cuba
And Beyond

Two years earlier, when Roosevelt had been looking for new horizons, he had turned to New York. He now saw his future back in Washington. The financial panic of 1893 was continuing and showed no signs of abating. Coupled with significant labor unrest, it made it likely that the Republican Presidential nominee would be elected in November. Roosevelt wanted to be an important part of his administration.

This would have been easy if the candidate had been Roosevelt's good friend, House Speaker Thomas Reed. Well before the Republican convention opened in June in St. Louis, however, it had become clear that the delegates instead would choose former Ohio Congressman and Governor William McKinley. An affable, outgoing man, his priggish character was well suited to this late Victorian era.[1] Roosevelt regarded him as a straddler "whose firmness I utterly distrust" and later would describe him as having "no more backbone than a chocolate eclair." What counted in St. Louis, however, was not only his popularity with the delegates, but also that he was the candidate of the powerful Ohio industrialist and political boss Marcus Alonzo Hanna, whose major goal in life was to make McKinley President.[2]

Roosevelt had previously been concerned that his position as a Police Commissioner would make it inappropriate for him to participate actively in Presidential politics. His desire to move to Washington was so strong, however, that he set aside both these doubts and his concern over McKinley's qualifications, and at once passed the word to the nominee's advisers that "I shall, of course, do everything in my power for him." [3] His appetite to campaign for McKinley was whetted by the surprise choice of populist Nebraska Congressman William Jennings Bryan as the Democratic nominee following his electrifying "Cross of Gold" convention speech. Roosevelt expressed the opinion of most of his economic and social class when he wrote to his sister Bamie that "[n]ot since the Civil War has there been a Presidential election fraught with so much consequence to the country." [4] Thus, after re-charging his mind and body with a three-week Western hunting vacation, in mid-September he plunged into the fray, speaking first in New York State and then across the upper Middle West as he closely followed Bryan's campaign train.* McKinley himself conducted a "front porch" campaign while, as Roosevelt later observed, Hanna "[m]arketed him as if he were a patent medicine." [5] With the Republicans warning of an economic disaster to both businessmen and their employees if Bryan were elected, McKinley won a close but nevertheless decisive victory.

❦ ❦ ❦

The Washington position that Roosevelt coveted was Assistant Secretary of the Navy. Ever since he had written his *Naval War of 1812*, he had been interested in naval matters. He was also a strong disciple of the influential historian Alfred Thayer Mahan, who had cogently argued that a strong navy was essential to national security. Immediately following McKinley's election, and through Lodge, he began to press his case, but soon came up against two major obstacles. The first was the President-elect, who voiced his concern with Roosevelt to the wife of an old Ohio colleague:

"I want peace and I am told that your friend Theodore – whom

---

* In the twentieth century, speakers who followed opposition candidates in order to refute their arguments would style themselves as "truth squads."

I know only slightly — is always getting into rows with everybody.
I am afraid he is too pugnacious." [6]

The second problem was Platt. The Easy Boss was not content with
his control of New York's Republican Party. Ever since his short time in
the Senate prior to his resignation during the 1881 Conkling-Garfield
debacle, he had hoped to return to that exclusive legislative club. The
Republican control of the New York legislature gave him his chance. In
1897, with the 17th Amendment to the Constitution still 18 years in the
future, in many states, including New York, United States Senators
were chosen by the legislature instead of the voting public. The only
person willing to challenge Platt in that arena was Manhattan lawyer
Joseph H. Choate.

The 64-year-old Choate was a long-time friend of the Roosevelt
family. After winning his first Assembly seat in 1881, Roosevelt wrote to
him that "I owe both my nomination and election more to you than to
any other man." [7] But Roosevelt was above all a realist and recognized
that his support of Choate would have no effect on the Platt-dominat-
ed Republican legislative majority. He also knew that with Platt in the
Senate he stood no chance of obtaining the Navy Depart-ment position
without the Easy Boss's support. Thus, when a prominent Republican
industrialist hosted a "harmony" dinner for party leaders on December
16, 1896, Roosevelt was one of the guests. The next day he wrote to
Lodge that "Platt was exceedingly polite." [8]

Throughout the winter, Roosevelt did his best to put himself in the
good graces of the new Senator. Nevertheless, despite the encouraging
efforts of Lodge and others with McKinley and his Washington associates, the Easy Boss continued to hold out. The official word to Roosevelt was that Platt had nothing against him but could not agree to
Roosevelt "receiving a place which ought to be credited to the organization." Privately, however, Washington insiders were saying that Platt
"hates Roosevelt like the plague." The frustrated suitor agreed, writing

to his sister on March 20 that "I have no ardent backers from New York State and the machine leaders hate me more than any other man." [9]

Platt's lieutenants, however, had become convinced that Roosevelt would be less troublesome to them if he was in Washington building up the Navy than if he continued to enforce public morality as a New York City police commissioner. Thus, just as Roosevelt was about to give up, they convinced the Easy Boss that he should not stand in the way if McKinley decided to appoint him. Meanwhile, help had come in the person of newly appointed Navy Secretary John D. Long, an indolent hypochondriac who was dreading the oppressive heat of the long Washington summer. When Roosevelt made it known that he would "stay in Washington, hot weather or any other weather" so that the Secretary could escape to his cooler Massachusetts home, Long went to bat for him. On April 6, McKinley sent Roosevelt's name to the Senate, and the exultant nominee telegraphed Lodge that "Sinbad has evidently landed the old man of the sea." When the Senate confirmed the appointment two days later, Platt was not in the chamber, hoping that by his absence he would demonstrate that he was not sponsoring his nemesis. [10]

❋ ❋ ❋

As might have been expected, as soon as Roosevelt arrived in Washington, he hit the ground running. Although he was always careful to show respect for his "boss," he at once made it clear that he was not one to operate only through official channels. He had no difficulty in bypassing Secretary Long to give often unsolicited advice to other members of the Administration. Perhaps because his upper story office in the east side of what is now the Executive Office Building looked down on the White House, the recipients of his missives included the President. Thus, on April 22, 1897, less than two weeks after assuming office, he wrote to McKinley, "In view of the dispatch by the Japanese of their protected cruiser *Naniwa* to Hawaii, I would like to inform you as to the vessels at Hawaii and those which could be sent there." * Four days later, he directed the President's attention to the other side of the world as he warned that it was "inadvisable to send a battleship to the Mediterranean unless we intend to make a demonstration in force, in which case we should send certainly three or four armored vessels, and not only one." He then listed the ships he had in mind.[11]

Roosevelt's views as to the uses of naval power were strongly colored by his firmly held opinion that the United States belonged in the ranks of the major world powers and that a strong navy was essential if that goal was to be achieved. The late 1890s were the high point of this imperialistic age, and the model for all aspiring nations was Great Britain, with its string of colonies on every continent, protected by a fleet larger than that of any other two powers. An important element of the imperialist doctrine was the Darwinian concept of the survival of the fittest. As British Prime Minister Lord Salisbury put it in an 1898 speech, " the nations of the world" could be divided between "the living and the dying" and:

"For one reason or another . . . the living nations will gradually encroach on the territory of the dying and the seeds and causes of conflict among the civilized nations will speedily appear. Of course, it is not to be supposed that any nation of the living nations will be allowed to have the monopoly of curing or cutting up these unfortunate patients and the controversy is as to who shall have the privilege of doing so and in what measure he shall do it. These things may introduce causes of fatal differences between the

---

* In 1897, Hawaii was an independent republic. The Harrison Administration had tried to annex it, but before the Senate could ratify the treaty, Grover Cleveland had become President and opposed the proposal. Partly because of the large Japanese population in Hawaii, Japan hoped eventually to acquire the islands and occasionally sent its naval vessel *Naniwa* there to show its interest.

great nations whose mighty armies stand opposed threatening each other." [12]

Roosevelt, however, viewed the spirit of the age with none of the concern felt by the cautious and careworn 66-year-old Prime Minister. Instead, as he proclaimed in a well-publicized June 2, 1897, speech at the Naval War College in Newport, Rhode Island:

> "No triumph of peace is quite so great as the triumphs of war . . . It may be that at some time in the dim future of the race the need for war will vanish, but that time as yet is ages distant. As yet no nation can hold its place in the world, or can do any work worth doing, unless it stands ready to guard its rights with armed hand." [13]

To Roosevelt and his fellow believers like Lodge, the testing time was at hand. In nearby Cuba, an insurrection had expanded into revolutionary war with Spain. Since its "discovery" by Columbus, except for a year's interval during the Seven Years' War in the mid-18th century, the "Pearl of the Antilles" had been under Spanish rule and was her richest colony. From the earliest days of the American Republic, Cuba's northern neighbor had recognized its strategic importance in the Caribbean and Gulf of Mexico, and in 1848 President Polk had offered to purchase the island but had been abruptly rebuffed.

By late 1896, the initial Spanish efforts to defeat the insurgents had failed, and they had expanded their operations, burning the island's most profitable sugar plantations. In October, Madrid's response was to send as the new governor general the ruthless General Valeriano Weyler, who herded the peasants into penned-up areas, where they could no longer assist the rebels and could themselves be held as hostages. Their food supplies were inadequate, and thousands soon died from starvation and disease. In the United States, the "yellow press," with William Randolph Hearst's New York *Journal* in the lead, lost no opportunity to dramatize the war in all its lurid details. Much of what it reported was overdrawn and some of it was untrue, but the public and the politicians generally accepted it without question. Among the American correspondents in Cuba was the renowned Richard Harding Davis, who in 1895 had reported favorably on Roosevelt's activities as Police Commissioner, and now movingly described the destruction of the countryside and the firing squad execution of at least one insurgent. Davis was accompanied by artist Frederic Remington to whom, in response to his report that there was nothing worth painting, Hearst reportedly replied, "Please remain. You furnish the picture and I'll furnish the war." [14]

Even before he took up his Washington position, Roosevelt had believed that the United States should aid the Cuban insurgents. His April 26, 1897, memorandum to McKinley itemized possible courses the Navy should take to be prepared for "complications," "trouble," or a "crisis" relating to the island. On August 3, he wrote to Lodge that "I do feel that it would be everything for us to take firm action on behalf of the wretched Cubans." [15] But McKinley as a Civil War veteran had personally experienced war's horrors, and was not prepared to commit the United States to actions that might involve it in war with what some still regarded as a major foreign power. The goal of his Administration was to further business prosperity — not to embark on a foreign adventure whose outcome was uncertain.

Nevertheless, Roosevelt lost no opportunity to impress on the President what, as he wrote to Lodge, "ought to be done if things looked menacing about Spain, urging the necessity of taking an immediate and prompt initiative." His proposals included sending an expeditionary force to Cuba and dispatching the Asiatic squadron to "blockade, and, if possible, take, Manila." The pace of his activities, if anything, increased during Long's two month 1897 summer vacation when, as described in a report in the August 23 New York *Sun*, he "has the whole Navy bordering on a war footing. It remains only to sand down the decks and pipe to quarters for action." As soon as Long returned to Washington, Roosevelt resumed his efforts to convince his placid chief of "the Navy Department doing all it can to further a steady and rapid buildup of our Navy" including six new battleships, six large cruisers and seventy-five torpedo boats. [16]

❀ ❀ ❀

Even as he was trying to put the Navy on a war footing and bring the United States into the Cuban conflict, Roosevelt continued his keen interest in New York politics and tried to maintain an amicable relationship with Platt. Thus, when the Easy Boss was having difficulty in obtaining membership in Washington's exclusive Metropolitan Club, on June 16, 1897, his old enemy wrote to the Club's Board of Governors to quash as "utterly unfounded" rumors that Platt "cares nothing for club life at home and would probably not care for it here but would use the club to put up constituents." [17] Shortly thereafter, the *Times* reported that the two men "had been seen together frequently in Washington of late," and suggested that this "re-established friendship" meant that Platt was considering running Roosevelt for New York City Mayor "to head off the boom" for Columbia University President and former Brooklyn reform Mayor Seth Low.[18]

Roosevelt was absorbed by his new position and had no interest in that idea, if indeed Platt had even proposed it. He watched with dismay as Low announced that he would run as the nonpartisan candidate of what Roosevelt regarded as the "ultra wing" of the New York Citizens Union, and Platt angrily rejected him as the Republican nominee in favor of former Navy Secretary Benjamin Tracy. [19] * Privately, Roosevelt supported Low for, as he wrote Lodge, he believed that the Republican ticket

---

* Platt had already turned down Mayor Strong for renomination because he had not sufficiently cooperated with the Republican machine.

"does represent exactly what the populists say, that is corrupt wealth . . . I am glad I am out of it. I would have no heart in a campaign against my own organization, and yet I could not with self respect support men who have done everything they could to nullify the work I did for two years."

With the anti-Tammany vote split between Low and Tracy, the result was a plurality of more than 80,000 votes for Democrat Robert Van Wyck, an obscure municipal court judge with a good Dutch name whom Croker had pulled off the bench to run for Mayor. When the result was announced, the Tammanyites paraded through the streets chanting, "Well, well, well. Reform has gone to Hell!" To Roosevelt the election was "an overwhelming disaster, partly because the reform or Citizens Union element behaved with such perversity, but infinitely more because the Platt machine were equally stupid, and a great deal more immoral." [20]

❁ ❁ ❁

The new year 1898, which was probably to be the most important in Roosevelt's life, dawned on a hopeful note with the beginning of a new and more conciliatory Spanish policy toward Cuba. Within less than two weeks, however, riots broke out in Havana, apparently instigated by Spanish army officers who opposed the partial autonomy that had just been granted. On January 24, the McKinley Administration sent the battleship *Maine* to Havana, ostensibly to support the new Spanish policy, but in fact to protect American lives and property. On the evening of February 15, the *Maine* blew up in Havana harbor with the loss of more than 250 of the 350 men aboard. Although the United States and Spain immediately began official investigations into the cause of the explosion, most of the American public, whose emotions were fanned by the press, had made up its mind: the Spaniards had blown up the *Maine* and the United States should go to war.

Officially Roosevelt maintained a noncommittal position; privately he expressed no doubt: although "it will go down an accident," in fact the *Maine* "was sunk by an act of dirty treachery on the part of the Spaniards." [21] * Even before the *Maine* left for Cuba, he had persuaded Long that the powerful North Atlantic Squadron should be sent to Key West so that it could attack Havana without delay in the event of war. [22] On February 25, when Long left the Navy Department in charge of the Assistant Secretary while he received a treatment by his osteopath, Roosevelt took advantage of his several hour's authority to arrange for large stocks of coal and ammunition, designate points where navy units could rendezvous if war was declared, make plans for a possible auxiliary fleet, and ask Congress for legislation permitting the unlimited recruitment of women. Roosevelt's most important act that afternoon, however, and the one for which posterity would remember him, was his telegram to Commodore George Dewey, ordering him to concentrate his Asiatic Squadron at Hong Kong and, in the event of the war with Spain, to "commence offensive operations in the Philippine Islands." As a result, as soon as war was declared, Dewey was able to sail immediately to Manila and destroy the Spanish fleet that was protecting the Philippines. The peace treaty signed later in the year awarded the islands to the United States, which, except for their occupation by Japan during World War II, retained them until it gave them independence in 1946. More than 50 years later, a noted historian commented:

> "The Assistant Secretary had seized the opportunity given by Long's absence to insure our grabbing the Philippines with- out a decision to do so by either Congress, the President, or least of all the people. This was important history made not by economic forces or democratic decisions, but through the grasping of chance authority by a man with daring and a program." [23]

---

* The actual cause of the disaster was never determined.

Throughout March and early April, as war fever in the United States mounted, Spain gradually made concessions that in time would almost surely have led to Cuban independence. It was a case of "too little, too late," however, as McKinley's advisers told him that he must lead the country into war or run a serious risk of destroying the Republican Party. On April 11, he sent Congress a message stating that "I have exhausted every effort to relieve the intolerable condition of affairs which is at our doors," and leaving to the legislators the issue of peace or war. On April 19, they responded by passing a joint resolution authorizing him to use military force to drive the Spanish from Cuba. McKinley signed it the next day. [24]

❦ ❦ ❦

On January 13, more than a month before the sinking of the *Maine*, Roosevelt had told Long that if war came, he planned "to abandon everything and go to the front." The same day he wrote a letter to the same effect to a friend who was Adjutant General of New York, adding that although "I believe I can get a commission as a major or a lieutenant colonel in one of the regiments, I want your help and the Governor's." He added that "I believe I would be of some use with the President in seeing that the New York troops, or some of them, were at once used in active service." [25]

When war actually came, however, Roosevelt would not serve as the officer of a New York regiment. Apparently at the suggestion of the territorial governor of what later became the State of New Mexico, the call for volunteers that Secretary of War Russell Alger prepared for McKinley's signature included a provision for three regiments "to be formed exclusively of frontiersmen possessing special qualifications as horsemen and marksmen." When Alger offered Roosevelt the command of the first regiment, the Assistant Navy Secretary surprisingly turned down the offer on the basis that he had no military experience. Instead, Alger accepted his suggestion that he would serve as lieutenant colonel under his friend Leonard Wood, who had won fame as victor over the Apache Chief Geronimo. [26]

When Roosevelt announced his decision, most of his friends were appalled. Henry Adams, among others, suggested that he had gone mad. One acquaintance concluded that "Theodore is wild to fight and hack and hew . . . of course this ends his political career for good." The press also was almost unanimous in questioning his decision, arguing that he would be most useful to the country if he stayed in the Navy Department, where he had been doing an outstanding job. The New York *Sun* struck the common chord: "Is not his work organizing war infinitely more important to the country than any part, however useful and glorious, which he could play as an officer in the field? We are convinced it is." [27]

Roosevelt, however, had made up his mind and would not change it. Even before McKinley sent his war message to Congress, he had written to his brother-in-law Douglas Robinson that

". . . it does not seem to me that it would be honorable for a man who has consistently advocated a warlike policy not to be willing himself to bear the brunt of carrying out that policy. I have a horror of the people who bark but don't bite."

To the editor of the *Sun*, which had praised the sense of chivalry and patriotism that had led him to go to war, he explained that although the Navy "is not of course in exactly the shape I should like to see it, . . . still it is in very good shape indeed, and will respond nobly to any demand made upon it." He added that "I don't expect any military glory out of this Cuban war, more than what is implied in the honorable performance of duty." [28]

If Roosevelt really believed this last statement, he was seriously deluding himself. His decision to go to war as the leader of a regiment of cowboys struck the country's fancy as nothing else could. If all this were not enough, he conceived the idea that among its Western cowhands and frontiersmen should be sprinkled a number of well known athletes and other young men from the East's most elite aristocracy. The result was that for the war's duration the press would provide the contingent's activities with coverage that was far out of proportion to their actual importance. Roosevelt would be the primary beneficiary.

Although Wood was officially in charge, as far as the public was concerned it was Roosevelt's regiment, and after he let it be known that he did not like himself to be referred to as "Teddy" in its popular title, it quickly became known as Roosevelt's Rough Riders. [29]*

❀ ❀ ❀

After several weeks of training at the San Antonio, Texas, fair grounds, the Rough Riders left for Tampa, Florida, where an expeditionary force was being formed to attack the Spanish position at Santiago, on Cuba's southeastern coast. At each stop during the four-day cross-country train ride, crowds clamored to see "Teddy." When the Rough Riders arrived at Tampa, they found the confused results of a country trying to put together a volunteer army overnight. During the evening of June 8, when the order came from Washington for the invasion force to board steamers in Port Tampa, nine miles away, it was every regiment for itself, and "first come, first served." Demonstrating their special tactics in a free-for all and unable to secure conventional transport, the Rough Riders commandeered a train of approaching coal cars and persuaded the engineer to take them there in reverse gear. On arrival, the soot-covered troops spotted the steamer *Yucatan*, which was just entering the harbor, but which had already been assigned to two other regiments. As Roosevelt recalled with relish:

"... I double-quicked the regiment up to the boat, just in time to board her as she came into the quay, and then to hold her against the Second Regulars and the [New York] Seventy-first,

---

* To his family and close friends, he was always called Theodore

Roosevelt as Assistant Secretary of the Navy
(Courtesy of the Corbis-Bettman Archives)

Roosevelt in his uniform as an officer of the Rough Riders
(Courtesy of the Corbis-Bettman Archives)

who had arrived a little late, being a shade less ready than we were in the matter of individual initiative." [30]

When the breathless New Yorkers came up a few minutes later, Roosevelt met them at the gangplank, announcing to their commanding officer, "We were here first, Colonel, and we intend to stay." Then, when he spotted a pair of photographers lugging a primitive 60-pound camera and tripod, who told him that "we are going over to Cuba to take moving pictures of the war," as one of them later wrote:

"Roosevelt's zeal for publicity was alive and roaring. He beckoned up. 'I can't take care of a regiment but I might be able to handle two men.' " [31]

After several stifling days during which the recently boarded expeditionary force was kept in port until it could be assured that it would not be attacked en route by a Spanish naval force, it finally sailed on June 14. Following an uneventful voyage in calm seas, its first units landed seven days later without opposition 18 miles east of Santiago and quickly pushed inland. Although he had not been scheduled to land until after most of the regulars, Roosevelt persuaded a former Navy Department colleague to let the *Yucatan* steam to within a few hundred miles of shore, where the Rough Riders, now horseless, disembarked that evening. [32]

Once on land, they were assigned to the division commanded by General Joseph Wheeler. A former Confederate cavalry general, who had won renown by "never staying still in one place long enough for the Almighty to put a finger on him," he disregarded orders and pushed some of his force, including the Rough Riders, ahead of other troops commanded by former Union war hero General Henry W. Lawton. Early on June 24, they attacked a 1500-man Spanish force that was protecting a mountain pass on the road to Santiago called Las Guasimas. After several hours of hard fighting, in which the Rough Riders distinguished themselves, but during which Wheeler had to call for help from Lawton, the Spanish retreated, causing the excited Wheeler to cry, "We've got the damn Yankees on the run!"

To Roosevelt, the victory was especially satisfying. As he wrote to Lodge three days later:

"Well, whatever comes I shall feel contented with having left the Navy Department to go into the army, for our regiment has been in the first fight on land, and has done well." [33]

❀ ❀ ❀

Several days passed while the American force readied itself for the final attack on the Spanish lines outside Santiago. To its west, between it and Santiago was a series of hills known as the San Juan Heights, the most prominent being San Juan Hill. The American plan was for Lawton first to capture a fortified hill to the northeast called El Caney and then join the main force, which included the Rough Riders, for an attack on the Heights. Unfortunately, although it had begun at 6:30 a.m. on the beautifully clear morning of July 1, by early afternoon Lawton's assault on El Caney had made little progress. Meanwhile, the American troops that were waiting to advance on the Heights were exposed to destructive Spanish artillery fire, but without any word from headquarters a mile and a half to the rear that would extricate them from their penned up position. [34]

Finally, around 1:00 p.m. they received the order to attack. Their's was not a charge as the public would idealize it, with bayonets fixed and in massed array. Instead, according to Richard Harding Davis' first-hand account, they "held their guns pressed upon their breasts and stepped heavily as they climbed, . . . slipping and scrambling in the smooth grass, moving forward with difficulty, . . . slowly, carefully, and with strenuous effort." [35] The Rough Riders were on the extreme right of the line. By now, due to the illness of his superiors, Wood had been placed in charge of a brigade. Thus, Roosevelt was now their commander, with the title of Colonel. Their goal was the summit of an elevation

to the east of the northern end of the Heights called Kettle Hill. They
quickly reached the top, but then came under fire from the Spaniards
on the Heights to the southwest. When they also saw other American
troops moving up to attack that position, "[o]bviously," Roosevelt
wrote later, "the proper thing to do was help them." For ten minutes
he directed a rifle fire on the Spanish position and then decided to add
his force to the attack. The Rough Riders and other dismounted cavalry followed him in a mad dash down Kettle Hill and up the grassy slope
beyond. By the time they reached the top of San Juan Heights, they saw
the defenders fleeing west toward Santiago. Not all of the enemy had
departed, however, and Roosevelt had his only opportunity for face-
to-face combat.

> "I was with Harry Bardshar, running up at the double, and two
> Spaniards leaped from the trenches and fired at us, not ten yards
> away. As they turned to run, I closed in and fired twice, missing
> the first and killing the second." [36]*

Contrary to the myth that soon developed, the Rough Riders did
not lead the American attack on the Heights, and did not actually attack San Juan Hill. It was small wonder, however, that the public had
this misconception in view of the press coverage that they received. Especially laudatory of their gallantry was Richard Harding Davis, who
had accompanied the regiment, and, according to Roosevelt, "gave us
our first opportunity to shoot back with effect" by spotting the exact
location from which the Spaniards had been firing on them. Roosevelt
cited Davis in his official report, and tried to get the Associated Press
correspondent to mention Davis in his account of the battle. Not surprisingly, particularly since the Rough Riders had indeed participated
in the attack, Davis was effusive in their praise. [37]

❁ ❁ ❁

---

* For the rest of his life, he would be known and addressed as Colonel Roosevelt.

For Roosevelt personally, the charge was to be the most important event of his life. As a close personal friend later observed, in spite of or indeed because of all its gore, to him it was a "glorious personal experience." For the moment, however, he was concentrating on what he believed was a failure in military leadership, centered in the expeditionary force's commander, the 63-year-old 300-pound General William R. Shafter. On July 3, the Spanish Atlantic squadron had been destroyed by the blockading United States fleet as it tried to escape from Santiago harbor. However, as Roosevelt wrote to Lodge two days later, in the case of the Army units, under the "criminally incompetent" Shafter: "The siege guns have not yet been landed! The mortars have not been started from the landing place. . . . There is no head; the orders follow each other in rapid succession, and are confused and contradictory to a degree." On July 10, he complained that "Shafter is tacking and veering as to whether or not he will close with the Spaniards' request to allow them to walk out unmolested." He added that "it will be a great misfortune to accept less than unconditional surrender." [38]

To some extent Roosevelt was correct. Shafter was so "panic stricken" that, following the taking of the Heights and prior to the naval victory, he had been considering a retreat. But the commanding officer's concerns were not entirely unfounded, since his July 1 victory had cost in casualties one-tenth of his 15,000 man army, and the normally aggressive Wheeler had predicted that a successful attack on Santiago would result in 3000 more. Shafter also worried that a long siege at the outset of the yellow fever season would lead to heavier losses than the Spanish army could inflict. Thus, when the Spanish commander proposed on July 9 to give up the city provided his troops could return to Spain, Shafter was receptive. After several days of negotiations with both the Spaniards and Shafter's hawkish superiors in Washington, who favored unconditional surrender, it was finally agreed that Santiago's defenders could "capitulate" rather than the more humiliating "surrender." On July 17, they did so in a ceremony that one reporter described as resembling "a meeting of old friends and not the acknowledgment of defeat." [39]

❊ ❊ ❊

At least one of Shafter's fears had been well founded. Malaria was already beginning to spread through his army. On August 2, he cabled the War Department that "at any time a yellow fever epidemic is likely to occur" and urged that his troops be moved as soon as possible. He hoped to send the major part of his army back to the United States. Washington's response, however, was anything but encouraging. Based on confusing earlier reports, Secretary of War Alger and his colleagues believed that, instead of worsening, the army's health was improving. Also, because they were unaware of the cause of yellow fever, they were afraid that bringing the sick troops home would introduce the disease into the United States. Thus, Alger's response was to suggest that Shafter move his army by train to the hills above Santiago and keep it there until the sickness had run its course. [40]

Alger's proposal was unrealistic. The railroad that he thought could transport the sick soldiers to the hills was no longer operative. In addition, the supposedly dry area to which the troops were supposed to move was even rainier than the army's present location. Shafter's response to the War Department's proposal was both prompt and alarming: if his army was not promptly shipped back to the United States, "I believe the death rate will be appalling." [41]

Due to his reputation for excess timidity, Shafter was far from confident that his superiors would approve his recommendation. Thus, after writing Alger, he called a meeting of his senior officers and included Roosevelt. After discussing what they believed was an impending catastrophe, they decided to take their case to the American public. In part because Roosevelt, as a volunteer, was not subject to charges of military insubordination, Shafter asked him to prepare a letter describing the medical situation and give it to the press. Looking out for his friend's future interests, Leonard Wood suggested that Roosevelt instead merely prepare a draft which would be signed by Shafter and all his leading officers. The result was an August 5 "round robin" letter that expressed the army's plight in the strongest possible language:

"We, the undersigned officers . . . are of the unanimous opinion that the army is disabled by malarial fever to the extent that its efficiency is destroyed, and that it is in a condition to be practically entirely destroyed by an epidemic of yellow fever, which is sure to come in the near future. . . .

"The army must move at once or perish. As the army can be safely moved now, the persons responsible for preventing such a move will be responsible for the unnecessary loss of many thousands of lives."

Roosevelt wrote Shafter a separate letter that expressed a similar opinion, and both were handed to an Associated Press reporter. Thus, when McKinley, Alger and the rest of the American public opened their newspapers the next morning, they were shocked by reports of an incipient disaster.[42]

This extreme action was unnecessary. Alger and his colleagues had been sufficiently frightened by Shafter's earlier warning that they had already prepared orders for him to move to the mainland all troops not required in Cuba "at once, using the ships you have to their limit." When Roosevelt's work on the "round robin" became public, however, the public gave him credit for saving the army from disaster and helped distance him from the reports of official mismanagement of the war that were already beginning to spread. Meanwhile, on the morning of August 7, the Rough Riders were included in the first contingent of troops that sailed for the United States.[43]

6

Waiting For Roosevelt

SINCE EARLY IN THE MORNING OF A SUNNY AUGUST 15, A CROWD HAD been gathering on the beach at Montauk, Long Island's extreme eastern end. Through the daily press, it had learned that later that morning, the first contingent of troops would be arriving from Cuba on their way to the nearby newly built Camp Wikoff, where they would be quarantined for yellow fever and other contagious tropical diseases. Among the units scheduled to land that day were the famous Rough Riders, and the ever-growing throng was especially interested in seeing them and their leader, Colonel Theodore Roosevelt.

At about 10:45 a.m., the transport *Miami* came into view about three miles offshore, and a half hour later she had docked at the pier. Wheeler, wearing a spotless half-dress coat, was the first man ashore. Then, to even louder cheers, he was followed by Roosevelt, clad in a new brown canvas uniform. Next came the Rough Riders. Thinned and weakened by inadequate rations and malaria and other diseases, their dispirited appearance shocked the onlookers who had come to give them an enthusiastic welcome. Roosevelt, however, was the picture of good health, with a ruddy complexion and apparently having suffered no loss in weight despite the rigors of the campaign. To questioning reporters, he seemed embarrassed by his condition, saying, "Really, I am ashamed of myself, feeling so well and strong, with all these poor fellows suffering and so weak they can hardly stand."[1]

On his first morning ashore, all that Roosevelt wanted to talk about was his regiment, "all a lot of crack-a-jacks. . . . It's the finest regiment that ever was and I'm proud to command it." Thus, as the *Herald*

reported, he "threw up his hands in a gesture of vehement depreca-
tion" and answered, "I won't say a word about myself" in response to
the question of the hour "shouted" by "half a dozen men in one breath
... 'Will you be our next Governor?'" [2]

✾ ✾ ✾

During his last weeks in Cuba, Roosevelt was aware of talk that he
might become a candidate for high office. On July 12, after "a long talk"
with the editors of the New York *Sun*, Lodge had written to him that
"what we want for you is the Senate but it looks as if the drift was very
strong to make you Governor and that may lead to the Senate next
winter." With memories of previous political experiences, however,
Roosevelt was skeptical. As he responded:

"... If I could get down to National politics instead of dealing
with sewers and police boards in New York, I should prefer it, but
I haven't any real knack of getting on in politics, and the favor of
the multitude (especially when extended about equally to our
regiment, which has an almost unequaled record, and the 71st
New York, which did very badly) is a matter of about ten days. The
good people of New York at present seem to be crazy over me; it is
not very long since on the whole they felt I compared unfavor-
ably with Caligula. By the time election comes round they may
have reverted to their former feeling, and in any event I don't
know how to get on with the New York politicians. If I had
enough money to keep in National politics it would not be difficult, because the average New York boss is quite willing to allow
you to do as you wish in such trivial matters as the war and the
acquisition of Puerto Rico and Hawaii provided you don't interfere with the really vital questions, such as giving out contracts
for cartage in the Custom House and interfering with the appointment of street sweepers."

"[W]hile this war lasts," he told Lodge, "the only thing I want to do is to command this regiment and get it into all the fighting I can." He hoped, after the Rough Riders had recuperated, to lead them in what he referred to as "the great Havana campaign." It therefore may have been a disappointment to their Colonel to learn, that three days before he landed at Montauk, on August 12, the warring parties had agreed to a cease fire, with peace negotiations to commence in several weeks. What his friend John Hay described to him as "a splendid little war" had ended, and with it Roosevelt's military career. Thus, he could now consider a possible return to politics with an entirely different mindset. [3]

❧ ❧ ❧

Just as Roosevelt's personal situation had changed, so also had the outlook for New York State's Republican Party. Incumbent Governor Frank S. Black was in trouble, and his reelection in November was becoming increasingly doubtful. Riding on McKinley's coattails, Black had been handily elected in 1896, carrying with him a Republican majority of more than two-thirds in both houses of the legislature. He had been a popular Congressman from Rochester, who previously had won fame as a lawyer in prosecuting election frauds in Troy and in sending the notorious murderer of a Republican election inspector to the electric chair. Black was also an effective speaker, with what was described as "originality of thought, aptness and piquancy of metaphor, and humor of a fresh and vigorous order." At the Saratoga nominating convention, there had been other strong candidates, including another up-and-coming Congressman, Benjamin B. Odell of Newburgh. Platt, who controlled the convention, initially leaned toward Odell, who was backed by most of his lieutenants. He quickly switched his support to Black, however, when he learned that Odell would be unlikely to support the New York City unification that was so dear to the heart of the Easy Boss. [4]

Black had hardly taken over the reins in Albany before he ran into trouble with New York's good government forces, including those who had supported him. One of his first actions was to appoint as Superintendent of Insurance Louis F. Payn, the Republican boss of Columbia County * and a key Platt associate of many years standing, who had been influential in securing Black's nomination. Payn was a notorious lobbyist who had promoted the interests of Jay Gould and other equally unscrupulous businessmen. As Roosevelt later wrote, in his new position,

> "Being a frugal man, out of his seven thousand dollars a year salary, he has saved enough money to enable him to borrow nearly half a million dollars from a trust company, the directors of which are also the directors of an insurance company . . . under his supervision."

Payn's selection had been rumored for several weeks, and was the subject of strong opposition, but, as the *Times* reported from Albany on February 1, 1897, after "a battle which has been bitterly waging for a month," the nomination was delivered to the Senate that evening "in a large blue envelope." By then the outcome was assured, for "[t]he programme for the completion of the job has been agreed on in detail, and its execution is in the hands of the ablest machine leaders." [5]

Other actions by the new Governor soon led many of his former supporters to agree with the editors of the Buffalo *Express*, who wrote on February 2 regarding Black's appointment of Payn:

> "He has made his own the low standard of political morals which bars honesty and fitness from consideration in the choice of public officials and looks upon the man who has been most unscrupulous in politics as the man most worthy of political rewards."

---

* When once accused of voting "tombstones" in that bailiwick, Payn reportedly replied that all he had done was cast the same votes the deceased would have registered had they lived: "We always respect a man's convictions."

Even as the Payn appointment was pending, Black named one of the lobbyist's cohorts, Rochester boss George W. Aldridge, to the patronage-laden post of Superintendent of Public Works. He next persuaded the legislature to amend the civil service law to add an examination of "fitness" to the existing "merit" qualification, thus allowing local bosses to involve themselves in the selection process. To add insult to injury, he announced that he would not extend this new provision to New York City, where the political leadership was likely to be Democratic instead of Republican. Then, after the Democrats had taken over power in most of the State's large cities following the 1897 elections, he obtained an opinion from the Attorney General that the "fitness" standard did not apply to municipal officials but only to State appointees. [6]

Black also suffered from the unhappiness of independents and many Republicans who were not closely allied with the party organization over Platt's refusal to support Seth Low in the 1897 New York City mayoral contest. Although Van Wyck had won with a substantial plurality, he had received less than half the votes cast. If Low had won most of the votes that went to the Republican candidate, they argued, he would have been elected and the city would have been spared a return to Tammany rule. [7]

The 1897 elections saw a sharp reduction in the Republican Assembly majority. Black seemed to read this as handwriting on the wall, and during the 1898 session, took pains to support legislation backed by the independents, including a bill regarding primaries that was supported by good government forces. At the same time, however, he risked offending Platt by not making the required visits to the Amen Corner, and by expressing increasing doubts as to the New York City unification legislation that the Assembly was considering. Although fear of reprisal led him to sign the measure, the fact that he was even considering crossing Platt on this issue troubled the Easy Boss. [8]

As spring turned into summer, knowledgeable observers expected nevertheless that the Governor would be renominated when the Republican convention met in Saratoga in late September. Shortly thereafter, however, two events transpired which transformed the political outlook. The first involved the Erie Canal. Its completion in the 1820s had been instrumental in the development of upstate New York, and its use to send products from the Great Lakes to the Atlantic had ensured New York City's preeminence as a business and financial center. The growth of railroads at mid-century reduced the Canal's importance, but by the 1890s it was still heavily used in the shipment of coal, grain and other products for which cost savings were more important than speed of delivery. The grain traders of New York and Buffalo recognized, however, that a major modernization effort was required if the Canal was to retain its economic viability. In 1894, based on an estimate that it would cost $12,500,000 to increase the Canal's depth from seven feet to nine, the voters approved a Constitutional amendment authorizing the legislature to proceed with the project. When it did so the next year, without any engineering advice and apparently out of a desire to save money, it approved spending only $9,000,000. [9]

From the outset the project ran into trouble. The work was turned over to Superintendent of Public Works Aldridge, who applied the recently enacted "fitness" standard to appoint as division heads such worthies as a man with a former prison record, who in turn selected as his subordinates men with similar backgrounds. An appalled State Comptroller withheld the salary payments of some of them. When the $9,000,000 was about to run out with the essential work less than two-thirds completed, he refused to release additional funds, stating that there was "no right to assume that the people would have authorized the expenditure of nine million had they realized that it would only half do the work." The resulting public hue and cry made an investigation imperative. When Black hesitated in ordering a probe, the clamor became even greater. [10]

The seven man commission that the Governor finally appointed labored from late March, 1898, to the end of July, taking testimony from many witnesses and personally inspecting several portions of the Canal. On Saturday, July 30, it delivered to Black its more than 50,000 page report, which was released to the press the following week. It concluded that there had been "improper expenditures of $1,000,000, exclusive of moneys paid out for ordinary and extraordinary repairs which amount to not less than $1,500,000." The "improper expenditures" included such items as the reclassification of certain excavated material as "rock," thus permitting the contractors, who were presumably friends of Aldridge, to charge more than they would have received for the "earth" listed in the project specifications. While there was no evidence that the Superintendent of Public Works had profited personally, the commission castigated him for a failure to take any action that would have prevented the improper expenditures. [11]

Although the commission's report contained no charges against Black personally, it reactivated the criticism that had been so acute early in his administration. In the public mind, Aldridge was Black's man, and thus the Governor bore responsibility for what was widely viewed as a scandal of major proportions. His prospects were further weakened by the fact that the Canal was dear to the heart of the farmers and other upstate voters who were a core Republican constituency, whose support was essential for the GOP to be returned to power in the upcoming November elections. [12]

❧ ❧ ❧

This brought into play the second factor that changed the New York political landscape: Roosevelt's highly publicized charge up the San Juan Heights. He already had earned a reputation for political independence and honesty, and could not be tarred with the alleged misdeeds of Black and his associates. Now, he had suddenly also become a certified war hero.

The apparently spontaneous Roosevelt boom began as soon as the public had time to digest the thrilling news from Cuba. On July 12, campaign buttons appeared carrying his picture in army uniform surrounded by the Stars and Stripes, over which were the words, "For Governor, Theo Roosevelt." Four days later, under the headline "ROOSEVELT FOR GOVERNOR," a *Times* article opened, "Theodore Roosevelt is coming forward very prominently in connection with the State campaign, and since the fall of Santiago politicians of all classes have been discussing him as a possible candidate for Governor on the Republican ticket." It later cautioned, however, "There are very few . . . who believe that Senator Platt would favor such a nomination." [13]

On July 20, the Republicans of western New York's 1st Assembly District became the first organized group to endorse Roosevelt. Several days later, the conflict between his supporters and Black's cohorts surfaced at an acrimonious meeting at Mott Memorial Hall, on Madison Avenue, of an organization that styled itself the Republicans of the County of New York. That group's leaders initially had hoped to pass a resolution endorsing the Governor for renomination, but apparently had not rounded up enough of his followers to assure themselves a majority that would defeat the vociferous band of Roosevelt men that were also in attendance. When the chairman adjourned the session for lack of a quorum, the Roosevelt supporters, with shouts of "Three cheers for Colonel Theodore Roosevelt, our next Governor!" and "Three groans for Black!," tried to remain and hold a rump session of their own, only to have the lights turned off, leaving them in the dark. When the organization next met on August 9, the resolution supporting Black was tabled and the only action was to condemn the "outrageous mismanagement" of the Canal project and praise "the Republican controller of this State," who first alerted the public to that "deplorable" episode. [14]

The growing popular support for Roosevelt was manifesting itself in different ways. One of them was poetry, as illustrated by a ballad that appeared in a northern New York newspaper. Reprinted in the *Times*, it was titled "Teddy's Prayer":

"Our Teddy called his Riders Rough
Before his tent one day,
And like the Pharisee of old
Thus laid him out to pray:

We thank thee, Lord, that we are not
Like other soldiers here,
We've got the sand and we can stand,
Though bullets whistle near.

We're worth ten thousand State Troops, Lord,
With their archaic arms;
Those fellows ought to know their place
Is home upon their farms.

We thank thee, Lord, we're no such chumps
As these poor regulars,
Who get no glory in this war,
And only bloody scars.

But if you read the papers, Lord,
You'll see your Teddy's name
Is getting well embellished
Upon this roll of fame.

And when this war is over, Lord
And we go home to stay,
You'll see that Teddy gets the votes
Upon election day." [15]

As soon as it was released, the Canal report sent shock waves through the Republican leadership ranks. Inside of a week, according to a front page *Times* article,

"... the outcome of the affair, so far, is that whoever had an idea of placing the name of Gov. Frank S. Black as a candidate for renomination before the coming Republican State Convention had abandoned it absolutely. Most of the Republican politicians are of the opinion that the Gubernatorial bee has buzzed its last buzz in Gov. Black's bonnet. It is considered doubtful even if his name will be mentioned when nominations are made."

During August, the oppressive heat of a New York City summer penetrated even the inner sanctum of the Fifth Avenue Hotel's Amen Corner. Accordingly, Platt had transferred his lodgings to the more salubrious air of the Oriental Hotel facing Sheepshead Bay on Manhattan Beach, at the eastern end of Coney Island. In the 1890s, before its development as a popular amusement area, it was what a mid-20th century guidebook described as the site of "a number of fashionable hotels and piers, immense pinnacled wooden structures benefitting from the imagination and wit of Victorian decoration." A London *Times* correspondent referred to Manhattan Beach as "the resort of the New York businessman, whose business will not suffer him to be at Newport, which is practically a day's journey distant, or the Adirondacks or other remoter haunts of leisured classes." [16]

For Platt, however, there was little time for rest and relaxation. Each evening, he received visits from frightened Republican politicians who brought him daily reports of impending disaster. By week's end, exhausted and discouraged, he fled the hotel with his wife for a hopefully peaceful few days at his son's summer home at Wilkes Borre, Pennsylvania. [17]

When he returned later the next week, however, his troubles reasserted themselves in even more acute form. In less than two weeks, the State Committee would be holding an already scheduled meeting, and, as always, its members would be looking to the Easy Boss for instruction. It was not just the difficult task of replacing a sitting governor who might not give up voluntarily. Equally difficult was finding a candidate who had no connection with the Black administration and would be willing to do Platt's bidding when it counted. Visitors to Manhattan Beach reported that the Easy Boss was considering the names of Secretary of the Interior Cornelius N. Bliss and former Minister to Spain General Stewart L. Woodford. Bliss, however, was happy where he was and would probably turn down a nomination. Even more important, the public would be unlikely to regard either man as an obvious candidate in his own right who would have been seriously considered for the position if he had not been Platt's hand-picked choice. [18]

In his conversations with his lieutenants, the Easy Boss seems to have avoided addressing the real question: What to do with Roosevelt and his increasing popular support? On Sunday, August 14, however, he had two visitors who confronted him directly with the issue. One was Quigg, now a second-term Manhattan Congressman facing a very tough reelection fight and also Chairman of the New York County Republican Committee. Quigg was a loyal Platt follower, and had assisted him in assuring that the Republicans would not back Seth Low in the 1897 mayoral contest. He was also a long-time friend of Roosevelt, and had been instrumental in persuading Mayor Strong to appoint him Police Commissioner. He was therefore in a position to mediate between the Colonel and the Easy Boss.

Quigg was accompanied by Benjamin Odell, now Chairman of the Republican State Committee. Although he was one of Platt's most important lieutenants, he carried a grudge toward the Easy Boss for abandoning him in favor of Black at the 1896 convention. He also saw himself as Platt's eventual successor and was already gradually and unobtrusively taking steps that would lead to that end. Odell could have presented himself as a possible gubernatorial nominee. He was, however, a thorough-going realist who had already shown an astute capacity to analyze and predict political events. Thus, he instinctively recognized that he was too closely associated with Platt to be a viable candidate. Instead, apparently unbeknown to Platt, he had persuaded a political associate to write to Roosevelt in Cuba "suggesting to him that if he would put himself solely in the hands of his friends, under the Organization standard, he could be nominated for Governor." Roosevelt replied that he would not "leave this regiment while the war is on, even for so [great] an office as that of Governor of New York." Apparently Odell believed that this response was sufficiently positive and he immediately started lining up support for the Colonel among prospective convention delegates. [19]

The message that Quigg and Odell delivered to Platt that Sunday afternoon was simple: Roosevelt was the only Republican who could possibly overcome the Canal scandal and win election in November. Predictably, the Easy Boss was hard to convince. He first questioned his visitors' claim that Roosevelt was a winner. The Colonel might gain solid reform support, but what about disgruntled Black loyalists as well as organization voters who feared that the candidate would be too independent? And weren't the Germans and the liquor interests still angry at Roosevelt because of his attempt to support the Sunday laws when he was Police Commissioner? Quigg and Odell countered by arguing that most Black supporters and organization Republicans would end up voting for the Republican nominee no matter who he was. They admitted that a few Germans might defect, but that their loss should be more than offset by church members and good government advocates. Finally, the Colonel's reputation as a war hero would gain him the support of many persons who would not otherwise vote for a Republican candidate. [20]

These questions, although important, were not what was really troubling Platt. The overriding issue was the extent to which Roosevelt would be willing to "play ball" with the Easy Boss and his organization if he was elected. Roosevelt's entire career had involved a tendency to operate independently of the machine, and a willingness – indeed, a zest – to do public battle with it. In addition, as Platt wrote to Roosevelt the next year during a period of relative harmony between the two men:

> "The thing that really did bother me was this. I had heard from a good many sources that you were a little loose on the relations of capital and labor, on trusts and combinations, and, indeed, on those numerous questions which have recently arisen in politics affecting the security of earnings and the right of a man to run his own business in his own way, with due respect, of course, to the Ten Commandments, and the Penal Code."

Platt had one more concern: Roosevelt's imperialistic urges. Now that he had become a Senator, the Easy Boss was directly considering issues of national importance, and, with his habitual caution, distrusted anyone who had what he considered to be overly ambitious goals. Thus, in the course of the Manhattan Beach meeting, he told Odell and Quigg:

> "Mr. Roosevelt's courage and sincerity are not to be questioned. . . But if he becomes Governor of New York, with his personality, he will have to be President of the United States, and nobody can foresee how the problems growing out of the Spanish War will work out, and aside from the question of whether he will be fair to me and to our organization, I am afraid to start that thing going." [21]

To these doubts, Platt's visitors could provide no satisfactory answers. They did convince him, however, that something must be done before the upcoming State Committee meeting. Roosevelt and his Rough Riders were due to arrive at Montauk the next day. Why not send Quigg to visit him and sound him out? There was not merely the question of his relationship with the organization; he might not be interested in running on any terms. If the answer to either question was negative, Platt could report the Colonel's response to the Committee and it could move on to other possible nominees. If it was positive, well, maybe the Easy Boss would have to swallow his feelings and make Roosevelt *his* candidate. For, as a New York City newspaper commented several days later, Platt had "the habit, when two unpalatable alternatives were presented to him, of choosing the least nauseous, smacking his lips over it and declaring that he [had] always liked it." He was not called the Easy Boss for nothing. [22]

Their course agreed to, Quigg departed, and, like the hotel's other guests, Platt and Odell could spend the rest of the afternoon in rocking chairs on its veranda overlooking the bay. For them, however, the view brought no peace, since, as a *Herald* correspondent wrote, "none of the ocean waves bore a message to them" from their troublesome newly-minted war hero. Like every other political observer, they were "waiting for Roosevelt." [23]

7

The Easy Boss Chooses
His Candidate

As Platt and his aides were conferring, still another problem was developing for the Republicans. Camp Wikoff, where Roosevelt would spend most of the next month, was in no condition to minister to the needs of large numbers of sick and undernourished men. Until the end of July, the government had not even acquired its Eastern Long Island site. The camp of 10,000 tents that had sprung up in only two weeks would have been an impressive sight as a home for battle-ready troops, but a shortage of hospital facilities and medical supplies as well as ambulances and other transport made it woefully inadequate for the suffering soldiers who were arriving in these mid-August days. Many of the troops had to walk the several miles from the landing areas to the camp. Some fell by the wayside, thus delaying the disembarkation of others. To make matters worse, the distribution of food was held up by bureaucratic red tape.

Needless to say, the press raised a loud hue and cry. With New York less than a hundred miles away, it was easy for reporters to reach the camp, and they took full advantage of their opportunity. Hearst's New York *Evening Journal* headline "Starving Men at Montauk Point" was typical. The public response was instantaneous, with ladies' aid societies and Red Cross groups hurrying to the rescue. William K. Vanderbilt and other wealthy New Yorkers sent their cooks to Montauk, together with such delicacies as pheasants and champagne, which would have been relished by healthy eaters but hardly provided the nourishment needed by the Rough Riders and the other recuperating men.

Fighting Joe Wheeler was put in charge of the camp and did his best to break the logjams that were caused by trying to send provisions and medical supplies over the single rail line to Montauk. By August 24, when Secretary of War Alger responded to the criticism by visiting Camp Wikoff, conditions had substantially improved. Alger tried to put the best light possible on the situation, asserting that the loss of only 126 lives out of 22,000 men was not a bad record. The press and public strongly disagreed, and the ensuing reaction against the McKinley Administration gave Republican politicians like Platt additional cause for concern as the November elections neared. [1]

❁ ❁ ❁

Shortly after reaching Camp Wikoff, Roosevelt, in obvious good health, was released from the medical quarantine that had been imposed on the majority of the Rough Riders. Thus, when Quigg asked to see him on the eve of the August 20 Republican State Committee meeting, he was able to oblige. On August 19, the Congressman arrived at the encampment and found his way to the Colonel's tent on Rough Rider Street. Roosevelt was waiting, and, presumably because he wisely wanted a witness to what he knew would be an important interview, had already been joined by his brother-in-law Douglas Robinson. As he wrote 15 years later in his *Autobiography*, in a friendly session that lasted two hours,

> "Quigg spoke very frankly to me, stating that he earnestly desired to see me nominated and believed that the great body of Republican voters in the State so desired, but that the organization and the State Convention would finally do what Senator Platt desired. He said that the county leaders were already coming to Senator Platt, hinting at a close election, expressing doubt of Governor Black's ability for reelection, and asking why it would not

be a good thing to nominate me; now that I had returned to the
United States this would go on more and more all the time, and
that he (Quigg) did not wish that these men should be discouraged and be sent back to their localities to suppress a rising sentiment in my favor." [2]

After this flattering introduction, Quigg put his cards on the table.
What he wanted Roosevelt to give him was

". . . a plain statement as to whether or not I wanted the nomination, and as to what would be my attitude toward the organization in the event of my nomination and election, whether or
not I would 'make war' on Mr. Platt and his friends, or whether I
would confer with them and with the organization leaders generally, and give fair consideration to their point of view as to party policy and public interest. He said he had not come to make
me any offer of the nomination, and had no authority to do so,
nor to get any pledges or promises. He simply wanted a frank
declaration of my attitude toward existing party conditions." [3]

Although Roosevelt had been back in the United States for only a
few days, he had already learned enough from friends to have a good
sense of the direction in which the political wind was blowing and
what Quigg was likely to ask him. He therefore did not hesitate in responding to Quigg, and, through him, to Platt

". . . that I should like to be nominated, and if nominated
would throw myself into the campaign with all possible energy. I
said that I would not make war on Mr. Platt or anybody else if war
could be avoided; that what I wanted was to be Governor and not
a faction leader; that I certainly would confer with the organization men, as with everybody else who seemed to me to have
knowledge of and interest in public affairs, and that as to Mr. Platt
and the organization leaders, I would do so in the sincere hope
that there might always result harmony of opinion and purpose;

but that while I would try to get on with the organization, the organization must with equal sincerity strive to do what I regarded as essential for the public good; and that in every case, after full consideration of what everybody had to say who might possess real knowledge of the matter, I should have to act finally as my own judgment and conscience dictated and administer the State government as I thought it ought to be administered." [4]

Roosevelt's answer pleased Quigg: it "was precisely what he supposed I would say; . . . it was all anybody could expect; . . . and he would report it to Senator Platt precisely as I had put it to him." Both men tried to keep the interview a secret, with Quigg refusing to tell a reporter whether or not the purpose of his visit to Camp Wikoff was to see Roosevelt. Others, however, had no compunction in talking with the press, even if the information they conveyed was only partially accurate. Thus, the August 19 *Herald* quoted "Colonel Roosevelt's friends" as making "no secret of the fact that he has long cherished the ambition to become Governor of New York." The same reporter asserted that "I have been told" that "Mr. Quigg's visit to the Rough Rider chief yesterday . . . can be construed in but one way. That is that Senator Platt and his friends have finally decided to nominate Colonel Roosevelt, and that he will be the choice of the Saratoga gathering." [5]

❋ ❋ ❋

A reader of these reports might reasonably have concluded that the forthcoming State Committee meeting would result in a decision by the party leadership that Roosevelt would be the nominee and that the next month's convention would merely ratify a fait accompli. This, however, was not the case. Although the majority of the attendees seemed to favor Roosevelt, Platt made clear that he would only listen and not decide. Black and his supporters, led by Insurance Superintendent Payn, were not about to concede, and the Roosevelt boom could weaken during the five weeks before the Saratoga convention. Thus, the Easy Boss quietly absorbed the reports that leaders from around the State were giving him. Meanwhile, his lieutenants were insisting that Quigg had visited Roosevelt on his own, without authorization by Platt or any member of the State Committee. [6]

During the afternoon of August 20, having obtained a four-day furlough, Roosevelt left Camp Wikoff for his Sagamore Hill home. When he arrived that evening at the Oyster Bay Station, with his train's whistle blowing at full blast, he was greeted by "a huge bonfire, the screeching of a steam whistle, and the firing of cannon, pistols, muskets, fireworks and torpedoes." What a *Herald* reporter called "the largest crowd ever gathered in Oyster Bay . . . seemed mad with enthusiasm. . . Women and children were brushed aside like feathers" and "a little girl who was caught in the crowd was literally stripped of her frock." It was only with the aid of the welcoming committee, made up of three clergymen, that the returning hero was able to make his way to the two-seated wagon that was waiting to transport him and his wife to their home. [7]

❈ ❈ ❈

Although Platt had been careful not to express any decision on his gubernatorial choice, the leaders who had conferred with him during the State Committee meeting acted as if they had little doubt as to who it would be. On August 22, only two days later, the Republican State Committeeman from Manhattan and three leaders in the Brooklyn organization declared their support for Roosevelt. The next day, at its headquarters on Grand Street in Lower Manhattan, the Republican Association of the 12th Assembly District became the first regular party organization formally to endorse the Colonel. The *Times* front page report concluded that since the group's chairman "is a pronounced Platt man of undisputed regularity," its action was likely taken "with the previous knowledge of Mr. Platt himself." Further, although some observers "distrust the sincerity of Senator Platt's apparent acceptance of Col. Roosevelt and . . . insist that it conceals a deep-held plot to play Roosevelt against Black at the convention with the object of running in a compromise man of his own at the last moment," even they were starting to "admit that the popular demonstrations in favor of the fighting Colonel are so marked as to indicate that the movement already has passed beyond the leader's control." [8]

❋ ❋ ❋

These Republicans were not the only men who wanted to harness the Roosevelt groundswell for their own political purposes. Others with similar designs were the leaders of a self-styled Independent Party headed by the idealistic John Jay Chapman. In temperament as different as possible from Platt, whose tactics he detested, Chapman was of a type unique to the romanticism that still influenced a few members of America's well-bred leisure class during the late nineteenth and early twentieth centuries. Four years younger than Roosevelt, and like him a graduate of Harvard and a Porcellian member, he had initially opted for a legal career, but soon abandoned it for a life in literature, where he would later develop a reputation as an essayist and poet.

Chapman made a singular first impression, standing tall, and in the words of his biographer, "with the commanding presence to which a prophet or poet might lay claim." He "dressed with something of the sweet neglect that sits best upon the well dressed and well formed, wearing a woolen scarf about his neck and shoulders in nearly all weathers." His appearance was especially unique because he lacked a left hand. While a student at Harvard Law School, he had beaten another man whom he believed was a rival suitor for the woman who was to become his first wife, and then, beside himself with revulsion and remorse, plunged the hand into a hard coal fire that was burning in his Cambridge apartment and held it there with his right hand for several minutes. Like nothing else, this impulsive act epitomized a man whom his biographer described as "a figure of passion, ferocity and tenderness, of extravagance in thought and deed, of violent contrasts, of an inward wildness needing to be tamed for almost any relationship of life. . . ." To a contemporary he was

". . .glowing and beautiful like fire, pure and purifying like fire, lambent, wayward, unshapable, mischievous like fire, uncontrollable like fire, destructive like fire, seeking heaven like fire."[9]*

During the 1890s, one of Chapman's major efforts was to try to weaken and perhaps even destroy the power of New York's political bosses of both parties. Unlike Roosevelt, he regarded the 1897 New York City mayoral election as a victory for good government, evidenced by the more than 180,000 votes that Seth Low secured in running solely as an independent. He saw Roosevelt's triumphant return from Cuba as an unequaled opportunity to advance his cause even further. If the Colonel would agree to run as the Independent Party candidate, Chapman hoped that Platt's interest in retaining the State House would be so strong that the Easy Boss would have no alternative but to swallow his pride and make Roosevelt the Republican candidate as well. The Independent ticket not only would be headed by Roosevelt but also would have as its nominees for the other elective State offices "decent men from both parties, men known to the whole state if possible, unknown men if necessary, decent men in any case. . . ." With these running mates Roosevelt would win more votes as an Independent than on the Republican line. Moreover, although his Independent Party running mates would likely not be elected, they would draw enough votes that the other Republican nominees would go down to defeat. Platt and his machine would be the real losers, and Roosevelt would be "the instrument of the citizen destroying the Boss."[10]

---

* On one occasion, Chapman's quixotic romanticism surfaced when, on learning of a particularly lurid lynching in a Southern community, he rented a small shop in the town where he then announced in the local press he would conduct "a service of atonement," which was attended only by a solitary elderly woman.

Chapman's views were shared by other leaders of good government groups, including the City Club and the Central Committee of the Citizens Union. Unlike these more practical reformers, he also admitted, in answer to the criticism of one of them, that he was "in love" with Roosevelt. As he later wrote:

"I shall never forget the lustre that shone about him. . . . I never before nor since have felt the glorious touch of hero-worship which solve's life problems by showing you a man. Lo, there, it says, Behold the way! You have only to worship, trust, and support him."

On August 10, he wrote to his wife:

"It would be the saving of Roosevelt's life to be nominated by the independents and forced upon the Republican machine — would leave him free. He is a strong Republican in his talk, with party loyalty, but in his actions he is an independent."

Chapman's allies mistrusted his romantic idealism. Thus, when Chapman visited Roosevelt on August 24, he was accompanied by one of them, political organizer Isaac H. Klein. Because Chapman was the Colonel's social acquaintance and equal and could present their case with greater enthusiasm, Klein let him lead the discussion. Chapman did so, explaining the reformers' plan to Roosevelt, "as it were with diagrams." He also conceded that, unlike himself, "the reform group was not nominating him because they loved him, but because they desired to make use of him." Especially since the Colonel had been back in the country for only a week and a half, the two men would give him "a week to think it over." [11]

With a caution that he had learned from previous political experiences, Roosevelt was only too happy to agree. He must have known that he had become involved in a political balancing act, and did not want to burn any bridges behind him. As he wrote to Low on August 27, "I am 'running' in the same way that you did; . . . like you I have a

fire on both flanks." Yet, he must also have realized that, as he had decided in 1884 and unlike Low in 1897, his entire life had been as a Republican, and that to abandon his party would be an act of political
suicide. Further, as he had written several years earlier, if a person

"... goes into politics he must go into practical politics, in order to make his influence felt.

He must be prepared to meet men of far lower ideals than his
own, and to face things, not as he would wish them, but as they
are. He must not lose his own high ideals, and yet he must face
the fact that the majority of the men with whom he must work
have lower ideals. He must stand firmly for what he believes, and
yet must realize that political action, to be effective, must be the
joint action of many men, and that he must sacrifice somewhat of
his own opinions to those of his associates if he ever hopes to see
his desire take practical shape."

Consistent with this philosophy, he wrote to Quigg on August 31: "If the
organization wants me to go before the convention, I will do it without
any regard as to whether Gov. Black puts up a fight," and added as a
handwritten postscript, "I entirely understand the Senator's position." [12]

Publicly, Roosevelt continued to "lie low." He was accepting the advice of one of his early backers: "For God's sake to say nothing – not to
talk to anybody." Thus, he wrote Quigg on August 27, "I have absolutely refused to say anything as you have doubtless seen," and in his letter
of the same date told Low, "I am just letting events take their course."
All this would appear to indicate that he was prepared to take the Republican nomination in the likely event that Platt agreed to accept
him. Yet, if Roosevelt meant what he said in a letter he wrote his friend
Francis Leupp on September 3, he was far from enthusiastic over the
possibility:

"... while on the whole I should like the office of Governor
and should not shirk it, the position will be one of such extreme

difficulty, and I shall have to offend so many good friends of mine, that I shall breathe a sigh of relief were it not offered to me.

". . . [I]f I should take it ...I should have to treat with and work with the organization, and I should see and consult the leaders – not once, but continuously – and earnestly try to come to an agreement on all important questions with them, and of course the mere fact of my doing so would alienate many of my friends whose friendship I value . . . I would not entertain any conditions save those outlined in this very letter – that, while a good party man who would honestly strive to keep in with the leaders of the party organization, to work with them, and to bring the Republican party into a better shape for two years hence, yet in the last resort I should have to be my own master, and when question of honesty or dishonesty arose I should have to pay no further heed to party lines."

Roosevelt closed his letter to Leupp by saying that as to whether or not he was chosen, "I can . . . say, with all sincerity, that I don't care in the least." He was undoubtedly sincere in dreading the necessity of working with Platt and his friends on a regular basis. In fact, however, his conversation and later correspondence with Quigg indicated that by now he wanted the nomination very much. His protestations to the contrary may have been primarily a defense mechanism that would allow him to hide his disappointment if it did not come his way. [13]

With this concern, Roosevelt was willing to continue to pursue an Independent Party candidacy even though he must have realized that it would lessen the chances of obtaining Platt's approval. Thus, when Chapman and Klein paid him a return visit on September 1, they apparently received a reply that they considered a "go ahead" to form an Independent Party ticket that he would head. Twenty years later, Chapman recalled that "all that we asked of him was that if he rejected the proposition he should reject it at that moment, – i.e. not take our nomination and then later throw us down by withdrawing from the ticket. Well, he allowed us to make the nomination . . ." On September 4, Chapman wrote to an associate, "We expect to put Roosevelt in the field at the head of a straight independent ticket next Friday," that the campaign "will be the noisiest thing since General Jackson" and that although it might be conducted under the aegis of the Citizens Union, "it will leak out that I am the whole of it." [14]

To the more politically astute Klein, Roosevelt's commitment was far from clear. On September 9, he told the *Times* that "[t]he impression I got from my conversation with the Colonel was that, having so recently returned to this country and being unfamiliar with present conditions, he was not prepared to say whether he ought to accept a nomination coming from any source in hostility to the regular political organization to which he belonged." Be that as it may, Chapman and other Independents were proceeding to form a ticket headed by Roosevelt, and on September 9 at a City Club meeting announced that they had chosen candidates for every position except Lieutenant Governor. Three of the six candidates were from upstate New York and, according to the committee that chose the slate, all six "have broken all ties with the machines that corruptly control their party organizations." Except for Roosevelt, all of them had committed themselves to run. [15]

❦ ❦ ❦

On September 3, McKinley visited Camp Wikoff, which by now was operating in reasonably good working order. As soon as the President arrived, Roosevelt rode up to make sure to be one of the first officers to meet him. He was successful, for McKinley spotted him and immediately called out, "Colonel, I'm glad to see you." Then, according to the *Sun's* account, Roosevelt was so eager to shake hands with the President

"that he forgot to make a formal dismount, but sort of fell off his animal in the way he does at the end of a race across the hills with a squad of his cowpunchers. At the same time the President did a remarkable thing for a President to do. He stood up in his carriage, pushed open the door, and jumping out, started toward Col. Roosevelt, who was coming toward him as fast as he could. The President held out his hand. Col. Roosevelt struggled to pull off his right glove. He yanked at it desperately and finally inserted the ends of his fingers in his teeth and gave a mighty tug. Off came the glove and a beatific smile came over the Colonel's face as he grasped the President's hand. The crowd which had watched the performance tittered audibly. Nothing more cordial than the greeting between the President and Col. Roosevelt could be imagined. The President just grinned all over."

Before McKinley moved on, they privately chatted for a minute or two. The subject matter of their conversation was never divulged, but it is at least possible that McKinley took the opportunity to tell the Colonel how pleased he would be if Roosevelt helped the Republican Party by running for Governor. In any event, the President's obviously friendly attitude would do Roosevelt no harm in convincing the Party regulars that he was *persona grata*. [16]

❧ ❧ ❧

During these early September days, Platt's associates had been active. By the end of August, State Chairman Odell had been able to sound out party leaders from nearly three-fourths of the State's counties. In the next few days he conferred with the leaders in Brooklyn's 21 Assembly districts. Quigg was equally busy. On September 8, he paid an early morning visit to the White House with a constituent who was seeking a military promotion for his son. An *Evening Post* correspondent speculated, that the real reason for Quigg's Washington trip was to try on Platt's behalf "to draw the President into a 'dicker' which will make up to the New York machine in federal patronage for what it would lose in State patronage if Roosevelt should become Governor." The Easy Boss supposedly hoped that McKinley's desire for the strong

Republican showing that a Roosevelt candidacy would provide would lead him to give favors to Platt in return for the Easy Boss agreeing to Roosevelt's nomination. The President, however, was no particular friend of Platt, who had opposed his Presidential nomination, and ,according to the *Post*, "thinks Col. Roosevelt so strong a party man that factional differences in New York would not be considered in making appointments to state offices." Indeed, one wonders if there was any truth at all to the report, since any perceptive observer would have recognized that if Roosevelt was not nominated, the Democrats would almost certainly win the Governorship and there would be no patronage for the Easy Boss to dispense. [17]

By now, Platt had reluctantly concluded that, if Roosevelt was willing to run on the Republican ticket and agreed to work with him, there was no realistic alternative but to support him. He recognized that Black was not about to surrender, but was confident that the Governor did not have the support of enough party leaders to derail the Roosevelt boom, once the Easy Boss had passed the word that the Colonel was his candidate. He must have laughed at talk of a possible compromise candidate: for the organization to reject both Roosevelt and Black in favor of some obvious party functionary would assure defeat in November.

Although Platt had reached his decision after taking advice from many quarters, the opinions of two men were especially influential. One was Judge John R. Hazel, the Republican leader in Buffalo and Erie County. According to Quigg, Platt's experience had taught him "that on election day the forces between Democratic New York City and its environment and the Republican country counties were so evenly balanced that Buffalo and Erie would decide the issue." Not surprisingly, the Erie Canal Commission's findings had a strong impact in that area, and Hazel told Platt in no uncertain terms that many voters would hold Black accountable and the Governor could not be reelected. [18]

The other man to whom Platt paid close attention was Chauncey M. Depew. At age sixty-four a year younger than the Easy Boss, Depew had had an even longer career at the highest level of New York politics. At an early age he had caught the eye of the influential Republican leader Thurlow Weed and in 1863 had been appointed New York Secretary of State. In 1866 Depew was about to be chosen United States Ambassador to Japan, but instead accepted Commodore Vanderbilt's offer to handle his political connections and those of his New York Central. Eventually becoming the railroad's president, his personal charm and political skill permitted him to play an influential role in both state and national Republican politics even during periods when the railroad's interests were in public disfavor.

Depew was renowned as a witty speaker, and the sight on a dais of his bald pate and sideburns that extended down over his choker collar ensured that a public dinner would be an enjoyable occasion.* Thus, Platt valued not only his political sagacity but also his sense as to what would hold the crowds at the political gatherings which were so important in this pre-radio and TV era. As Depew later recalled, in late August, as soon as he had sat down with the Easy Boss at Manhattan Beach, Platt

" . . . entered at once upon the question at hand by saying: I am very much troubled about the governorship. Frank Black has made an excellent governor and did the right thing in ordering an investigation of the Canal frauds. But the result of the investigations has been that the Democrats have been able to create a popular impression that the whole State administration is guilty . . . Benjamin Odell, the chairman of our State committee, urges the nomination of Colonel Roosevelt. As you know, Roosevelt is

---

* Even at age 82, his 45-minute remarks would help calm the fractious delegates at the 1916 Republican National Convention.

no friend of mine, and I don't think very well of the suggestion. Now, what do you think?"

Depew's immediate reply carried more than 40 years of experience:

"Mr. Platt, I always look at a public question from the view of the platform. I have been addressing audiences ever since I became a voter, and my judgment of public opinion and the views of the public are governed by how they take or will take and act upon the questions presented. Now, if you nominate Governor Black and I am addressing a large audience – and I certainly will – the heckler in the audience will arise and interrupt me, saying: 'Chauncey, we agree with what you say about the Grand Old Party and all that, but how about the Canal steal?' I have to explain that the amount stolen was only a million and that would be fatal. If Colonel Roosevelt is nominated, I can say to the heckler with indignation and enthusiasm: 'I am mightily glad you asked that question. We have nominated for governor a man who has demonstrated in public office and on the battlefield that he is a fighter for the right and always victorious. If he is selected, you know and we all know from his demonstrated characteristics, courage and ability, that every thief will be caught and punished, and every dollar that can be found returned to the public treasury. Then I will follow the Colonel leading his Rough Riders up San Juan Hill and ask the band to play the 'Star Spangled Banner.'"

Platt had only one response: "Roosevelt will be nominated." [19]

❀ ❀ ❀

Once he had made up his mind, Platt's role involved more than listening to reports of Roosevelt's strength. Although publicly he continued to maintain a neutral position, he had begun working behind the scenes to undermine Black's possible support. The September 8 *Tribune* reported that Lieutenant Governor Timothy Woodruff, who had been considered a Black ally, "has made no effort to hold the Brooklyn men in line for the Governor." The next day's *Herald* carried a "strange story" that a Platt aide had boarded a train at Poughkeepsie and "waylaid" Woodruff on his way back to Brooklyn from Albany and

> " . . . on behalf of Senator Platt, offered assurances that if the Kings County delegates were peacefully turned over Mr. Woodruff would be placed on the ticket with Colonel Roosevelt. The further assurance was given, it is said, 'that Colonel Roosevelt would leave the executive chamber for the United States Senate and thus place Mr. Woodruff in the Governor's chair.' " [20]

The fact that Woodruff vigorously stated that he was and "always had been" for Black did little to quiet the rumors.

Although he had been unable to persuade the Governor to withdraw, by September 10 Platt felt sufficiently sure of Roosevelt's success that, undoubtedly with his authorization, Quigg sent Roosevelt a long letter outlining the Easy Boss's position. At the outset, he reported that against his own advice Platt would "make one more effort to induce Governor Black to withdraw," but that this last try would almost certainly be unsuccessful since "everything has been done that human ingenuity can suggest to convince Governor Black of the folly of insisting upon remaining a candidate; but he will not listen to anybody." Whether or not Black withdrew, however, Platt's only recourse was to ditch him, for it had become clear

> "that . . . the Governor would be beaten if nominated; that he could be nominated only as a result of great machine exertion; that the sentiment throughout the State is genuine and universal; and that for him (Platt) to disregard the expressions of public feeling that have come spontaneously from every county, except for the most serious party reasons, would be foolish leadership, and that he is not prepared to assume such a responsibility."

Nevertheless, Roosevelt should understand that the nomination

decision was entirely in Platt's hands. Ever since Quigg's August visit to
Camp Wikoff,

"... perceiving that the sentiment at 49 Broadway [Platt's business office] was favorable to you, ... the organization leaders ...
have acted accordingly. Instead of an effort to restrain the public
sentiment, it has been cultivated and developed, and with the final result that the Senator is convinced that it will scarcely be
possible for Black to obtain more than one hundred and fifty
votes out of a total of nine hundred and seventy-one."
Even so,

"The invariable answer that he [Platt] receives when he asks
how a delegation will stand is substantially this, 'We are organization men and we will support you as the leader of the organization. We will cast our votes for any ticket that you recommend. If
you say Black, we will be for Black; if you say Roosevelt, we will
say Roosevelt. We prefer Roosevelt. We think that his nomination
will help our local ticket and enable us to make a thoroughly successful campaign. We doubt whether Black can be elected, but we
will act on your judgment and take your advice.' There is not a
single county delegation, with the exception of those controlled
by State officeholders, which has not placed itself in the Senator's
hands in just this way."

With the stage thus set, and based in part on the understanding of
his conversation with the Colonel at Camp Wikoff, Quigg described the
basis on which Platt would give Roosevelt the nomination:

"... that if you were nominated it would be as the result of his
support; that you were not the sort of man who would accept a
nomination directly out of the hands of the organization without
realizing the obligation thereby assumed, to sustain the organization and to promote and uphold it; and that you were perfectly
prepared to meet that obligation and to discharge it justly; that if

you were Governor you would not wish to be anything else than Governor; that you would not wish to be a figurehead or to accept any position before the public or in your own mind which was not in keeping with the dignity of the office or which would not allow you to discharge your duties in the light of your judgment and conscience; but that you would take the office, if at all, intending in good faith to act the part of his friend personally and politically, to acknowledge and respect his position as the head of the Republican organization and as the Republican Senator from the State of New York; that you would not be led into any factional opposition to the organization. But that to the contrary you would aim constantly to make its interests identical with the public interests; that you would consult with the Senator fully and freely on all important matters; that you would adopt no line of policy or agree to no important measure or nomination without previous consultation, and that you wanted him to agree to the same things on his part, so that both you and he could meet in consultation with minds free and open, each intending to reach a conclusion satisfactory to both, and in that way preserve complete harmony in the organization and among the supporters of the party. I said that you did not mean by this that you would do everything that was wanted precisely as it might be originally suggested, but that you did mean in good faith and honest friendship to enter with him upon the consideration of all matters proposed, without prejudice and with the intention to reach a conclusion which the Senator as well as yourself would deem wisest and best. I told him that it would be helpful to you to have Mr. Odell or some man of similar position near to you at Albany, in order to facilitate intercourse and for the purpose of supplying general information about the conditions of the state; and finally that while in the end, as an honest man you would have to act on your best judgment and in the light of your oath, you would seek with him to keep the party united and the organization intact."

All that remained was to close the deal, and for that purpose Platt summoned the Colonel to see him. In negotiations with Quigg that had preceded his writing Roosevelt this long letter, the Colonel had agreed to a meeting in about two weeks time, after the Rough Riders had been mustered out. Several months later, Roosevelt referred in a letter to a friend to "mysterious negotiations" in which it had been suggested that "if necessary we could meet at some out of the way place in the evening." The Colonel rejected this idea and responded that he would "call upon" Platt "with the utmost pleasure in broad daylight at the Fifth Avenue Hotel." Although this may not have been the Easy Boss's first choice, he must have derived satisfaction that as a matter of appearance Roosevelt would be coming to see him rather than the other way around or meeting at a neutral location. [21]

Even though Quigg's letter was apparently the result of careful negotiations, Roosevelt did not want him to "take silence for consent," and immediately telegraphed him that his description of what the Colonel had previously said "was substantially right, that is, it gave just the spirit." He then followed up with a letter that questioned the "wording of some of your sentences," i.e., "instead of saying that I would not 'wish to be a figurehead' you should have used the word 'consent.'" There "were also other similar verbal changes to which I think you would agree." As another example,

> " . . . you could have brought out the fact that these statements were not in the nature of bids for the nomination or of pledges by me, and that you made no effort to exact any pledges, but that they were statements which I freely made when you asked me what my position would be if nominated and elected (you having already stated that you wished me nominated and elected)."

"However," Roosevelt continued, "I need not go into the matter more in detail, and I am not sure that it was necessary for me to write this at all, for I know that you did not in any way wish to represent me as willing to consent to act otherwise than in accordance with my conscience. . ."

To a less nervous man without an intense concern as to his square-dealing reputation, the letter could have stopped there. Roosevelt, however, insisted upon a postscript "to make clear that there was no question of pledges or promises, least of all a question of bargaining for the nomination . . ." As if this was not enough of a protestation, he added:

> "I was not making any agreement as to what I would do in consideration of receiving the nomination; I was stating the course which I thought it would be best to follow, for the sake of the party, and for the sake of the state – both considerations outweighing infinitely the question of my own nomination." [22]

Quigg responded with alacrity: "There is no difference between us as to that report. It is perfectly understood and understood just as you indicate." As Roosevelt later put it, Quigg "did not ask for any pledges," the wording of his letter was no "Apostles Creed," and all he had been trying to do was determine Roosevelt's "mental attitude toward the office." The negotiations were now complete. All that remained was the official "laying on of hands," to take place on September 17. [23]

❀ ❀ ❀

Knowing that at some point he would be meeting with Platt, Roosevelt wanted the public to know his position on the nomination in advance. Accordingly, on September 10, after a visit to Montauk, Colonel Lovell H. Jerome, a nonorganization Republican who had been actively promoting the Colonel's nomination, read a statement that Roosevelt had authorized:

> "That he was and always had been a Republican in the broadest sense of the word. While he was not seeking the Republican nomination for Governor, should it come to him he would

The Bronco Buster
(*New York World*)

Shaking Hands
(Courtesy of the Theodore Roosevelt Birthplace)

accept it as an honor and duty, recognizing, as he does, the dignity and honor of the position. He means the regular nomination
of the Republican Party by the delegates to the Saratoga Convention. Should he receive the nomination and be elected, he would
be a Republican Governor – a Governor of the entire party – and
he would most earnestly hope to receive the support of Republicans throughout the State, irrespective of faction. An endorsement from the independents would be most flattering and
gratifying to him, and he would certainly hope for their loyal
support toward his election should he be honored with the
nomination." [24]

The Independent Party leaders immediately focused on Roosevelt's
statement that he "would be a Republican Governor – a Governor of
the entire party." Where did that leave them and their nomination?
Their concern must have been heightened by statements of other visitors to Montauk quoted in the next morning's *Herald* that "under no
circumstances" would Roosevelt be an independent candidate, and an
oral comment attributed to him by the *Times* that implied that he
might become the Independent Party standard bearer only if he was
not the Republican nominee.

Immediate clarification was called for, and Independent leader Meyer D. Rothschild left at once for Montauk to see the Colonel. On September 12, he wired back to New York the heartening word that
"Roosevelt stands where he did when Chapman and Klein saw him."
The next day, Rothschild confirmed this advice as an evening meeting
of the Citizens' Union that had been called to consider endorsing
Roosevelt if the Independents nominated him. "Roosevelt," he said
"had not used the especially partisan language referred to." Rothschild's message was apparently consistent with a note that Roosevelt
sent another Independent leader the same day. Referring to a public
statement that a member of the City Club had made on September 9

supporting Roosevelt as an Independent Party candidate although "we do not know his desires," it read, "That address was all right. I have just seen Rothschild." With these apparent assurances, the Citizens Union, in what the *Times* wrote gave "the independence movement an importance which it did not before possess," endorsed an Independent ticket headed by the Colonel. [25]

The reformers were refusing to face reality. Platt would probably not object if the only issue was Roosevelt running as an Independent. But the Easy Boss would never consent to his appearance on a ticket otherwise made up of candidates who would draw votes away from the different names that would appear on the Republican slate. As Quigg put it to a newspaper reporter on September 13:

> "By nominating a full State ticket with him at the head, they are simply compelling him to deny their nomination out of necessary loyalty to his associates on the Republican ticket." [26]

❋ ❋ ❋

Roosevelt himself may not yet have focused on the practical impossibility of running at the head of two separate tickets. During these early September days, he was busy arranging the demobilization of his beloved regiment. At 1:00 p.m. on September 13, as he was working in his tent prior to the formal mustering out later that afternoon, he heard shouts and the movement of large numbers of men. A few minutes later he was summoned outside and was led into a hollow square of several hundred Rough Riders, in the center of which was a table on which a blanket covered what turned out to be a bronze Remington statue of a bronco buster. A gift from the regiment's rank and file, it was presented to the Colonel by a private who in civilian life had been a judge in the New Mexico Territory. He had been chosen to make the gift because "while you held your officers in the highest esteem on account of their gallantry, bravery and ability, your heart of hearts was ever with your men . . . ." The *Herald* reporter wrote that when Private

Murphy had finished, "[t]he cowpunchers' yell was strong enough to round up a bunch of horses on the hill a mile away and it grew in power when Colonel Roosevelt stepped forward, patted the mane of the statued bronco, and, speaking with effort which was apparent in every word," thanked and praised his "men of every occupation – men of means and men who work with their hands for a livelihood" and expressed his gratitude "to know that I have you for friends." With evident emotion, he said that his appreciation for the gift was "tenfold" because "it comes to me from you who shared the hardships of the campaign with me, who gave me pieces of your hardtack when I had none, and who gave me your blankets when I had none to lie upon." The statue, he said, "is something I will hand down to my children, and I shall value it more than the weapons I carried through the campaign."

During his remarks, the Rough Riders were joined by a group whom the *Herald* reporter described as "colored men" from two cavalry regiments that had fought alongside them in Cuba. When Roosevelt spotted them, he interposed in his thanks to his own regiment what he was "sure" were "the sentiments of every man and officer in this assemblage . . . that between you and the other cavalry regiments there is a tie which we trust will never be broken." As soon as he had finished, the Rough Riders gave the African-Americans a cheer, and followed it with three more for Roosevelt. Then one of his officers, whom the *Herald* described as "a free silver democrat of the most fervid type" let out a yell, "Three cheers for the next Governor of New York State," and the troops lustily responded. [27]

Roosevelt's remarks reflected his consistent public posture of minimizing his own role in the Rough Riders' exploits and praising the deeds of his men. He must have appreciated, however, that this evident affection for his troops and their equally obvious feeling for him would pay political dividends even though his aristocratic background might

otherwise have made him unacceptable to the diverse New York electorate that he was about to face.

❊ ❊ ❊

Shortly after the mustering out, Roosevelt returned to Oyster Bay. On
Saturday, September 17, he took a late morning train to Manhattan,
and after attending to private matters, was joined by Quigg. The two of
them arrived by taxi at the Fifth Avenue Hotel just before 3 p.m.

His meeting with Platt was no secret. In fact, it was front page news,
with the *Times* suggesting that it was "the desire of the Republican
politicians to advertise as widely as possible the fact that the 'Hero of
Santiago' was coming to call on the party leader." As a result of this
publicity, and since this would be Roosevelt's first appearance in New
York City since the war, by the scheduled hour of 2 p.m. a large crown
of local politicians, newspapermen and generally curious onlookers
had thronged the hotel lobby. Fearing a demonstration, on their arrival
Quigg smuggled Roosevelt through the ladies' entrance, and, not waiting for the elevator, rushed him up the side stairs to the State Committee's headquarters.

For two hours, the growing crowd in the lobby waited expectantly
while Roosevelt talked with Platt, who had arrived earlier from Manhattan Beach. Finally, shortly before 5:00 p.m. there was a stir as someone reported, "He's going." Almost at once, the Colonel came down
the main stairs into the lobby opposite the clerk's desk. According to
the *Times*, " . . . he wore civilian clothing, but his hat was of the army
type, which gave him a semi-military air." The throng immediately
crowded around him and blocked his passage as it volleyed questions
about what had occurred upstairs. When he began to reply, "I have had
a very pleasant conversation with Senator Platt and Mr. Odell —," he
was interrupted by the only question that really counted: "Will you accept the nomination for Governor?" His reply was quick and decisive:
"Of course I will. What do you think I am here for?"

Then, before it was asked, Roosevelt answered another inquiry that he knew was on everyone's lips: Would he act independently of the Platt machine? His reply was intended to dispel any rumors to the contrary: "I desire to say, so that you all may hear, that not a condition of any sort or kind has been suggested in connection with my acceptance of the nomination." Then, after repeating his disavowal in slightly different language, but with even greater emphasis, he elbowed his way through the throng and left the hotel to join a nearby gathering of some of the just discharged Rough Riders. As he departed, he was given a loud "three cheers for the next Governor of New York." The *Times* reported that "the Colonel simply smiled." [28]

8

"I Cannot Accept The So-called Independent Nomination"

O NLY AFTER R OOSEVELT AND HIS ADMIRERS WERE WELL OUT OF SIGHT did Platt leave the Fifth Avenue Hotel. All he would say to the waiting reporters was that the meeting had been "satisfying and interesting" and that the Colonel was "a thorough-going Republican." State Chairman Odell, however, made it clear that Roosevelt would be the organization candidate: "I believe Colonel Roosevelt will be nominated and elected. I am for him and expect to vote for him, and there are 700 delegates to the State Convention who will do the same thing." [1]

Like his candidate, Odell went out of his way to emphasize that "[T]here were no conditions and stipulations, and no intimations of any character that could lead to the suspicion of a condition." At least for the moment, some independent observers seemed to be convinced, with the reform-minded E.L. Godkin's *Evening Post* portraying the meeting as a "painful experience" for Platt, which the Easy Boss "went through . . . in an extremely creditable manner." It suggested that "his misery must have been intense":

"He was abdicating his chief function as the 'nominating power' of the party, and was allowing the people to exercise it in favor of a civil service reformer. Quigg and a few other faithful agents of the old system of state government . . . had seen the 'old man' give the high-toners many a strong dose, but they never expected to live to see him administer a dose like this to himself." [2]

Another noted reformer saw matters very differently. On September 30, Dr. Parkhurst returned to New York after a long European mountain-climbing holiday, with restored strength to assail the forces of evil from his pulpit at the Madison Square Presbyterian Church. He expressed great pleasure when the reporters who met him at the pier told him of Roosevelt's candidacy, but became incredulous when he learned of the Colonel's meeting with Platt:

> "He is a brave and honorable man. I cannot bring my mind to believe that he has done anything ignoble. I cannot conceive of Theodore Roosevelt going to Thomas C. Platt and humiliating himself before the 'boss.' I remember that when he was Police Commissioner, he and I talked about Commissioner Parker's conduct as unwise and improper as tending to strengthen Platt's power, which was already too great. It is possible that Mr. Platt, recognizing his need of Col. Roosevelt, sent a messenger to him with an urgent invitation and that in that way they met. But that he could go submissively to Mr. Platt, I cannot bring my mind to believe. Col. Roosevelt is too big, too courageous a man for that." [3]

❦ ❦ ❦

Platt's endorsement finally forced Roosevelt to confront the Independent nomination. On leaving the Platt-Roosevelt conference, Odell had told an inquiring reporter that the Colonel had not been asked to decline it and "[t]hat is a matter I suppose he will settle for himself," adding "I don't imagine he will reject any endorsement that may come to him." That statement notwithstanding, it is almost impossible to believe that in their two hour meeting the question did not arise. It was a *sine qua non* of the Independent nomination that the remainder of their slate would consist of nonorganization men who would draw off enough votes from the Republican ticket so that Roosevelt, as the sole

joint candidate, would be the only man elected. Since this strategy was
intended to weaken and perhaps even bring down Platt, it is unlikely
that the Easy Boss did not demand that Roosevelt turn down the Independents as the price of his endorsement. His parting comment that
Roosevelt was "a thorough-going Republican" indicates that he was
satisfied on the matter. As a biographer wrote ten years later, "Roosevelt was in the position of a coquette who had engaged herself to two
suitors and found their joint attention embarrassing." With no choice
and "rather in sorrow than in anger," he "proffered back the ring" to
Chapman. [4]

Roosevelt knew that this unavoidable step would be unpleasant,
writing to Lodge on September 19, "The first installment of trouble is
already on hand, for I cannot accept the so-called independent nomination and keep good faith with the other men on the Republican ticket, against whom the independent ticket is really put up." He wasted no
time in biting the bullet, writing the same Monday to, "Dear Jack":

"I do not see how I can accept the independent nomination
and keep good faith with the other men on my ticket. It has been
a thing that has worried me greatly; not because of its result upon
the election, but because it seems to be so difficult for men whom
I very heartily respect as I do you, to see the impossible position in
which they are placing me." [5]

Chapman's reaction was a combination of shock and anger.
Notwithstanding the press reports that Roosevelt would decline the
Independent nomination, he had continued to believe that the Colonel
was committed to accepting a dual candidacy. Only a few days earlier,
he had boasted to an associate that "he had gotten up on the whole
Roosevelt independent movement and never had so much fun in his
life watching others in convulsions of fear lest it was a blunder." Thus,
on receiving Roosevelt's note, he immediately sent "Dear Teddy" an
anguished reply:

"You will remember that you told Klein and myself that you would, if nominated by the Republicans, be glad of our nomination, as it would strengthen your hands, and Tucker tells me you said the same thing to him, and that simultaneous nominations would be satisfactory. . . .

"I know that you are the least astute of men, and this led me into an almost brutal frankness in explaining the situation, and in giving you a week to think it over. As a practical matter, our petitions are now being signed in every county in the State, and the returns are coming in by each mail. We expect to conclude the work by the middle of next week, and if by that time you are convinced of your duty to decline our nomination, it will be an easy matter for you to file the certificate of your declination. Our committee for filling vacancies will on October 1st be in a position to place another man at the head of our ticket and proceed with the canvass.

"I am satisfied, however, that you misapprehend the situation and that you will never decline. . ." [6]

❋ ❋ ❋

Before Chapman received Roosevelt's letter, his associates were busily proceeding on the basis that the Colonel's meeting with Platt had not affected their plans to place him at the head of the Independent ticket. On September 19, Klein among others radiated confidence that there wasn't "the slightest doubt" of his accepting the nomination: "It is such an improbable thing that we have given no thought as to who will fill the vacancy. There will be no vacancy." That evening the Citizens Union Central Committee met at that organization's headquarters to hear reports of progress in organizing the city's assembly districts for the coming campaign. The group received a report that working groups had already been organized in 28 of the 37 districts in Manhattan and the Bronx. [7]

To these men, the news of Roosevelt's September 19 letter to Chapman came as an unexpected shock. Like Chapman, they believed that Roosevelt had given them his word and that he would not go back on it. One of them, George E. Waring, Jr., had agreed to run as the Independent candidate for State Engineer on the assumption that the Colonel would head the ticket. Waring later contended that at one point Roosevelt had suggested to him that

> " . . . he could not run against a candidate of his party, to which he [Waring] had replied . . . that if he ran only on Platt's ticket his name might be used to help fill the legislature with 'Yellow Dogs' who at Platt's bidding might elect even Quigg to the U.S. Senate — that if he ran also on the Independent ticket, Platt would be bound to put up good men for every place; that he need not accept the Independent nomination, but that he should not decline it; and that it would suffice if he would say, in accepting the Republican nomination, that he was glad to become the candidate of his own party and of all others who might choose to vote for him."

Waring stated unequivocally that he "received in reply a letter which began: 'With what you say in your letter I cordially agree. . . .'" [8]

❋ ❋ ❋

On September 22, the Independents received a body blow. Following his strong showing in the previous year's mayorality election, Seth Low was probably the man who best symbolized to the public the New York City reform movement. On September 22, the New York morning newspapers, in the case of the *Herald* under the headline "SETH LOW'S BOMBSHELL," published the text of a letter that he had recently sent to the Citizens Union in which he rejected that group's request that they support the Independent ticket. Their proposed action, he wrote, "is the one thing that can cause the defeat of Col. Roosevelt and the possible loss of a sound-money Senator from New York, as well

as sound-money representatives in Congress." He could "see absolutely no benefit from the course which has been taken and which is proposed." To him, it looked "as unreasonable and unprofitable as the
attitude of the prohibitionists, who sacrifice all practical results year after year for the sake of a theory." [9]

Even while he was in Washington, Roosevelt had kept in close contact with Low, and the Columbia University president sent a copy of
the letter to the Colonel, who promptly saw that it made its way into
the hands of the press. It made an especially strong impression, since it
was the first time that Low had publicly expressed the conclusion he
had reached after his 1897 defeat that that year's separate ticket policy
was a mistake which he would never again endorse. [10]

Low's position was quickly endorsed by former Mayor Strong. Their
stance reflected the fact, as the *Times* editorialized under the caption "A
QUESTION OF INDEPENDENCE," that the Citizens Union and
City Club group headed by Chapman and others

". . . can hardly claim to be the keeper of the conscience of
those who are opposed to the Platt machine on the one hand and
the Croker machine on the other. It is not a representative body.
It has not received authority from any number of citizens known
to be considerable to act for them or fix a policy for them. The opposition of the members of the committee to the machine does
not make them the leaders of all anti-machine men, Republicans
and Democratic alike. They are, so far as we are informed, gentlemen of honest intentions and public spirit, but they have no monopoly of these by no means rare virtues . . . ." [11]

❧ ❧ ❧

Meanwhile, Roosevelt was mulling over his public position regarding
the Independents. On Tuesday, September 20, he visited the city and
met with Depew, who was to make the nominating speech for him at
the next week's convention, and with Odell. Although the announced

purpose of the conference with the State Chairman was to consider the balance of the Republican slate and the party platform, it is likely that the two men also discussed the Independent nomination. The next day the Colonel was feted at a rousing official welcome-home, nonpolitical "Peace Jubilee and Roosevelt Reception" by his Oyster Bay neighbors and hundreds of others from surrounding communities. [12]

That evening, Roosevelt was visited by Preble Tucker, an emissary of the Citizens Union group. Although he reportedly told Tucker that he would think over the Independent nomination further, the next day he prepared a letter to Chapman that would set forth and explain his final decision and would be made public. Dated September 22, it read:

"My name will probably be presented for Governor at the Republican state convention in Saratoga on the 27th. If I am nominated then it will be on the same ticket with those who are named for the other state offices. The Republican Party will also have congressional and legislative tickets in the field. National issues are paramount this year, very few municipal officers are to be elected. The candidates will be my associates in the general effort to elect a Republican Governor, Republican Congressmen to support President McKinley, the cause of sound money, and a Legislature which will send to the Senate a Republican United States Senator.

"It seems to me that I would not be acting in good faith toward my fellow candidates if I permitted my name to head a ticket designed for their overthrow, a ticket moreover which cannot be put up because of objections to the character and fitness of any candidates, inasmuch as no candidates have yet been nominated.

"I write this with great reluctance, for I wish the support of every Independent. If elected Governor, I would strive to serve the State as a whole and to serve my party by helping it serve the

State. I should greatly like the aid of the Independents, and I appreciate the importance of the Independent vote, but I cannot accept a nomination on terms which would make me feel disloyal to the principles for which I stand, or at the cost of acting with what seemed to be bad faith toward my associates.

"Again expressing my hearty appreciation of the honor you wish to confer upon me, and my regret that it comes in such a shape that I do not see my way clear to accept it." [13]

Undoubtedly embarrassed and ashamed at the position into which he had put many of the independents, Roosevelt did not immediately deliver the letter to Chapman. Instead, he held a series of conferences with the Independent leaders, in which he tried to make them understand his position and they still attempted to get him to change his mind. Roosevelt left no record of what was said, but Chapman wrote his wife that in a "two hour talk" on September 23 at the City Club "there is nothing that has not been said — no point not covered. . . . I want to save Roosevelt. . . . He hadn't an idea of the forces he was to encounter . . ." Almost more in sadness than in anger, he continued:

"The resource remains to get Roosevelt to let us lay the matter before friends of his — politicians or otherwise in whom he has confidence. They would see his ruin clearer than he can himself. At any rate, the more desperate the situation, the heavier and stronger we will lay it on. You will say why do it. The reason is that Roosevelt is a boy — a child — he is honest — in spite all he is honest. He hadn't an idea of the forces he was to encounter . . .

"A mere collection of the correspondence without a word of comment would damn him . . . Show him the letter endorsing an address — he says he glanced at it — but didn't understand. And yet he is good — by Jove you can't help saying he is good. Of course half of our men say he deceives himself, he did understand — he did commit us, and let us go ahead. . . . I see in him only a very muddleheaded and at the same time pigheaded young man, who needs to be shoved right at this crucial point. . . ." [14]

The next day, September 24, the discussions continued. According to Chapman, Klein met with Roosevelt in New York and "talked with him for an hour", during which the Colonel reportedly "cried like a baby — I don't mean in a babyish way." Another reformer, Fulton Cutting, "dismissed him like a French noble dismissing a lacquey." A third participant in a meeting with persons whom Chapman called "eight of the best heads in town" reported that "it was the most terrible thing he ever saw." [15]

After enduring this barrage and already deeply troubled by a question that had just arisen as to his ineligibility as a potential Governor, Roosevelt took a late afternoon train for Oyster Bay. Even there, however, peace and quiet were denied him. Waiting in his home was Chapman, who had taken an earlier train in order to make a last plea. As that uninvited guest later described "what was not a pleasant evening":

"... I was not going home leaving any misunderstanding in the air as to how the Good Government Club group viewed the situation. But I went further. I unloaded the philosophy of agitation upon Roosevelt and pictured him as the broken backed half-good man, the successor of the dough face and Northern man with Southern principles of Civil War times, the trimmer who wouldn't break with his party and so, morally speaking, it ended up by breaking him."

Chapman later praised what he recalled was Roosevelt's receipt of "all this with a courtesy, deference, and self-control which were absolutely marvelous. I never expect to see such an exhibition of good breeding as Roosevelt gave that night." His host had a somewhat different recollection, telling a mutual friend of the two that Chapman had used "such harsh language" that he

"... grew very wroth and told him that he had no right to say such things to him, an able-bodied man who could not hit back (Jack had only one arm), and ordered him off the place. Half an hour later Jack returned, having missed his train, and rather sheepishly asked to be allowed to spend the night — and might he borrow a toothbrush."

Roosevelt was "disarmed and amused" at Chapman's discomfiture, and invited him back in. [16]

Chapman returned to New York early the next morning. He need not have wasted his time. Before he returned to Oyster Bay, Roosevelt had delivered to the reform leaders his September 22 letter declining their nomination. Its text appeared the next morning in the September 25 Sunday newspapers. [17]

For all practical purposes, this ended any impact that the Independent Party might have had on the election. With a Rochester lawyer quickly substituted for Roosevelt at its head, as Chapman later put it, "Our ticket staggered, but was kept in the field." But just barely, for, as he bitterly described his reception as he tried to win votes on an upstate tour:

> "One man cannot help us because he feels conscientiously bound to stand by the Democrats for one more election, having protested his Democracy against Bryan. Another also with us in spirit, but his brother has a chance of being Congressman on Platt's ticket and his hands are tied. Almost every single business-man or man of consequence in Syracuse is tied up by some such tie. The uniformity of it is ludicrous."

In the end, the Independent candidate, Theodore Bacon, would receive only 2103 votes. [18]

In his standard speech during his upstate swing, Chapman would suggest that "ambition has addled the brain and rotted the moral sense of Theodore Roosevelt." It was not until 20 years later, after the death of Chapman's son Victor and the loss in France of Roosevelt's son

Quentin, that the two men were once more drawn together during the short period before Roosevelt's death. [19]

❦ ❦ ❦

Some reformers never forgave what they considered to be a betrayal of both themselves and their ideals. For example, a less than friendly 1908 biographer wrote:

> "If a cleverer piece of political manipulation can be located in the history of the United States, it has escaped our notice. . . . What would have been rank trickery in Platt, Quay or Gorman,* might be quite laudable in a gentleman of high and holy motives seeking an end much to be desired. . . . Roosevelt in proud consciousness of his own rectitude wondered why his old friends among the Independents felt aggrieved. Surely nothing could be wrong that would promote so important a thing as Theodore Roosevelt's progress to high place in the 'governing class.'" [20]

Later and more objective historians have been more tolerant. In his prize-winning 1979 biography, Edmund Morris noted the possibility that Roosevelt's "own youthful idealism, mingled with sympathy for many of the Independents" led him to keep up their hopes, but then concluded that the "more likely" alternative was that "he wished to take on as many Independent voters as possible before nudging Chapman overboard." In 1997, H.W. Brands suggested the possibility of "simple inadvertence." Roosevelt himself, in his 1913 *Autobiography*, did not directly address the matter, merely referring to "extremists who had at first ardently insisted that I be forced on Platt," and then, "as soon as Platt supported me themselves opposed me *because* he supported me." [21]

There is another and equally plausible possibility. Roosevelt may

---

* In 1898, Matthew Quay was the Republican boss in Pennsylvania and Arthur Pue Gorman was the Democratic boss in Maryland.

have assumed that on the basis of his refusal to bolt the Republican Party following Blaine's 1884 Presidential nomination, the Independents
would recognize that he would run on a Republican ticket if he was
satisfied that Platt would lay down no compromising conditions to his
nomination. Once he believed that had occurred, he hoped that he
could convince the Independents that, as the *Evening Post* had suggested,
if any concessions had been made, it had been Platt rather than he who
had surrendered. Perhaps he could not believe, as Seth Low had feared,
that the Independents would once again "sacrifice all practical results .
. . for the sake of a theory."

What is clear, after the passage of more than a hundred years, is that
there will never be an entirely satisfactory explanation. Meanwhile, another concern quickly pushed the matter aside from public attention:
would Roosevelt actually receive the Republican nomination?

9

Decision At Saratoga

By Thursday, September 22, Benjamin B. Odell should have been a contented man. His efforts to persuade Platt to offer Roosevelt the Republican nomination had been successful, and he and the Easy Boss were assured of the support of at least 700 of the 971 delegates to Monday's State Convention. Earlier in the week, the platform and the balance of the ticket had been agreed upon. All that remained was the actual voting.

Nevertheless, as the Republican State Chairman boarded a late afternoon train that would take him to his Newburgh home en route to the convention city of Saratoga, he was worried. The Black forces should have realized that with the strong support of the Platt organization, Roosevelt's selection was assured. Yet they were still fighting, and Lou Payn, who was not known for shooting off his mouth, had declared only the day before that the Governor's renomination was "as sure as there is a heaven," and he and other Black supporters reportedly were backing up their words by making substantial bets. Payn was also quoted as saying that he had "surprises" to spring. What did he have up his sleeve?

As his train steamed north, Odell contemplated the possibilities. By the time he reached Newburgh, his fears had centered on whether, on some basis or other, Roosevelt might not be eligible to run for Governor. He recalled that the State Constitution required several continuous years of residence for anyone to hold that high office. He also remembered hearing rumors that someone had been in the New York City tax office examining Roosevelt's tax records, but he and other Re-

publican leaders had laughed them off. Thus, before proceeding on
from Newburgh to Saratoga, he first telephoned Roosevelt: Did the
Colonel know of any problem? *

Roosevelt's answer sent Odell back to New York. That spring, in response to a New York City property tax assessment, he had filed an affidavit stating that he was not liable since he was a resident of
Washington, D.C. After consulting by phone with Platt, Odell immediately summoned the Colonel to a late Friday afternoon meeting at the
Fifth Avenue Hotel. All that day, as they waited for their candidate to
arrive and explain his apparently damning statement, the Republican
leaders, as the *Herald* reported, "saw in imagination all their work going
for nothing and the triumph of Governor Black in the Convention."
Finally, at 6:00 p.m., armed with extensive documentation, Roosevelt
arrived and explained his affidavit to Platt, Odell, Quigg and others, including several judges. [1]

❊ ❊ ❊

Roosevelt's tax history was far from simple. During the 1890s, New
Yorkers were subject to both real and personal property taxes. In 1897,
Roosevelt's Oyster Bay real estate assessment had been quintupled
from $15,000 to $75,000, and his personal property valuation had
jumped from $2,000 to $12,000. Considering these increases "perfectly
absurd," he asked his lawyer uncle James Roosevelt whether anything
could be done about them. Uncle Jim replied that since Roosevelt had
voted in New York City during his term as Police Commissioner, he
need not pay Oyster Bay taxes at all. On his uncle's advice, he filed an
affidavit dated August 27, 1897, that took this position. On October 1,
however, his lease on his sister's town house expired, and since the

---

* Article IV, Section 2 provided, "No person shall be eligible for the office of Governor
or Lieutenant Governor, except a citizen of the United States . . . who shall have been
five years next preceding his election a resident of this State."

Roosevelt family was by now living in Washington, there was no reason to renew it.

Matters rested there until January 10, 1898, when the New York City real estate tax assessors, now again under Tammany domination, notified the Assistant Navy Secretary that his New York City personal property was being assessed at $50,000. Since Roosevelt's only residences were in Washington and Oyster Bay, this was patently ridiculous, but instead of challenging it on that basis, Roosevelt, who regarded Sagamore Hill as his real long-term home, asked his cousin Emlen Roosevelt to send the city authorities a statement asserting that he no longer had any "personal property subject to taxation in the city of New York," and that he now lived in Oyster Bay. The statement apparently was never sent, however, for on March 5, he wrote to his brother-in-law Douglas Robinson:

> "I don't know what to do about my taxes . . . I did not vote in New York, and could not have voted, and abandoned my residence there, and had no intention whatever of resuming it. Could I not make an affidavit that on November 1st my interests in New York ceased; that I did not vote there and have no residence there; and that I then intended, and now intend, to make my residence at Oyster Bay, where I shall vote and pay all my taxes this year?"

If Roosevelt had followed his inclination, he would not now be facing possible political disaster. Another lawyer relative, John E. Roosevelt, thought differently, however. Believing that the best course was for Roosevelt to avoid paying New York City taxes by claiming that he was a resident of Washington, D.C., he prepared and sent to his client an affidavit which took that position: "In October last my family came on here from Oyster Bay, L.I., and since then I have been and now am a resident of Washington, D.C."

It was this document that raised the issue of Roosevelt's eligibility.

Roosevelt had sensed that this was not the right approach, and asked his lawyer whether it was "practicable to alter matters so as to have me taxed at Oyster Bay?" If not, he was prepared to pay New York City taxes, since "I don't want to sneak out of anything, nor do I wish to lose my vote two years in succession." Apparently receiving no reply, by March 31, he concluded that his affidavit was a mistake, and wrote John Roosevelt:

> "I ought to have expressed myself more clearly . . . that I did not want to take any step that would cause me to lose my vote this coming year in New York. Don't you think that I could fix the matter up at Oyster Bay? Can't I pay the taxes there now?"

Perhaps because Theodore was not suggesting that he should be subject to continuing New York City taxes, John Roosevelt did not focus on the statement in the affidavit that he had become a resident of the District of Columbia, did nothing to change it and filed it with the authorities. Meanwhile, Uncle Jim, who handled Theodore's Oyster Bay affairs and apparently was supposed to put his nephew's name back on the Oyster Bay tax rolls, died before he could take any action. With other more compelling things on his mind, Theodore never followed up on the matter. Thus, as of late September, the official position of the organization candidate for New York Governor was that he was not subject to any New York taxes because he resided outside the State. [2]

❋ ❋ ❋

Roosevelt had not had time to completely document his position during the less than 24 hours between Odell's call and Friday's late afternoon meeting with the party leaders. What they did hear from him, however, led them to conclude that their candidate had enough of a case that they should not abandon him, particularly since there was no viable alternative. They had just made this decision when Platt received word that a delegation of Black supporters was outside and wanted to see him. Excusing himself, he went to another room at the party headquarters, where he was confronted by a group headed by Payn and former Republican New York County Chairman Edward ("Smooth Ed") Lauterbach, who had met with Black in Albany earlier that day and then had come to New York "to make things fast." They had with them the Roosevelt affidavit, which apparently had been given them by Tammany Hall insiders who saw Roosevelt as a major threat whose candidacy should be derailed.[3]

There followed what must have been one of Platt's finest hours. As he later recalled, Payn and his cohorts "asked me to read" the affidavit "and explain how in the face of such a declaration it was possible to proceed with the plans for his Gubernatorial nomination." With a bravado that he could not have felt, the Easy Boss replied that he had known all about the matter for some time, for "I have had some rats burrowing myself," and that "if they were possessed of all the facts, they would view the matter differently, and that later I hoped to apprise them of such facts." He stuck to his guns even after Payn made it clear that the text of the affidavit would appear in the next morning's papers. Seeing that they were not going to convince Platt to withdraw his support for Roosevelt, the group departed. According to the next day's *Herald*, Lauterbach at once

> ". . . went up to the Savoy Hotel, where he found Richard Croker and all the Tammany leaders except Mayor Van Wyck. He told them what Governor Black and his friends had discovered, and furnished them with a copy of the affidavit, which the democratic leaders at once had typewritten for distribution."

According to Platt's account, as soon as his uninvited visitors had left,

> ". . . I then rejoined my friends in another room, and reported to them what Mr. Lauterbach and his associates had presented for my consideration.

> "At this juncture, Mr. Roosevelt took me aside and said, with a

trepidation I had never before and have never seen him display: 'I cannot remain in this fight. I must withdraw from the race.'

"His desire to withdraw was made apparent to everyone in the room. The fatal effect of his withdrawal was to me so manifest that I replied: 'You must not withdraw. You must trust to me to solve the problem and elect you Governor of this State.'

"In order to emphasize my determination and to restore his courage, I said with brutal frankness: 'Is the hero of San Juan a coward?'

"He replied with his customary vehemence: 'No, I am not a coward!' " [4]

After further discussion the meeting adjourned. To the press, Platt struck the same posture that he had taken with Payn and Lauterbach: "You can say for me that Colonel Roosevelt will be a candidate at the Convention and that he will be nominated." Roosevelt did likewise when a reporter cornered him that evening: "There is nothing in the charge of any kind or description. I voted last in New York." He added, "I am going through a great turmoil as I did in Santiago, and I will come out of it the same way." [5]

❋ ❋ ❋

Although Platt publicly exuded confidence that Roosevelt's affidavit would pose no obstacle to his nomination, in his own mind he knew that the Colonel's explanation itself would not suffice. The Easy Boss needed the best talent available to sustain the legal position that Roosevelt had kept his New York residence.

Fortunately, the man for the job was among those in the Fifth Avenue Hotel room with him and Roosevelt. By general consensus, if one wanted the best New York lawyer available, you could choose no better than Elihu Root. Now 53 years of age and at the height of his professional career, Root was perhaps the first of the great turn-of-the-century lawyers epitomized by a client's reported praise: "I have had many lawyers who have told me what I cannot do; Mr. Root is the only lawyer who tells me how to do what I want to do." With this skill, he was in increasingly great demand by clients who were involved in the organization and reorganization of the large corporations which were revolutionizing the conduct of United States business in the late 1890s.

Unlike many of his fellows, however, Root also believed that a lawyer had a civic duty to involve himself in public affairs. In his case, this meant the Republican Party, and especially its element that believed in the importance of municipal reform. Nevertheless, with an acute instinct as to the ways that power is and can be exercised, he had always maintained friendly relations with Platt and his associates. Thus, it was Root who, as New York County Republican Chairman, helped convince Roosevelt to run for Mayor in 1886 and diligently worked for his election.

Impressive though these qualities were, however, they probably were not what led Platt to choose Root as the man to convince the Saratoga convention that Roosevelt was eligible to run for Governor. Before he had turned to his now primary role of corporate adviser, Root had been renowned for his skill as a litigator. With the slit eyes and waxen cheeks of a Chinese mandarin, and hair cut Roman style with bangs (he was an admirer of "Roman virtues"), his appearance was not that of most courtroom lawyers. But this was of no matter to judges and juries, for with his logic and clarity of argument, ever-present wit, and a phenomenal memory of detail, "he gave off the impression that he understood everything there was to understand in any human situation." And he could be tough as nails, for, as New York lawyer Henry Stimson was to observe, "on cross-examination his eyes seemed to burn with a red glow" which reminded Stimson of a description of "a similar red light . . . in General Sherman's eyes when he went into battle."[6]

❋ ❋ ❋

Although he had his doubts as to the strength of the case, Root was more than willing to take on the assignment. While he had previously turned down McKinley's request that he serve as Minister to Spain, he undoubtedly harbored a desire to perform some important public service, and the next year would accept the President's invitation to become Secretary of War. In this connection, he was fully cognizant of the importance of Platt's support. Moreover, Root was a long-time friend of Roosevelt, and sympathized with his position. As he recalled many years later:

> "Roosevelt was a youngster. He didn't know much about business or business affairs. He got caught in a little inconsistency of an affidavit about his tax. Jack Roosevelt, who was looking after his affairs, had made the affidavit as strong as he could and it was open to a possible, but not a natural interpretation which would have disqualified Roosevelt for the governorship." [7]

❀ ❀ ❀

With the care that had been instrumental in securing his leadership position, Platt was not content with leaving Root to his own devices. Perhaps on the theory that two good lawyers would be better than one, he suggested that Root consult with Joseph Choate and "obtain his views in the premises." The 66-year-old Choate was by now an elder statesman of the New York Bar, and was probably the equal of Chauncey Depew in his ability to sway a large audience with a mixture of oratory and wit. Perhaps the combination of his charm with Root's logic was what would persuade the delegates at Saratoga.

Choate was spending a few days at his country home at Stockbridge, at the southern edge of Massachusetts' Berkshire Hills, and would not return to New York in time for Root to meet him there before the convention. Accordingly, Root had no choice but to take a train to Stockbridge, and then ride by carriage the short distance to *Naumkeag*, the Norman-style hillside "cottage" that Stanford White had designed twelve years earlier, where Choate was spending an increasing amount of time.

By the time that Root arrived, Choate had undoubtedly read the morning newspapers and was generally acquainted with Roosevelt's problem. Thus, he had time to reach at least a preliminary opinion on his response to the questions he knew Root would ask him. He surely recalled how, less than two years earlier, Roosevelt had refused to back him for United States Senator against Boss Platt. But as the two old friends sat overlooking the valley with its foliage about to erupt into autumn splendor, it is doubtful that there was any mention of recriminations. Instead, Choate bluntly told Root that his only chance was to push Roosevelt's nomination through the Convention by political pressure since as a legal matter the case was hopeless: "I don't see anything to it, Root, but for you to go up to the Convention and force it on them." If Roosevelt managed to be nominated, Choate would probably lend a hand to elect him. For now, however, Root was on his own. [8]

❁ ❁ ❁

As soon as the public had had a chance to read its Saturday morning newspapers, the question of Roosevelt's eligibility was the talk of the entire state. The issue was seemingly a simple one: "Had Roosevelt changed his New York residence or had he kept it?" It was a matter on which even the most poorly educated citizen could and did opine. As in most political matters, however, the answer frequently depended on the political preference of the individual expressing his or her opinion.

The press, of course, was eager to weigh in with its own views and advice. Under the heading "PROOFS, NOT OPINION", the *Tribune* noted that certain "eminent lawyers" were said to "have fully examined the case and have decided that Mr. Roosevelt's residence in Oyster Bay can be absolutely shown." But, the editors continued:

"... the opinion of these distinguished men, influential though it may be, is not proof, and there will be great disappointment

Elihu Root
(Courtesy of the New York Public Library)

A Low Down Santiago Trick
(*New York Herald*)

among the delegates and among the Republican masses if the absolute proof, which so convinces the lawyers, is not immediately forthcoming."

If Roosevelt was to be the Republican candidate, "he should run with his eligibility settled beyond a reasonable doubt."

The *Times* took a similar stance: ". . . it will be difficult to overcome the impression, which Col. Roosevelt's opponents will strive to make general, that he made the Washington affidavit in order to get rid of paying his taxes." It concluded by warning "Mr. Platt and his associates" that "a candidate is harassed and the labors and anxieties of his managers are very much increased by a campaign attack that cannot be met and silenced." [9]

The reform-minded *Evening Post* took a different tack, which may have caused any convention delegates who read it to have second thoughts about abandoning Roosevelt in favor of Black. Without passing on the legal merits of the case, it attacked Black, Payn and Lauterbach for having "assailed" Roosevelt "as a gang of thugs would fall upon a victim in a dark alley." It continued with language that its Democratic readers must have relished as they realized how they could use it against Black if the Roosevelt residence issue led to his defeat and the Governor's renomination:

"So the Governor of the state conspires with Payn, Aldridge, Lauterbach and some of Croker's men for the purpose of defeating Col. Roosevelt's nomination by a trick. Lou Payn gives the proper name to the proceeding by telling everybody that he has 'something up his sleeve' that will prevent the Colonel's nomination, and offering to bet $10,000 on it. Lauterbach gets the documentary evidence from Tammany officials upon which the trick is based . . . And they are all so delighted with what they are doing that they give away their game in advance. They forgot for the moment that they were playing tricks with their own boss, who taught them all the tricks they have ever known, and just as they were ready to produce their card, the boss himself disclosed it to the world. This is a fine game for the Governor of a great state to be engaged in! What is to be said of the intelligence, to say nothing of the moral sense, of a man who thinks his chances for renomination to high office can be benefited by such methods." [10]

❧ ❧ ❧

As soon as the news of Roosevelt's affidavit had been made public, both sides began intensive efforts to gain public support for their positions. On Saturday, the Black forces in Albany issued a statement arguing that when Roosevelt went to Washington to be Assistant Secretary of the Navy, "he no doubt expected to remain in Washington for four years, and there was perfect propriety, therefore, in his choice of Washington as the place for the payment of his personal taxes . . ." Later in the day, Black himself, stung by the charge that he had participated in a conspiracy to undermine the Roosevelt nomination, denied that he had known about the matter "for several weeks." In fact, "[t]he question of such ineligibility was first presented to the Governor on Thursday night." [11]

For their part, the Roosevelt adherents asserted that Payn and his friends had had a copy of the damaging affidavit in their possession for some time, but had delayed using it until shortly before the convention so that it would have maximum effect. They made public a copy of Roosevelt's July 31, 1898, acknowledgment of the receipt of his commission as Colonel, in which he stated, "I was born in New York on October 29, 1858, and have resided in New York ever since." Roosevelt himself was generally unavailable to reporters except to reiterate that he had told his lawyer "that I had no intention of changing my domicile" and "I would much rather pay the tax than have any question about it, though I did not think that as a non-resident of New York City it was just that I should be assessed." [12]

The one point on which both the Roosevelt and Black forces seemed to agree was that the legal issue was whether the candidate had given up his New York "domicile." The word is generally synonymous with "permanent residence," "final abode," or a place at which a person intends to live for an indefinite period of time. * Under a common law doctrine established in English law well before the first colonists arrived in the New World, a domicile is retained until a person demonstrates by statements

---

* Seventy-two years later, the New York courts would rule that a candidate for New York State office does not lose his residence by reason of service in Washington as a United States government employee. The State Constitution at the time provided that the Comptroller and Attorney General must "possess the qualifications" required for the State's Governor and Lieutenant-Governor, i.e., five years of New York residence. From 1966 to 1969, Adam Walinsky, a candidate for the 1970 Democratic nomination for Attorney General, had worked in Washington as an attorney in the Justice Department. During that time, he lived with his family in McLean, Virginia, where he registered his automobiles, obtained a Virginia driver's license and made plans to build a house. In response to a challenge by a primary opponent, the New York Supreme Court held that the issue was whether Walinsky had changed his New York domicile and that:

> "All of these acts show intent to make Virginia his permanent residence. On the other hand he was a bona fide domiciliary of New York when he accepted a position in the United States Attorney's office. He was engaged in the practice of law in New York City, he and his family lived in New York City, he was a member of the New York State Bar, and he was historically from birth a resident of New York. Based on these facts a reasonable man could find that he had shown an intent to change his domicile, but a reasonable man would also ask what other course he had. He had a family, and is it not a man's desire to have his family in close proximity. Should he have left his family in New York? Would this be reasonable. I do not think so."

The court concluded that Walinsky "did not cross the invisible line of residency via intent," and its decision was affirmed on appeal. In the *Matter of Robert L. Meehan, Petitioner, v. James P. Lomenzo, as Secretary of State of the State of New York, Adam Walinsky et al, Respondents,* 63 Misc. 2d 490 (May 24, 1970); *affirmed,* 34 App. Div. 2d 1024 (June 1, 1979), *affirmed* 27 N.Y. 2d 600 (June 4, 1970).

or other actions that he or she intends to establish a new domicile elsewhere. In some situations, the abandonment of a long-term "domicile of origin" may be more difficult to prove than the surrender of a short-term domicile of choice. Thus, the editors of the New York *Sun* were on solid ground when they argued in the paper's September 27 issue:

"It is remarkable that the question should now be whether a Roosevelt is a citizen of New York, and therefore ineligible to office in this state, for the Roosevelt family from the earliest days of New York has been associated with its noblest undertakings."

After listing the civic accomplishments of several earlier-generation family members, commencing with Isaac Roosevelt in the mid-18th century, the editorial concluded:

"Roosevelt is a name for all New Yorkers to be proud of, a name honorably and usefully associated with the history of the city and the State from the earliest colonial days. It has never sought the cheap glare of social prominence and display. Yet, now, political sophistry has sought to delude people into the belief that Theodore Roosevelt, one of the brightest examples of public devotion in that family and in any family of America, is not a New Yorker. The idea is absurd." [13]

❧ ❧ ❧

Although the Republican State Convention was not scheduled to open until the next Tuesday, September 27, by Saturday evening a large number of delegates had already checked in at their hotels. For many years, Saratoga had been a favorite destination for politicians, and these Republicans were no exception. Prior to the Civil War, the area had been the summer home of many Southern planters, who enjoyed the combination of its temperate climate and the supposedly medicinal qualities of the mineral water that flowed from its springs. During the Civil War, with this source of revenue gone, the city fathers built a track, and the lure of racing, including the fun of betting on one's

favorite horses, soon led Saratoga to rival Newport as an August
location for both patricians and social climbers to see and be seen. Large
hotels were built to attract the visitors, and, before long, the politicians
arrived, especially the "Tammany Boys," headed first by Boss Tweed,
later by Big Tim Sullivan and then by Richard Croker, who habitually

> ". . . walked at his gorilla trot, swinging his long arms, from
> horse to horse under the trees, and once appeared, as drays and
> victorias bowled in from the course, sitting beside a famous cour-
> tesan in her English cart, so scared of her effulgence that his one
> remark was: 'I think your check-rein's too tight, Ma'am.'" [14]

By late September, the horses had been gone for weeks and the Tammany Boys has been replaced by the minions of Platt and Payn. The two
men and their closest associates arrived on the same train, but there is
no evidence that they gave each other anything more than the most
cursory greeting. The rank and file, who until Friday had expected a
pleasant gathering at which Roosevelt would be easily nominated,
were now unsure which way to turn. Indeed, according to the *Sun*, "the
fact that Gov. Black and his friends had obtained the affidavit concern-
ing Col. Theodore Roosevelt's eligibility as a citizen of the State of New
York from Tammany Hall has made many old friends on both sides
sore and angry." The word from the Platt camp was, "No quarter to the
enemy." To everyone he saw, the Easy Boss exuded confidence. Meanwhile, his assistants were distributing to anyone who would take them
buttons to which were attached miniature rabbit's feet and bearing the
inscription: "You can't stop Teddy's luck. This rabbit was killed at midnight in the dark of the moon on the grave of a cross-eyed Spaniard on
San Juan Hill, Cuba." [15]

❋ ❋ ❋

September 25, 1898, was a Sunday, but for the politicians congregating
at Saratoga, it was far from a day of rest. Platt was in continuous conclave,
trying to put together a ticket that would include several candidates

who were sufficiently independent so that what emerged could not be dubbed a Platt slate. Under the caption, "Mr. Platt Enjoying His Supper," a *Herald* artist sketched a picture of the Easy Boss trying to eat a meal, but instead turning to speak with three frock-coated gentlemen who had interrupted his repast.

Rumors were flying that Platt had offered the Attorney General slot to Payn if he would withdraw his opposition to Roosevelt, but that he had been rebuffed. Fearing that it was too late to placate Roosevelt if he was nominated and elected, the Black forces saw no alternative but to fight to the end. They probably were influenced by reports that Roosevelt had vowed not to reappoint Payn as Superintendent of Insurance when his term expired. For his part, Payn turned down the suggestion of Platt's son Frank that his father meet with him: he didn't have the time. Meanwhile, "Smooth Ed" Lauterbach was walking back and forth along hotel corridors and piazzas, telling any delegates who would listen that, as a *Herald* reporter wrote, "the Republican party would sink itself into everlasting shame if it should make the Rough Rider their candidate and he called forth a goodly portion of the vituperative adjectives of English to make his argument picturesque." At one point, he managed to corner Platt, arguing to him that Roosevelt was at heart only a publicity seeker:

"He organized a regiment for the notoriety he would get out of it . . . He led his men into an ambuscade in Cuba in order to further this ambition . . . He risked other men's lives to gain his end."

Platt listened patiently to what the *Herald* called "only mild samples of the charges and harshness that are characterizing the prologue of what seems certain to be one of the most exciting political conventions of the history of the State." He then dismissed his visitor with his stock answer: "Roosevelt will be nominated." [16]

Meanwhile, after Chapman's early morning departure, Roosevelt spent a quiet Sunday at his Sagamore Hill home, not even venturing

Mr. Platt Enjoying His Supper
(*New York Herald*)

out to go to church. His only visitors were a number of Rough Riders, who had come to say good-bye before returning to the West. Later, he took a long walk around his property with his wife and enjoyed a family dinner with her and the children. The combination of the attacks on him by the Independents and the sudden raising of the eligibility issue had created a strain that even a man of his fortitude found almost impossible to bear. The next day, he wrote to Lodge that "I have, literally, hardly been able to eat or sleep during the last week, because of the pressure upon me." He was especially annoyed at "[t]he Citizens Union or Independent Movement," and "their exceedingly tricky conduct to me." [17]

❋ ❋ ❋

On Monday morning, with the convention due to open in less than 24 hours, the Black forces sprang one more surprise. Without warning, the Governor arrived in Saratoga on the 11:25 a.m. train and went directly to the headquarters of the Rensselaer County delegation, where he conferred with Payn, Lauterbach and other supporters. He then held court into the early evening while a stream of visitors, including delegates pledged for Roosevelt, came by to pay their respects. There was no precedent for an active candidate, especially the Governor, to seek votes in this manner, and, as a *Times* reporter wrote, Black's appearance "lent a new and sensational interest to the fierce struggle going on here." The delegates who visited with the Governor reported that he had not specifically asked for their votes but instead had emphasized that Roosevelt was not a New York resident and hence could not become Governor.

Before Black arrived, Platt and Payn finally met, but neither man would budge from his position. After Platt had left, Payn issued a statement that he had "positive evidence" that the Easy Boss did not mean to nominate Roosevelt, but "at the last moment" would substitute former Ambassador to Spain Stewart Woodford and "throw Mr. Roosevelt out." Platt's angry response was that the story "is the foolish outpour-ing from bewildered and defeated men."

Although they were outwardly confident, the Platt forces were counting on the convincing evidence of Roosevelt's eligibility that Root had promised them, and he had not yet arrived. The tension proved to be too much for Quigg. Shortly after noon, this notoriously suave and unflappable man blundered by mistake into Payn's cottage on the grounds of the United States Hotel, thinking it was Platt's. Payn was sitting in the parlor with his son. As Quigg rushed by, apparently intent on providing important information to Platt, whom he thought was in a back room, Payn stood up and exploded: "Who was that? Was that Quigg?" Quigg tried to apologize, but the clearly furious Payn without a word used his index finger to point the interloper to the exit. As the dazed Quigg tried to leave as fast as possible, he ran into Black, who was just arriving. According to the next day's *Herald*, Quigg, "al-most running, sought seclusion for the rest of the day." [18]

❀ ❀ ❀

Following his return to New York from his Stockbridge visit to Choate, Root had been avoiding the reporters as he worked full time on his presentation to the convention. In reviewing the items of correspon-dence and other evidence that the Colonel and his friends had located for him, he was assisted by Congressman George W. Ray, a respected lawyer who was later to chair the House Judiciary Committee and close his career as a United States District Judge. Even before he saw Choate, Root had prepared a letter from Roosevelt to him, dated September 24, explaining that "the residence in Washington" referred to in the Colonel's affidavit

"... was the temporary official residence incident to my service as Assistant Secretary of the Navy. My permanent residence was then and has been ever since I gave up my house in New York City on the 1st of the previous October at Oyster Bay, Queens County,

New York. That is now my home and that of my family and has
been so continuously for many years with the exception of the
two years I was Police Commissioner of New York."

Armed with this letter and other documents they believed would be
helpful, Root and Ray fashioned what they hoped would be a convincing legal argument, although Root planned to appeal to the delegates'
emotions as well. [19]

Perhaps because he believed he needed all the time possible to fashion his presentation, but also perhaps because he thought that a last-
minute arrival might heighten its dramatic effect, Root did not leave
New York that Monday until mid afternoon, and did not reach Saratoga until nine o'clock that evening. Even though he had not yet eaten
dinner, he immediately went to Platt's United States Hotel cottage,
where the Senator was waiting for him. He took Root to the nearby
State Committee headquarters, where his close associates, including
Depew and Odell, were waiting. Behind locked doors, they met for
nearly three hours. They emerged after midnight, all confidence and
smiles. Platt expressed their collective view: "The bottom has been
knocked out of all charges against him [Roosevelt]." Although Root refused to make public the "proofs" of Roosevelt's residence until the
next day's convention, Platt called them "conclusive evidence" of the
candidate's eligibility, which the group had "gone over carefully, so
that there would be no possibility of error."

Well before Root's arrival, the tide was running strongly in Roosevelt's direction. As the latecomers mixed on the broad high-roofed pi-
azza of the United States Hotel with the delegates who had arrived over
the weekend, it became clear, according to the *Tribune* correspondent,
that

"... the movement to nominate Colonel Roosevelt was a popular one, reflecting the voices of the constituencies behind the
delegates. No machine could bring together such a tremendous

vote for one man over the head of the State Administration who, with many creditable acts in his favor, was also a candidate for Governor."

Not even Black's personal appearance could change the result. When his managers met at 10:30 that Monday evening, they quickly realized that, despite all their efforts, they could round up the votes of no more than 200 of the more than 900 delegates, and that the balance would go to Roosevelt. Therefore, when they received word that the highly respected Root was prepared to furnish the Colonel's backers with clear and convincing proof of his eligibility, most of them were ready to concede defeat. With the issue all but decided and the bar of the United States Hotel still open after midnight, a *Herald* reporter observed "the Black men and the Platt men . . . amicably drinking cocktails together in the wee small hours." [20]

❦ ❦ ❦

If these delegates had hoped that a late morning's sleep would refresh them from their nocturnal activities, they were to be disappointed. Shortly after dawn, late-arriving delegations, preceded by brass bands, were parading down the usually quiet streets to their hotels. There was nothing for them to do but rise, breakfast with the newcomers, and ready themselves to partake of the activities of this September 27, which they were sure that they would long remember.

Although the first session would not convene until noon, the visitors' galleries in the large, multi-turreted Saratoga Convention Hall were filled long before the first gavel fell. With its red, white and blue bunting, the auditorium could have been mistaken for the site of a national convention, except that the official standards that designated the seats of delegations bore the names of counties instead of states. When word spread that the only visible portrait on the platform was a large picture of Governor Black, a late-arriving delegation quickly produced a banner showing Roosevelt in his Rough Rider uniform. When they carried it in, the assemblage rose to its feet and let out a loud yell that would have done proud the most uninhibited of the Colonel's cowboys.

During the late morning, the band entertained the waiting audience with what the *Sun* reporter called "all the patriotic airs that anyone had heard for the last fifty years." When the Roosevelt banner was carried in, as if on cue it switched from "The Battle Cry of Freedom" to "Tramp, Tramp, Tramp, the Boys Are Marching." With their long experience that political conventions never start on time, Platt and Depew were among the many late-comers. As soon as they were recognized, they were loudly welcomed. Undoubtedly aware of the direction that the political wind was blowing, Payn delayed his appearance until the roll was being called, and took his seat without attracting attention. [21]

As at all other political conventions, the first session dealt mainly with organizational matters, and was only a warmup for what was to follow. Indicative of the leaders' plan to avoid the Erie Canal scandals, temporary chairman Sereno Payne's keynote address stressed national issues, and drew resounding cheers as he praised the President: "that statesman, that warrior, that foremost citizen, William McKinley." After conducting some routine business, the convention adjourned until 3:30, and the entire assemblage quickly dispersed to find places to fortify themselves with a meal that would sustain them through what promised to be a long afternoon.

At 4:00 o'clock the second session was called to order, and this time all the delegates were in their seats. There were smiles all around when the chairman of the Credentials Committee happily reported that, presumably because the organization had done its work well, there were no contests to resolve. By now, the delegates were avid to commence their real business, and as the permanent chairman moved into his traditional address, he was constantly interrupted by cheers for Black and Roosevelt, with the supporters of each candidate trying to outshout the other. When it came time for the platform to be adopted and the chairman of Committee Resolutions could not be located, the impatient throng would brook no further delay. "Depew, Depew!" the Roosevelt delegates shouted. "The platform can wait." Probably just as pleased to have his candidate chosen as soon as possible, Quigg rose and obtained unanimous approval to move directly to the nominations. [22]

Although the pressure for the nominating speeches had come largely from Roosevelt backers who were anticipating one of Depew's polished performances, Black had already been scheduled to be the first candidate to be presented. The former upstate judge who had nominated him at the 1896 convention did so again this year. At his first mention of the Governor's name, the Black delegates rose with loud cheers as the speaker praised "the strong and faithful man, the same unswerving man and devoted patriot that you have always known him to be."

For the large majority of both the delegates and the galleries, Judge Cady's effort was mercifully short. When Depew followed him to the dais, the enthusiasm for Roosevelt exploded before he could even mention his candidate's name. There was a cry of "Three cheers for Roosevelt," which were repeatedly given. Depew was in his usual good form, drawing uproarious laughter as he suggested that when San Juan Hill was stormed, Roosevelt was "an influential citizen of Santiago de Cuba." When he spoke of how the Colonel bore "a charmed life" as he was spared by "bullets whistling by him" which were "rapidly thinning the ranks of these desperate fighters," he was interrupted by three men who, as the next morning's *Herald* recorded, burst through "the crowd that was massed in space in front of the door," which "parted in terror" as "a large piece of canvas on a frame" was "carried over the heads of the newspaper men and on to the platform." There, after it "fell on the heads of three women and ruined some exquisite millinery, it gave a half dozen men a vicious rap on the head." At last, after several failures, it was finally righted to display to the startled but relieved audience a large picture of Roosevelt in his military uniform. To mixed laughter and cheers, a bemused Depew announced, "That is the entrance into this Convention of a Rough Rider."

When Depew had concluded his remarks to wild cheers, it was time for the seconding speeches. * New York City's Abe Gruber, a short man with a broad smile who had not been noted as a crowd pleaser, drew cheers and laughter as he argued for Black that the voters "do not expect the Executive Mansion to be turned into a shooting gallery." The Roosevelt supporters joined in the general hilarity when he argued, "Let us say to Governor Black, well done, good and faithful servant," not "good and faithful servant, we will see that you are well-done." [23]

Finally, it was Root's turn, and the audience listened with rapt attention as he made the case for Roosevelt's eligibility. It was the sound argument of a man renowned for his legal advocacy, but it also contained what Root later referred to as "a lot of ballyhoo." At one point, after quoting from a letter from Roosevelt to Douglas Robinson asking his brother-in-law to see that his "just taxes" were paid, even though "I shall be horribly over my income," Root looked up from the letter and to wild cheering observed:

"Yes, horribly over his income because he was spending his money to raise the troop of cavalry with which he fought at San Juan and because he was about to abandon the position and salary of Assistant Secretary of the Navy for the meager pay and high expenses of a lieutenant colonel of cavalry.

And so, overwhelmed with this great burden of raising his regiment, he went to the front thinking that these taxes were paid, as he had directed them to be, and he never knew to the contrary until his return from Santiago . . ."

---

* As Depew recalled in his memoirs, he had made such speeches "many times in conventions, but have never had such a response."

By the time that Root ended by stating that Roosevelt has never intended to abandon "the State of his nativity, his ambition and his pride," even the most committed Black supporter knew that the fight was all over. Although it was time for the balloting to begin, the convention chairman first recognized Lauterbach, who mounted the platform to wave the white flag of unconditional surrender. After confirming his activity in obtaining and using on Black's behalf Roosevelt's affidavit of non-residency, and suggesting that his action had been a result of the training of Platt — "a hard taskmaster and a good teacher" — he announced that he "frankly and fully" accepted Root's explanation: it was "as clinching as though the Court of Appeals had decided it" and "as clear as the noonday sun." Undoubtedly fearing the continuing wrath of Platt and his cohorts, to the laughter of his audience he tried to make belated amends, concluding:

"... I wish to say I wish to be forgiven. I have been a bad boy, perhaps, and have felt cold chills all day."

The voting that immediately followed was an anticlimax. Erie County's (Buffalo) 53 to 2 vote for Roosevelt jumped him into a formidable early lead, and when Kings County (Brooklyn) added its 83 vote plurality, there was no longer any doubt. New York County's 172 votes put him over the top. When the roll call was completed at 7:41 p.m., the final tally was 753 for Roosevelt and 218 for Black. Lauterbach tried to gain the floor to make the vote unanimous, but he had already had his say, and the chairman recognized Black's nominator Judge Cady, whose motion was enthusiastically adopted. [24]

❧ ❧ ❧

Following his weekend return to Oyster Bay, Roosevelt had remained at Sagamore Hill, catching up on correspondence and relaxing with his family. His house was not connected to the outer world by telephone, and there had been no attempt to string up a telegraph wire from the village, three miles away. Late Tuesday afternoon, as the delegates were

He Went Right Through It
(*New York Herald*)

listening to nominating speeches, a group of reporters who had come up the hill to his home observed him in white flannels "calmly sauntering over the lawn with his wife, seemingly unconcerned about the doings in the Saratoga convention."

That evening, the candidate and his wife changed into evening attire and after a family dinner went into their library where, lighted by the rosy glow of a wood burning fireplace, they waited for the news from Saratoga. Before too long, a messenger bicycled up the hill with a telegram stating: "READING BY ROOT OF TAX CORRESPONDENCE PRODUCED PROFOUND SENSATION AND WILD ENTHUSIASM." Shortly thereafter another telegram reported Lauterbach's concession, and there soon followed several more announcing Roosevelt's nomination, including one from Lieutenant Governor Woodruff, whom the Convention later chose as his running mate.

When the reporters were shown into the room about 8:45, Roosevelt greeted them with the customary gratitude of a successful candidate for his nomination and an appreciation of "the heavy responsibilities it entails." But, still feeling the effect of the eligibility controversy, he also had "a word to my enemies":

> "When they find what they deem a mistake or error of judgment on my part let them go ahead, but when it comes to a question of my probity or honor, they may just as well make up their minds at the outset that they need to make extremely sure of the facts before they say anything, for I shall never wish more than to have all the facts known."

With that warning, the nominee was ready to put the past battle behind him and plan for the fight that lay ahead. [25]

10

Croker's Syracuse Surprise

THE NEXT DAY, SEPTEMBER 28, THE DEMOCRATS MET IN SYRACUSE. With the Erie Canal scandals fresh in the voters' minds, they were optimistic that after four years of Republican rule they would return one of their number to the State House. The scandals were not their only issue. There was also continuing urban unhappiness with the excise laws that kept the bars closed on Sundays, and anger over the administration of the New York National Guard, with widespread complaint over poor equipment and training and the failure of the Republican Adjutant General to bring home several regiments that were still suffering disease in southern camps. Unlike their opponents, however, who hoped that their war hero nominee would lead the electorate to forget if not forgive past mistakes, the Democrats had no obvious candidate.

Following Grover Cleveland's accession to the Presidency in 1885, Democratic politics had been dominated by his successor, Lieutenant Governor David B. Hill. A former Assembly Speaker and Mayor of Elmira, Hill had first won public recognition as an ally of Samuel J. Tilden in his efforts to expose the misdeeds of Tammany and its boss, William Marcy Tweed. After four years as Governor, in 1891 he persuaded the Democratic-controlled legislature to elect him to the United States Senate, which he used as a base to launch a campaign against Cleveland for the 1892 Presidential nomination. Although unsuccessful, he continued to wield political power in the Empire State until the

Republican legislature replaced him with Platt when his term expired in 1897. By 1898, following the Democratic defeats in the 1894 and 1896 elections and Tammany's 1897 triumph in the New York City mayorality contest, the party's center of gravity had shifted downstate, but Hill hoped that at Syracuse he might be able to control the choice of the gubernatorial candidate.[1]

Richard Croker, however, saw no reason why he could not rule the state as he did the city. When he arrived in Syracuse on September 27, it was as a conquering hero. According to the *Herald*, he

"...flushed with pleasure. . . as the first section of the Tammany train, with 1500 braves on board, entered the city on its way to the station. Sidewalks were lined with men and women, who cheered lustily for Mr. Croker and his army of tigers. . . When he alighted from his parlor car, Mayor James K. McGuire's bluecoats cleared a path for him, and with uplifted clubs drove the curious away. . . The crowd ran before and behind his carriage, and when it reached the Yates a great cheer greeted the leader from a throng of delegates and sightseers gathered in front of the hotel."

On his arrival, Croker met with Hill and U.S. Senator Edward Murphy, a Croker ally who nevertheless was on friendly terms with Hill. Neither side had an obvious candidate for Governor. Hill made several suggestions, but emphasized that he would be happy with anyone who was experienced in State affairs and was "a man of character." Croker expressed no particular interest in any of these names, and Hill was equally unimpressed by Croker's mention of an Albany judge.[2]

The next day, as the delegates awaited instructions from their leaders, the convention held an unexciting first session. While the speakers droned on, there was talk everywhere of a Hill resurgence, as his candidates, with the support of Brooklyn boss Hugh McLaughlin, won contests for disputed seats in the Buffalo and Rochester delegations. These victories were misleading. During the day, Croker, McLaughlin, and

Murphy had put together a combination of 238 delegates, 12 more than
a majority, who would do their bidding on the crucial gubernatorial
vote. Thus, when Hill met with Croker and Murphy that evening, it
gradually began to dawn on him that he was not in the driver's seat. He
did not give up easily, however, arguing vigorously, on the basis of his
broad experience, that any candidate from New York City would bear
such a Tammany taint that he could not be elected. On this basis, he
was able to veto the choice of Mayor Van Wyck, for whom a boom had
been developing.

At 2:00 a.m. without reaching agreement, the conference adjourned, and the exhausted Hill retired to his quarters for a few hours'
sleep. While he rested, in the words of a *Herald* reporter, he "was shorn
of the locks that made him a man feared in the Democratic party." For
as soon as Hill was seen taking the elevator to his room, Croker, Murphy and representatives of Brooklyn boss McLaughlin reassembled and
in only a few minutes agreed that Mayor Van Wyck's brother Judge Augustus Van Wyck would be the party's nominee. At this point, according to the *Herald's* account:

> "Because Hill was tired, they concluded that they would not
> spoil his slumber, but their work had been so neat and kept so
> well away from Hill that they could not long refrain from telling
> him that he had gone to sleep and lost. They woke him up at six
> o'clock in the morning and he was the most surprised man in the
> gathering of delegates."[3]

When Hill learned what had been done to him, his initial reaction
was to continue to fight. He quickly changed his mind, however, when
he realized that McLaughlin, a former ally, had deserted him. When
Croker then agreed that a Hill man would be the candidate for Lieutenant Governor and that his choice would head the State Committee,
he reluctantly conceded. Thus, on September 29, when the convention
was finally called to order nearly an hour and a half late, the delegates

were presented with a fait accompli. Against only token opposition, they docilely nominated Judge Van Wyck. Some in their number probably thought that they were voting for his brother, the Mayor, not realizing that Croker had made a last-minute sibling switch. Unlike the Republicans in Saratoga earlier in the week, they showed no enthusiasm as they completed their work. For, as the next morning's *Times* reported, "The shadow of the 'slate' rested like a pall upon the convention and chilled all efforts at nominating oratory."[4]

For most of the delegates, the primary question related to the background of the man they had just chosen. Now 52 years old, Augustus Van Wyck was a New York native who had been educated in New Hampshire, North Carolina and Richmond, Virginia, where he practiced law before moving to Brooklyn in the 1870s. He soon became involved in local Democratic politics, initially opposing McLaughlin, but later becoming his good friend and legal adviser. He was elected a City Judge in 1884, and later became a Supreme Court Justice when the legislature consolidated the two courts. He was no intellectual giant, but was respected as an upright, competent jurist of pleasing manners. More important for a gubernatorial candidate, he was honest and reputedly a good public speaker.

Van Wyck's term was about to expire, but he was looking forward to running for reelection in November, and, with the backing of McLaughlin and his organization, was sure to remain on the bench. He was visiting his brother at City Hall when word came that he would be the Democratic candidate. He quickly left for his Brooklyn residence. To say that he was surprised and bewildered would have been an understatement. After a *Tribune* reporter allegedly quoted him as saying that he would not accept the nomination, he remained in his house and refused to make any statements. On reflection, however, he soon realized what was expected of him as a good party man, and agreed to make the race.[5]

Despite the continuing ill feelings between Hill and Croker, the Democrats left Syracuse in good shape. Hill could legitimately claim victory except in the naming of Van Wyck, and Croker could gloat that with one Van Wyck in the State House and another in City Hall, he would be the master of all that really counted in New York. There was a good chance he would get his wish, for with his candidate a reputable member of the judiciary, he would be able to focus the voters on the recent Republican scandals and away from the Tammany crimes of bygone days.

The apparent wisdom of his choice was evidenced in the next morning's *New York Times.* Following its purchase two years earlier by Tennesseean Adolph Ochs, it had abandoned the staunch Republicanism it had displayed ever since it had supported Abraham Lincoln during the Civil War's darkest hours. Its September 30 editorial page, under the heading "FOR THE VOTERS CHOICE," praised Van Wyck's "service on the bench, where he had enjoyed the respect of the bar and of the community," which "gives ample assurance of his qualification in point of learning, capacity, and uprightness, for the office of Governor." Because he had been chosen as the result of a compromise reached behind closed doors by Croker and Hill, Ochs' editors were able to assert that Van Wyck was not the candidate of either, but instead was "one upon whom all factions and leaders united," and that his "sober judgment" and "sober, diligent, conscientious habit of work will commend him to the choice of the business community more strongly than the more brilliant but less safe temper of his opponent." They predicted that voters otherwise impressed by Roosevelt's "former position of political independence. . . . will decline to be fooled by Mr. Platt's adroit efforts to perpetuate his power in the State and shelter his party behind a good name from the storm of public wrath its misdeeds have provoked."[6]

The *Evening Post* assessed matters quite differently. It saw the issue as

Richard Croker
(Courtesy of the New York Public Library)

Van Wyck Chorus — 'My, But He's Good to our Family'
(*New York Herald*)

"which candidate for Governor is more likely, in case of election, to act independently of the boss who nominated him." But unlike the *Times*, it viewed Van Wyck as Croker's choice just as much as Roosevelt was Platt's. Roosevelt's nomination, however, "was made in response to a very powerful popular sentiment, and . . . if elected, he will go into office as the candidate of the people, permitted to stand for election by favor of Platt." By contrast,

> "When we come to examine the conditions of Judge Van Wyck's nomination, we find a very different state of things. . . Probably not a delegate in the body had heard of him as a possible nominee. . . In fact, he had never been heard of at all as a nominee till word came out of Croker's room that he was to be the man . . . Every delegate recognized the fact that he was merely recording Croker's will, and that neither he nor the people who had sent him to the convention had exercised a particle of choice in the matter."

Van Wyck's character, the *Post* agreed, was as "completely above reproach" as Roosevelt's. But if Van Wyck were elected:

> "We should then have one Van Wyck chosen personally by Croker as Mayor of New York City and another Van Wyck, chosen in the same way, as Governor of the State. Can anyone imagine Gov. Van Wyck opposing legislation for New York City which Mayor Van Wyck desires? And does Mayor Van Wyck desire anything except what Croker desires?"

Roosevelt would at least "prevent either Croker legislation or Platt-Croker legislation."[7]

11

"The Canvass Is Not Looking Well"

WHILE THE DEMOCRATS WERE MEETING IN SYRACUSE, ROOSEVELT spent most of his time at Sagamore Hill, reading the many letters and telegrams that were continually arriving and responding to some of them. His major concern at this point was that the impression that he was Platt's candidate might cause the defection of many of the good-government advocates who would otherwise support him. On September 30, referring to the 1897 mayorality contest, he wrote Quigg, "It is very important that we should get the idea firmly established that the forces which were divided last year, are united this year, . . ." To that end, he had already emphasized in a letter to Seth Low, "I particularly want to make my first speech with you at the meeting with me, . . . I think this is very important. I very earnestly want you to be with me when I make my first speech."

Several days earlier, Low had written to Roosevelt, offering to help "in any way, or at any time, . . ." Thus, when he told Roosevelt that he had a conflict and could not attend the campaign kickoff if, as initially suggested, it was held that Saturday, October 1, it was quickly rescheduled for the following Wednesday. As Roosevelt wrote Quigg, in a "long talk" on September 29, Low had said that he felt "very strongly that the first meeting, and especially the first meeting which he attends, should be an organization meeting, at which you speak, but that not merely he, but a number of prominent Republicans not connected with the organization should be present."

Joseph Choate was among the prominent nonorganization Republicans Low suggested should attend the first Roosevelt rally. Roosevelt undoubtedly recalled how Choate had refused to help him on the residence eligibility issue, and at his request Low agreed to see what he could do. On September 30, Low wrote to Choate that he would be on the platform and "[f]rom a conference I had last night with Mr. Roosevelt, I am confident that there is no one whom he would so like to keep me company as yourself." Reflecting that "the changes which time brings in political situations are most amusing," he asked, "Who would have believed, a year ago, that within twelve months I should be in cordial conference with Mr. Quigg and his staff?" He closed with the "sincere hope that you and I may again meet on the stage of the Carnegie Hall next Wednesday, and that as we recall the meeting of last year in the same place we may be able to maintain our countenances!"[1]

Low's effort, coupled with a visit to Stockbridge by an emissary, was successful. Even before Choate had replied, however, when the Republican leaders met with Roosevelt at Party headquarters the afternoon of September 29, they could not conceal their hope that, as the result of the support of Low and many of his friends, most of the 159,000 votes the reform ticket had received the previous year would go to Roosevelt.[2]

❧ ❧ ❧

By ordinary standards, life at Sagamore Hill could hardly ever have been regarded as calm, but for the next few weeks the house would rarely be a haven of rest. The incoming flow of mail was so intense that the Roosevelts had no choice but to hire a secretary to deal with it. Working in the house's Gun Room, she was frequently assisted by Edith and also by Roosevelt's oldest child, Alice, who had refused to go to boarding school and miss the excitement of her father's campaign.

With public interest heightened by the issue of Roosevelt's legal residence, the newspapers were eager to give their readers a description of his home and of his family life. Thus, several days after the Saratoga Convention, subscribers to the *Tribune* could read of a dwelling overlooking Long Island Sound, situated at the top of a small hill, with walls of "red brick to the second story, and above that of wood, painted in many colors." Within, it was "beautifully furnished from cellar to attic" and in "nearly every room are trophies of the Colonel's life on the Western plains. . ." A *Times* correspondent called it "a man's house throughout" with its many books and "rich, glossy skins" that served as rugs. He was especially impressed by the master of the house: his "athletic figure," his "action, spring, energy, enthusiasm," and his "restless eyes, half hidden by the gold-rimmed spectacles." The children's "romping, out of door life" was "making athletes of them all." They themselves seemed to take all the excitement in stride, although they wished that they could see more of their father now that he had returned from the war. When a reporter answered, "somewhere" to nine-year-old Kermit's query if he knew where his father was, the boy's response was a serious, "Father has to work hard to get us all food."[3]

❀ ❀ ❀

On September 30, a New York Supreme Court judge signed an order that would lead to the discontinuance of the proceeding that Roosevelt's lawyer had brought seeking to vacate his New York City tax assessment. Roosevelt's supporting affidavit stated that the case had been brought without his knowledge or consent while he was in Cuba. On Monday, October 3, his lawyer delivered Roosevelt's check for $885.28 in payment of the liability. Although some Democrats had threatened to challenge his eligibility in the courts, they never did so. His opponents tried to exploit the issue on the campaign trail, but Root's Saratoga arguments proved just as effective when delivered by others as they had at the convention.

That evening, Republican leaders held a "harmony dinner" at the

Fifth Avenue Hotel. Governor Black used a need "for a rest of a few days in the country" as an excuse for his nonattendance, and Platt, who had been expected, could not be located. Roosevelt, however, was very much in evidence, arriving shortly before 9 o'clock followed, probably to the astonishment of the attendees, by 20 uniformed Rough Riders. The day before, he had replied to McKinley's letter of congratulations that "my nomination seems to have brought the party closer together than has been the case for some time." As he shook hands and chatted with such former opponents as Lauterbach and Gruber, there was good reason to believe that he was correct.[4]

❧ ❧ ❧

The next day, both candidates received official notification of their nominations, and both formally accepted. In Roosevelt's case, the ceremony took place on Sagamore Hill's broad west veranda, overlooking Long Island Sound. Except for the candidate for Secretary of State, the entire ticket was present, but Platt did not attend, pleading an "indisposition." While Chauncey Depew in a brief speech delivered the formal notification, the *Herald* reporter observed that "Mrs. Roosevelt leaned against the balustrade, with her hands clasped." The candidate's wife had mixed feelings about a future in which she as well as her husband would constantly be in the public eye, and during Depew's remarks "she smiled with her eyes cast down. Barely did she look at her husband, who stood with his right hand on his thigh and his left holding his typewritten speech." When it was time for him to accept, in what the *Herald* headlined as "ROOSEVELT REFUSES TO WEAR PLATT'S COLLAR," the nominee in an obvious bid for the support of independent voters, made clear that if elected he would stress "the interests of the people as a whole, . . . knowing full well that by so doing I best serve my own party." He also indicated the course his campaign would take by stressing that "national interests are paramount this year."

Van Wyck accepted his nomination at a brief evening ceremony at his Brooklyn residence. He honestly admitted that his choice was "not intended as a personal compliment," and, speaking in the third person, that "[i]t was so unexpected and so foreign to his aspirations that he paused for a time to consider the advisability thereof and his action thereon." However, in words that must have amused anyone who was aware of the manner in which the party bosses had picked him, he explained that "he had soon reached the conclusion that the judgment of the democracy of this great commonwealth, manifested in State Convention assembled, could not and must not be disobeyed. . ." As he urged the need for "better government in the Empire State," his onlookers, according to one newspaper account, "were relieved to note that there was no weakness in his voice, as had been reported."[5]

❈ ❈ ❈

By 7:30 on the evening of October 5, an audience of several thousand men and women had packed Carnegie Hall to "ratify" Roosevelt's nomination. While a band played patriotic airs, they let out loud yells as a detachment of Rough Riders marched to seats reserved for them on the platform, above which hung a large picture of Roosevelt in his field uniform. When the candidate entered at 8:20, according to the *Herald*:

> "The floor trembled with the earthquake of stamping feet and swaying men, and from above came the thunders of delirious multitudes in the galleries."

Only slightly less enthusiastic had been the audience's response to Low's appearance on the stage. There was sustained laughter and applause when he referred to Croker's summer sojourn at his racing stable in the British Isles by joking: "It is true that both Colonel Roosevelt and Mr. Croker spent last summer on an island, but Colonel Roosevelt rode his own horses." Choate not only showed up, but, at the end of Roosevelt's address, held the crowd for more than 40 minutes as he

Dr. Depew Notifying Colonel Roosevelt of His Nomination
(New York Herald)

'We have discovered in Mr. Roosevelt the missing link. — Joseph H. Choate'
(*New York World*)

humorously praised him as "the missing link" who had succeeded in uniting the "regulars" and the "volunteers" who had backed separate mayorality candidates the year before. Somewhat surprisingly for a gubernatorial candidate, Roosevelt's speech concentrated on national issues. He sounded like a presidential or senatorial candidate as he spoke of "the time in the affairs of a nation . . . when it must face great responsibilities, whether it will or not" and of how "[t]he guns of our war ships in the tropic seas of the West and the remote East have a-wakened us to the knowledge of new duties." Claiming that his defeat would be a repudiation of the McKinley Administration's policy of annexing the Philippines, he argued that where the American flag "has once floated, there must and shall be no return to tyranny or savagery."

The only Republican objection to what was otherwise a perfect evening was that, as the *Times* noted, "it was too fashionable:"

"Magnificently dressed women occupied the boxes in the galleries and men in evening dress sat or stood beside them. It looked like a grand opera night, one of the Republican leaders said – and that was the only fault he could find with the splendid assemblage. 'This is not vote-getting, but it is magnificent.'"

Fortunately for Republican hopes, the less patrician crowd outside the hall was just as vocal in its praise for Roosevelt as the audience within. From three to four thousand persons packed and completely blocked West 57th Street as they listened to speeches of their own. The master of ceremonies was the national president of the United States Goldbeaters Union. He first introduced "Matt" Harrington, who predicted that Roosevelt would "charge up Capitol Hill in Albany, and, as the Spaniards fled before his gallant band, . . . so the Democrats will flee before his approach on January 1." Harrington was followed by M.J. Neary of Troy, "a workingman from top to bottom," and then by Tom Rouse, a six-foot sawmill worker otherwise known as "the Bowery

Peach," who attacked Tammany for trying to establish one more political "royalty," this one of Van Wycks.[6]

❉ ❉ ❉

Despite the apparent success of the Carnegie Hall meeting, the Republican leaders were uncertain as to the course the campaign should
take. The Saturday October 8, *Times* reported that upstate visitors to
party headquarters were asking State Chairman Odell when "the 'Hero
of San Juan Hill' would make a brilliant and dashing campaign, sweep-
ing the State from end to end with his fire and fervor." But although it
had reportedly been agreed that Roosevelt would tour the state in a
railroad car from which he would make short speeches at every stop,
Odell was now telling his visitors that nothing would be decided until
the middle or even the end of the following week. The upstaters
protested that with Election Day only a month away, this might be too
late, but Odell held his ground and refused to be budged even after
more pressure was put on him.

Odell had been an early Roosevelt backer and had been influential in
getting Platt to support him. Now, however, he worried that Roosevelt
would get himself into trouble if his campaign involved a large number
of unrehearsed speeches. Because the Colonel was inexperienced on
state issues, Odell feared that he was likely to make damaging miscues.
Odell's sense of political propriety was also offended by the band of
Rough Riders that seemed to materialize whenever Roosevelt made a
public appearance. He feared that the voters would soon tire of what he
viewed as a blatant attempt to capitalize on Roosevelt's wartime hero-
ics that had no bearing on his fitness for state office. The next Thursday,
a conclave of party leaders was scheduled to take place at the Fifth Avenue Hotel. The question could be decided then in plenty of time to
mount a strong campaign in the more than three weeks before the
November 8 election.[7]

❉ ❉ ❉

While his campaign role was being debated, Roosevelt did what politicking he could in the New York City area. The morning after the Carnegie Hall rally he met with Odell and others at the Fifth Avenue Hotel headquarters, from which Odell took him downstairs to join forty members of the Republican Editorial Association of the State of New York at its annual luncheon. That Thursday evening he attended a "smoker concert" in his honor at the Union League Club, which at that time had its headquarters at Fifth Avenue and 39th Street. It was a late evening, as Elihu Root did not escort Roosevelt in to meet the members until 11:00 p.m. After the candidate had shaken hands with the attendees, the group adjourned for supper in the main dining room, where they were joined by Mark Hanna and Vice President Garrett Hobart.

Although the group did not disperse until the wee morning hours, Roosevelt was up early the next day, and, after dictating a number of letters, left the Fifth Avenue Hotel for Sagamore Hill, where, he said, he planned to spend a weekend of "absolute idleness." He was not entirely accurate, for in the late afternoon, he went to Brooklyn, where he attended a reception at the Union League Club on Bedford Avenue. After dinner, at which Platt made a brief appearance, the clubhouse doors were thrown open, and for two hours, in the words of a *Times* reporter, "the Colonel did nothing but turn his strong right arm into a pump handle." The throng included women as well as men, and one young lady, encouraged by a club officer, "came along fully determined to kiss the Colonel," but when she grasped his hand "her courage failed." When the club doors were finally closed, Roosevelt went outside, where another 2000 people were waiting for him and cheered loudly as he promised to "carry out to the fullest extent those principles . . . in the Ten Commandments and in the Golden Rule . . . that thou shalt not steal, nor allow anyone else to steal."[8]

❀ ❀ ❀

At this point, except for an evening speech before an Afro-American group on Friday, October 14, the Republican leaders had scheduled no public activity for Roosevelt before a major speech in Brooklyn on Wednesday, October 19. Although the candidate officially expressed pleasure at being able to spend time resting at Oyster Bay, inwardly he was seething with frustration. As soon as the weekend was over, he returned to the city, and spent much of his time at party headquarters. He wrote a number of letters, including one responding to the inquiry from a stranger as to the pronunciation of his name:

" . . . it is pronounced as if it was spelled 'Rosavelt.' That is in three syllables. The first syllable as if it was 'Rose.'"

Meanwhile, efforts to persuade Odell to turn him loose continued unabated. Not all the pressure came from politicians. One of Odell's visitors, the respected Irish-American journalist Joseph I.C. Clarke, warned him that the vote would be very close, and that even if Roosevelt did create a "flare-up," it likely "will be to the good." At last, the State Chairman finally agreed that "Teddy must have his way," and by mid-week plans were announced for the Colonel to begin his upstate campaign starting the following Monday. Presumably reflecting the views of his would be "handlers," however, he emphasized that his tour "is not going to be a hurrah campaign from the rear platform of a special train."

It was about time. Under the headline "APATHY MAKES REPUBLICANS LAG," the October 14 *Herald* reported:

"That Colonel Theodore Roosevelt's canvass for the Governorship is lagging is admitted by Republicans with alarm and heralded by Democrats with joy . . . To all outward signs it has been at a standstill since the Saratoga Convention. The day Colonel Roosevelt was nominated his election was regarded as certain, and the Republican State Committee decided to keep him 'bottled up.'"

Almost immediately, however,

"...doubt arose when the Syracuse Convention adjourned and it was seen that Judge Van Wyck, against whose reputation and character nothing could be said, had been nominated for Governor, and each of the other State candidates had been located in some doubtful section to fan the fires of Republican dissatisfaction."

The *Herald's* Albany correspondent reported a looming Republican disaster: "Information received within the last twenty-four hours indicates that if the election were held tomorrow the Republican vote would run at least twenty per cent behind that cast for McKinley." Although McKinley had swept the state by more than 250,000 votes over William Jennings Bryan, a swing of this magnitude would give Van Wyck a greater than 70,000 vote plurality.

The Republican campaign was also weakened by Quigg's sudden indisposition. The strain of serving as New York County Chairman and running for Congressional reelection was apparently too much for him, especially since his House seat was in jeopardy. He had fainted at the Saratoga Convention and, on October 14, collapsed shortly after arriving at party headquarters and was sent home in a carriage. Party leaders were blaming his illness for the apathy in the Manhattan campaign. Although the city was for the most part Tammany territory, they had hoped that Roosevelt might be able to dent the usually large Democratic majority.[9]

❉ ❉ ❉

The Republican problems were not limited to the Erie Canal scandals and Van Wyck's surprising popular appeal. There was also increasing public dissatisfaction with the conduct of the Spanish-American War by the McKinley Administration. Initially, although such luminaries as former President Grover Cleveland had not believed that Cuba was worth a war, an overwhelming majority of Americans felt otherwise, with a million men answering McKinley's initial call for 125,000 volunteers. Following Dewey's easy triumph at Manila Bay and the surrender of the Spanish at Santiago, public enthusiasm had reached an unprecedented level.

Shortly thereafter, however, disillusionment began to set in. Even before the Santiago victories, there were increasing complaints over the canned, half-raw meat that the Army had purchased in large quantities, which was the principal ration of the troops in the trenches outside Santiago. Although it rarely was actually spoiled, by the time it had been subjected to the intense heat of the storage holds of naval vessels and the tropical sun of Cuban commissary dumps, it often emerged from opened tins as a slimy red mess that was refused by even the hungriest soldiers.[10]

Complaints regarding the Army's food, however, paled by comparison with the horror stories that the press was reporting from Wikoff and other military camps. Criticism centered on the War Department, and military officers, Democratic politicians and the press joined in centering their fire on Secretary of War Alger. Across the country there were widespread calls for McKinley to fire him. The President, however, believed that much of the criticism was unjustified, and refused to bow to the insistent warnings of Republican politicians that their party would lose control of Congress unless he were relieved before the November elections. Instead, in late September, McKinley appointed a nine-man commission to conduct a thorough investigation. It was obvious that it would not complete its work until early the next year.

His well-publicized authorship of the "round robin" letter urging the Administration to act to avoid a yellow fever epidemic was enabling Roosevelt to distance himself from much of this criticism. So also was the obvious admiration and respect his Rough Riders were showing for their commanding officer. Nevertheless, this widespread unhappiness with his party meant that, as its standard bearer,

Roosevelt must make an especially vigorous personal effort to pull both himself and the rest of his slate through to victory.[11]

❀ ❀ ❀

On Tuesday night, October 11, Roosevelt spoke at a meeting in the assembly district which he had represented at the start of his political career. After he had finished his prepared speech and noted several of his Rough Rider comrades sitting on the platform, he unexpectedly extended his remarks to speak of their efforts in words that the audience enjoyed much more than his formal address.[12]

Thereafter, until his first upstate tour that would start the following Monday, Roosevelt's only scheduled appearance still was his speech to his Afro-American supporters on Friday evening. Now that Odell had released him to make an active campaign during the three weeks before the election, he probably was pleased to have several "days off" to ready himself for that intensive effort. On Thursday evening, however, Odell received a telephone call from John Knickerbocker, a young politician in the upstate city of Troy, on the east side of the Hudson several miles north of Albany. He told Odell that if Roosevelt came up to Troy the next day, he would be able to address a crowd of several thousand at the Rensselaer County Fair. Since Governor Black had suggested a few days earlier that Roosevelt should speak in Troy at some time during the campaign, Odell seized what appeared to be a golden opportunity and telephoned Roosevelt at Oyster Bay: although it was very short notice, if possible he should make the trip.[13]

Although Roosevelt told Odell that it would be inconvenient, he agreed to go, and at 5:30 the following morning, left for New York. At Grand Central Station, he was met by Queens District Attorney William ("Billy") Youngs, who was to accompany him on the journey, and by Odell, who discussed with him the speech he was to deliver. When the train arrived in Albany, Governor Black was not there to meet him, and several of the men who welcomed him seemed surprised that he was coming on such short notice. Hoping to find Black at his office, the candidate took a carriage to the State Capitol, where the Governor greeted him cordially and apologized that he had received no official word of Roosevelt's visit. Although he had heard rumors earlier that morning that something might be afoot, he had dismissed them as unfounded until he was told that Roosevelt had arrived at the Executive Chamber. Unfortunately, a prior engagement made it impossible for him to accompany the Colonel to Troy.

This did not stop Roosevelt, who went by trolley to Troy and then by carriage to the fair grounds. By now apprehensive as to what his reception might be, he told the welcoming committee Knickerbocker had assembled that he would only speak for about five minutes, and that he would talk about the war and not politics. His worst fears were realized, for, as the *Times* described what ensued:

"When the grounds were reached, at 1:15, a band preceded the party in carriages and a parade was made around the track. There were less than 500 persons present, and scarcely one-third of them appeared to be aware of the personality of the visitor. A few men raised a cheer, and then Col. Roosevelt, pulling out his watch, said: 'I will not speak. It is late, and I must catch the 3:10 train from Albany.'

"Mr. Knickerbocker of the local committee asked him to say a few words from his carriage, but he declined with some asperity and the carriages were ordered to drive on. He was driven rapidly to Rensselaer, where he caught the train to New York."

Even before he had gone to Troy and learned the extent of his trip's fiasco, Roosevelt had told Odell that from now on he would take personal charge of his campaign. Before he could do so, however, one more embarrassment was in store. During the day, several New York newspapers had reported that the candidate would not return to the city in time for that evening's Afro-American rally, and that it would have to be postponed. Thus, although the auditorium where the gathering was to take place was capable of seating 3000, when it opened at 8 o'clock only 40 were sitting in the still only party lighted hall. When the candidate finally arrived an hour later, he was welcomed by an impatient audience of no more than 170 men and women.

When Roosevelt had finished speaking, his praise for the black regiments that had taken part in the Cuban campaign had mollified the crowd, and to that extent the meeting was a success. By the time he had arrived at the Manhattan home of his sister Corinne, where he was to spend the night, he had calmed down and jokingly described his experiences as "Little Rosamond's day of misfortunes," referring to the unlucky heroine of a novel by early 19th century Irish author Maria Edgeworth.* It was no laughing matter to his supporters, however, when they read their Saturday morning papers. Although the strongly partisan Republican *Tribune* spoke only of cheering crowds on the trip to Troy, the more balanced *Herald's* headlines reported, "ROOSEVELT IN A TROY AMBUSH" and "ROOSEVELT ON A WILD GOOSE CHASE." It also called the Afro-American meeting a "failure." More calmly, but with equal accuracy, the *Times* told its subscribers, "TROY SLIGHTS ROOSEVELT," and cited "SIGNS OF REPUBLICAN ALARM."

Thus, even before Roosevelt arrived at Republican headquarters the next morning, the Odell forces were blaming Black for slighting him, and the Governor and his friends were attacking Odell for not giving them advance warning of the Troy expedition. For his part, Roosevelt did not have the time to criticize either group; he needed the active support of both. Before he left for Oyster Bay, however, he again emphasized that, as the candidate, it was his campaign to run and he would do so from now on.[14]

---

* For the rest of the campaign, his family nickname was "Little Rosamond."

❋ ❋ ❋

Roosevelt spent much of the weekend preparing for his upcoming upstate swings and immersing himself in other campaign details. Earlier
in the week, when he was at headquarters, he had asked Odell to direct
Quigg to see to it that an upcoming Cooper Union meeting "the Germans should be properly recognized," and that a "Mr. Kunhardt is a
bright young man . . . and would make a good presiding officer." He
had also sent notes to the ailing Quigg asking whether an unidentified
gentleman "is a man with whom I should go" and suggesting that "we
can do something to help" a "Blaine Club" which in a previous election
"did . . . better work than the Regular Organization did." In a Sunday,
October 16, letter, after saying that he was "glad to hear that you are on
the mend" and "hate to bother you about business matters," he asked
the county leader how he should respond to a letter he had received
from a "longshoreman" and continued:

"It seems to me that there should be an immediate effort to
arrange, especially in the German, Jewish and Scandinavian communities, meetings at which not only the organization men, but
. . . all of the local leaders in each Assembly district who were with
Low last year should take part. I very much wish that at the meeting next Thursday where I am to speak we could have one or two
men who are not identified with the organization. We ought to
have men like Jacob Schiff, like Paul Goerel and others in with us
at these meetings. The registration does not look as well as it
should, and no stone should be left unturned."

Then, if this was not enough for poor Quigg to handle, there was a
postscript:

"In the *Evening Post* of last night it is asserted that we have put on
as election inspectors, five men who were indicted last year. If
they really were indicted, I think it is an outrage, and that they
should at once be taken out."[15]

To the press, Roosevelt's posture was that all was going well. In a letter he wrote that Sunday to his close friend Cabot Lodge, however, he was realistic in assessing his chances:

"This may be the last letter I shall write you for the canvass is not looking well and I shall evidently have to work like a beaver for the next three weeks. At first all the managers were anxious that I should do nothing, should take as little personal control of the canvass as possible and should make very few speeches but the result has shown that they were wrong and they have changed their minds. On the very point where they ought to have done the best work, that is, in the matter of organization, they have failed signally . . . Senator Platt and Congressman Odell are doing all they can for me and I could not wish the canvass to be in better hands, but in the city all of the vote-getters, and all of the men who can influence the doubtful vote which is not corrupt, have partly by their own fault and partly through the fault of the machine, left the party and it is exceedingly hard to get into touch with them. The Gold Democrats have returned to Tammany, being perfectly satisfied if only their party will dodge the issue of honest money. The Germans are inclined to be against me and the Independents care very much less for honest government than they care to register themselves against my views of expansion and of an efficient Army and Navy. In addition to this, Algerism is a heavy load to carry, and Lou Payn and Aldridge and the canal business . . . make up another burden with which it is difficult to deal. In fact, taking it as a whole, New York cares very little for the war now that it is over, except that it would like to punish somebody because the Republican administration did not handle the War Department well . . . The result is that I am not having an entirely pleasant campaign. I may win yet, and I am going to do everything that can be done, but there is great apathy among the Republicans, and, as for the Independents and the Democrats, their feeling is precisely Croker's, viz.: they wish me well as a good soldier, but that they intend to vote against me as a Governor."[16]

What Roosevelt needed was a state issue that would permit him to take the offensive, stop Republican apathy and rally the independents to his side. Fortunately, Croker had just handed him one.

12

"You May Take These, But You Shall Go No Further!"

By early October, Richard Croker could look back on an extraordinarily successful career, with hopes for an even brighter future. During his 55 years, he had advanced from boyhood as a member of a recently arrived immigrant family who lived in a shanty town in what is now the western part of New York's Central Park to a status so exalted that many referred to him as "Master of Manhattan."

His rise had not been easy. At 13, after his family had moved to an East Side Tammany neighborhood, he left school to work as a locomotive machinist. He soon joined a group of juvenile toughs known as the Fourth Avenue Tunnel Gang. With brawn and strength to match, he won local fame as a boxer, and after several years his pugilistic prowess had made him its leader. It also brought him to the attention of local Tammany leader Jimmy "The Famous" O'Brien, who by the time Croker was 21, had started him up the machine's leadership ladder.

Croker's ballot-box stuffing and other skills were so impressive that another Tammany leader, City Comptroller Slippery Dick Connelly, got him a job as a court attendant to a judge who was one of Boss Tweed's poker playing friends. Next, when Jimmy "The Famous" was elected County Sheriff, he saw to it that Croker succeeded him on the Board of Aldermen. But, in the early 1870s, after O'Brien had helped expose Tweed, Croker astutely saw which way the political wind was blowing and supported Honest John Kelly in his successful leadership fight against O'Brien for Tammany leadership. His reward was election to the lucrative post of City Coroner, where he was able to pocket annual fees of up to $25,000.

On Election Day, 1874, Croker's rise nearly came to an end. O'Brien was running for Congress against Abram Hewitt, whom Kelly, in a desire to rehabilitate Tammany's reputation, was supporting. In an encounter at an East Side street corner between a ballot box-stuffing gang headed by Croker and another that included O'Brien, the two men first traded insults of "loafer" and "thief" and then came to blows. In the general fracas that followed, an O'Brienite received a pistol wound, and, before dying, accused Croker of firing the fatal shot. He denied the charge, and after hearing conflicting testimony from witnesses from the rival gangs, a "hung" jury split six for conviction and six for acquittal. Croker was never retried. There had been testimony that one of his friends had fired the shot but, following the "law" of the streets, he never "ratted" on his colleague.

Even though he had escaped conviction, the public voted Croker out of office at the next election. He had spent most of his new-found wealth at the racetrack and, according to one press report, was now living "in almost abject poverty." With Kelly's backing, however, the Mayor made him a fire commissioner, and from then on his rise was rapid. He became Kelly's most trusted aide, and when it came time to replace Kelly, Croker was the obvious man to take over. He consolidated his position by his adroit championship of Hewitt in the 1886 mayorality election. By the early 1890s, his power in both the organization and the city was absolute. A British editor described him as "a kind of mundane Pope, with the Executive Committee as his College of Cardinals." His leadership, according to an associate, was based on three qualities:

"An inner determination, an ability to judge men, and an almost sacred observance of his promise once it was given. Once he made up his mind, nothing could change it . . . once he gave his word, that word was kept, no matter what the cost or consequences."

After the good government forces united to elect Mayor Strong in 1894, Croker gave up his leadership and moved to England. On September 7, 1897, however, in what the press called his "Return from Elba," he sailed into New York harbor in time to reassert his authority and elect Robert Van Wyck as Mayor. In a few months, his power was as complete as if he had never left.

Before he first took over the Tammany leadership, Croker had lived modestly in a house in Harlem. By the mid-1890s, however, he had moved to a fine home at 5 East 79th Street, just off Fifth Avenue, which had reportedly cost $80,000, with furnishings worth more than $100,000 and serviced by a staff of servants appropriate to his new station. He also owned a private railroad car and interests in horses and in stock farms in the United States and England which had cost him roughly $350,000. Yet, apart from the post of City Chamberlain which paid a $25,000 annual stipend, and which he resigned in 1890, he held no salaried positions.

The answer to how all this came about was contained in an expression coined by one of Croker's predecessors, George Washington Plunkitt: "honest graft." This was to be distinguished from "dishonest graft," i.e., bribes to carry on otherwise illegal activities such as gambling, blackmail and other forms of vice. His associates were free to feather their nests in such ways, but the boss was above all that. He instead would make killings from buying up land when he received inside word that an area was about to be developed or from stock market tips given by men who wished to be potential beneficiaries of his favors. As one example, Croker for little or nothing obtained shares of stock in a street transit company, laughingly nicknamed "The Huckleberry Railroad", that was to run through a rural area in the Bronx. In a few years, the route had become heavily developed and he made a killing on his "investment." Thus, whether the graft was honest or dishonest, there was money to be made, for, as another Tammany insider observed: " 'Tis a great game, is politics, and can be made to pay like a bank."[1]

❋ ❋ ❋

In extending its tentacles throughout the city government, Tammany did not exempt the judiciary. As Croker testified during an 1899 legislative investigation of municipal corruption, he had once told a judicial candidate who had come to visit him that "the Finance Committee [of Tammany Hall] at that time would exact about $10,000 as a contribution, and he said he was perfectly willing that it should be paid toward the election." If a check came in that was drawn to the order of Croker or someone else in the organization, it was returned with instructions that it be made out to "bearer." The "contributions" were never recorded on any account books, so that there was no indication in either Tammany's records or a judge's papers that these transactions had ever taken place.[2]

In the fall of, 1898, Supreme Court Justice Joseph F. Daly's term was about to expire and he planned to run for reelection. Now 58 years old, in 1870 he had been appointed a judge of the Court of Common Pleas and 20 years later became its Chief Judge. He retained that position until he was named a Supreme Court Justice in 1896. He was generally respected as a careful and honest jurist who merited reelection. He also was highly regarded outside the courtroom as a leading Roman Catholic layman and a well-known authority on the theater, where he was a founding member of the Players' Club.[3]

Probably, like other New York City judges of a Democratic persuasion, Daly had made the required "gift" to the appropriate Tammany leader. Despite his reputation as a fair and honest jurist, there was no evidence that his decisions had been offensive to Tammany or contrary to its interests. Twice, however, he had defied Richard Croker: first, by refusing to appoint a man recommended by the boss as court clerk and then by failing to enter an order that Croker had told him involved a "personal matter." This was unacceptable behavior, and Croker decided that it was time to replace him with a more amenable Democratic nominee.

By early October, Croker's decision was common knowledge. He apparently was unprepared for the amount of pressure that lawyers' groups and the Catholic clergy exerted to persuade him to change his mind. At an October 8 "harmony reception" at the Manhattan Club, to his surprise the evening's chairman greeted him with words of praise for the Judge. As the *Herald* described what followed:

"When he was not sitting at the banquet table, wherever he went he heard requests that Judge Daly be made the candidate of the democrats. To arouse Mr. Croker to angry mood it is necessary only to mention the name of Judge Daly, and so he had at the Manhattan Club an evening that began with gratification and ended in the request that he advocate his pet aversion."

The Republicans were watching Croker's performance with undisguised glee. On October 10, Roosevelt wrote to Quigg: "Don't you think we ought to nominate Daly! I think it would be a great card for us." Quigg and his associates needed no persuading. On October 11, after conferring with bar association representatives as to the qualifications of its likely choices, the Republican County Committee included Daly as one of its judicial candidates. As its members probably expected, this was the last straw as far as Croker was concerned. The next night, the Democrats picked a slate that excluded Daly. They replaced him with lower court Judge James Fitzgerald, who was chosen partly because of hope that his strong Catholic connections would minimize the defection of Daly supporters.

When he formally accepted the Republican nomination on October 13, Daly was in a fighting mood. He framed the issue as nothing less than "the sanctity of the judicial office, for to assail the independence of the bench is to attack the most sacred institution this land can boast." To the cheers of his audience, he then leveled his fire directly on Croker:

> "Mad indeed is the brain that conceives the punishment of a just judge. No subterfuge can disguise the wickedness of the purpose nor conceal the threat to corrupt the one thing the people respect most. No labored effort to put up what is called a good ticket against him can hide the true design. It is not a question whether you can get lawyers as learned or men as popular to take his place. It is simply and solely a question whether the freedom of the judicial office is assailed. The judge who has done his duty fearlessly and has been deaf to any consideration but justice stands for an immutable principle; and any nomination of candidates against him for the purpose of defeating him is none the less calculated to destroy the independence of the judiciary and is a menace to public safety."[4]

❦ ❦ ❦

In 1870, several hundred of New York City's most distinguished lawyers had formed an organization that they named the Association of the Bar of the City of New York. Its primary goal was to advance municipal reform, particularly in the city's court system, and its initial target was the corruption that under Boss Tweed and his Tammany cohorts had penetrated even the judiciary. After the Bar Association and other outraged citizens had brought him down, it served as a rallying point from which other reform groups, such as the Citizens Union, were organized to fight for good government in areas outside the legal system. Its leadership was drawn primarily from what later came to be known as Wall Street lawyers, most of them Republicans. Among them were

Joseph Choate, who had been its president ten years earlier, and Elihu Root.

One of the Bar Association's most important roles was to examine the character and ability of candidates for judicial office and report to the public whether, without regard to political affiliation, it considered them to be "qualified." At a special meeting on Saturday evening, October 15, held in the large meeting room at its imposing recently built headquarters on West 44th Street between Fifth and Sixth Avenues, it endorsed Daly for reelection. Also, after a stormy debate, it adopted the recommendation of its Committee on Judicial Nomination, chaired by Root, that it declare Supreme Court Democratic nominee David Leventritt unfit for that office. During the discussion, Democrats who had asked Croker to back Daly joined Republicans in denouncing the Tammany boss who, as one of them charged, had assailed "the integrity of our judiciary" to "gratify" his "personal spite."

Croker's immediate response was to attack the Bar Association as "nothing more than a partisan machine, run by Elihu Root. . . . What right has he to select a man for us to endorse." He then turned his fire on Choate, who had "assisted in his manipulation of this machine" and "who is also a Republican and who is attorney for most of the big corporations and trusts in this State, and I would like to know if he is a fit man to dictate nominations to Tammany Hall." He concluded his angry remarks to a group of fellow Democrats by suggesting that "it is about time that a bar association was organized that won't have to consult with Platt and Lauterbach before they take action on any matter." Croker should have known that it was a mistake to trade words with Choate, whose reply in a public letter turned the boss's proposal into a laughing matter:

"I cordially approve of Mr. Croker's proposition for the formation of a new Bar Association, which shall be all his own. Then all who want lawyers who know the law will know where to go, and those who are in search of advocates who know the Judge will be equally well provided."[5]

❧ ❧ ❧

If Croker had limited his public comment to an attack on the Bar Association, he might have escaped from the controversy reasonably unscathed. Already, however, he had shown his true colors so vividly that the public outcry went far beyond the legal community. On learning that the Republicans had nominated Daly, he reminded an inquiring reporter that it was "the Democratic organization" that had kept the judge on the bench for 28 years. Personally, however, "I never – absolutely never – asked him to do a single favor."

"Only the organization asked him to do favors. . . . When Democrats ask a favor – a thoroughly legitimate one – one to which they are entitled – he refuses to grant it, and when disappointed tries to make people believe that he was asked to do something dishonest."

"I suppose he refers to the time he was asked to appoint Michael T. Daly clerk of his court. . . . But it is not for this action alone that Tammany has no further use for him. . . . He turned his back on the men who made him time and again."

"But even that is not all. A political organization has the right to name for office the men who are most satisfactory to a majority of its members. Judge Daly in no way has given satisfaction. . ."

"Legitimate patronage is legitimate politics. If a victorious party can present for office men better than or as good as those whom it has conquered, why should it not be entitled to some favors at the hands of the men it has made. Judge Daly took everything and turned his back on the men who gave him his position."[6]

The public response was swift and crossed party lines. A Committee of Fifty was organized and scheduled a mass meeting at Carnegie Hall for the evening of October 21. Its choice of day was inauspicious, for as the *Times* recounted, "[t]he evening set in with a dreary downpour of rain" and, "[a]s the night advanced the rains became heavier, and the managers of the meeting began to despair of not having much of an audience to listen to the speeches of prominent members of the bar, who were to address themselves to the question of the refusal of Tammany to renominate Judge Daly." They need not have worried, "as long before 8 o'clock the hall was filled to overflowing." Men were forced to stand in the aisles, and the crowding in the upper levels was even worse. Although there were no flags or other decorations, the audience was just as enthusiastic as "at any political gathering." The cheering began as soon as it heard the opening words of John M. Bowers, a Democrat who was chairing the event: "The call for this meeting was issued by Richard Croker."[7]

Five men had been scheduled to speak that evening, but it was only one, W. Bourke Cockran, who could have claimed credit for helping to assemble a full house on such a stormy night. Born in 1854 in Ireland's County Sligo, he rejected the entreaties of his parents to enter the priesthood, and at age 17 made his own way to New York's Westchester County, where he became a public school principal in the village of Tuckahoe while studying law at night. He began his legal practice in the lower Westchester city of Mount Vernon, but soon moved to New York, where he became an advocate of note. Honest John Kelly took him under his wing and he became active in Tammany Hall, which helped elect him to three House terms. In 1896, however, although retaining his Democratic affiliation, he broke with the party over the "free silver" issue, and actively campaigned for William McKinley.

By 1898, Cockran was renowned as one of the most outstanding orators of his generation. A tall and commanding figure with deep-set eyes in a leonine head, his voice, which had retained its Irish brogue, was deep and resonant. He had been a friend of Winston Churchill's mother Jennie Jerome, and in late 1895, en route to serve as a military observer in Cuba, that future statesman spent a week as a houseguest in Cockran's spacious Fifth Avenue apartment. Many years later, Churchill told two-time Democratic Presidential candidate Adlai Stevenson that it was Cockran "who taught me how to use every note of the human voice like an organ" and with it "how to hold thousands in thrall."*

Although Cockran was suffering from an unidentified illness, he made what to many of his auditors who had heard earlier speeches on which his fame rested was "the greatest effort he has yet put forth." As the *Herald* reported:

> "His patient air of tolerance when he described the inevitable nature of bossism, his thunderous eloquence against any tampering with the judiciary, the last guardian of the people's rights and liberties, the rapier-like thrusts of his sarcasm and the sledge hammer blows of his denunciation raised that sedate legal crowd to the highest enthusiasm."

The cheers of the audience were especially loud and prolonged when Cockran praised Daly: "a faithful judge, in the language of the courtiers who surround the boss, . . . turned down because, forsooth, he has been loyal to his duty and faithful to his trust," and when he stressed that if "judges be taught that their prospects of renomination and of promotion depend not only upon loyalty to the people, but upon loyalty to the boss, . . . then our rights and our privileges are no longer ours to be enjoyed but become the favor that we may enjoy through the forbearance or favor of a boss." As he concluded his effort and collapsed into his chair, the throng, according to the *Times*, "rose

---

* In his 1946 Fulton, Missouri, "Iron Curtain" speech Churchill quoted Cockran, "a great Irish-American orator, a friend of mine: 'There is enough for all. The earth is a generous mother: she will provide in plentiful abundance for all her children, if they but cultivate her soil in justice and peace.'"

Bourke Cockran Speaking at Carnegie Hall
(*New York Herald*)

wildly to their feet, mounted chairs, and shouted and waved their handkerchiefs for more than five minutes," so deeply moved were they by his peroration in which he had urged an aroused citizenry to

"...proclaim with a voice as potent at that which the Almighty regulates the movement of the mighty sea to their boss: 'Our municipal chamber is yours to dominate and control; our streets are yours to pave, to sweep, to light, to confer upon your favorites for special privileges, but the judiciary you shall not touch. You may take these, but you shall go no further.'" [8]

❀ ❀ ❀

Between them, Croker and Cockran had dramatized an issue that had seized the attention of the many citizens who saw in Tammany's opposition to Daly a blatant attempt to extend political influence and corruption to the courts. The uncertainty facing Roosevelt was whether he could harness their anger to his own advantage. His opponent was not Croker, but Van Wyck, whose probity no one questioned. Even Cockran, for all his dislike of Croker, remained a Democrat at heart and, except in the case of Daly, planned to vote for his Party's ticket.[*] In the three weeks that remained before the election, the task that Roosevelt faced was formidable. The question was whether he could pull it off.

---

[*] Even so, the Republican State Committee distributed more than 100,000 copies of Cockran's speech outside New York City.

13

"The Speech Was Nothing, But The Man's Presence Was Everything"

A T 9:10 A.M. ON MONDAY, OCTOBER 17, ROOSEVELT ARRIVED IN NEW York by train from Oyster Bay. He was driven at once to the Forty-Second Street ferry, where he had a brief goodbye chat with his sister Corinne and her husband Douglas Robinson. Two minutes later, the boat pushed off and carried him and a few other passengers across the Hudson to Weehawken, where he boarded the two-car special train that was to carry him and his party north for a three-day campaign swing. Accompanying him were three men who would take turns introducing him and help with the speaking: Lieutenant Governor Woodruff, former Ambassador to Spain Stewart Woodford, and John Procor Clarke, a lawyer friend and leading independent. Also on board was "Billy" Youngs, who was in charge of the travel arrangements.[1]

The party also included several news correspondents and six Rough Riders in full uniform. According to that evening's *Post*, they "would have no speaking to do: when the train stops, they are to form a background for the Colonel; and they are to make themselves generally conspicuous." One of them, however, did have a special assignment. Emile Cassi, an Italian "soldier of fortune," carried a bugle, which as the train neared each stop he would loudly blow to announce their arrival. After a five-to-ten minute stop during which Roosevelt and one or two others would make brief remarks, Youngs, who, unlike many twentieth century campaign managers, managed to keep his candidate on schedule, would pull a bell rope, and the train would start off for the next stop.[2]

By 6 o'clock, when the Roosevelt Special pulled into Glens Falls two minutes early, it had made 16 stops and the candidate had said a few words at each. The first was West Nyack, where, from the platform of the rear car, he attacked the Democrats for refusing to nominate Judge Daly, which "indicates the principles on which they will run the State, as they have already run the City, if you give them the power." At Odell's home town of Newburgh, he promised to revitalize the State National Guard, and at Kingston, before 5000 people who filled a grandstand near the station, he spoke of the "grave question" that "has arisen as to the management of the canals of this State" and promised "the most thorough investigation."

At every stop, the Roosevelt party was greeted by large and enthusiastic crowds. Before the day was very far advanced, the excitement became too much for Rough Rider "Buck" Taylor, who persuaded Youngs to let him say a few words just before the train pulled out of the station. Buck's standard line, delivered in his southern drawl after Roosevelt had introduced him was "Mah fellow citizens – This is the proudest moment in my life." When he had repeated these identical sentiments at several stops, Clarke suggested that he was "having a great many proud moments on this trip." "Every time I talk for mah Colonel," came the quick reply, "I am prouder than I was before."[3]

The throngs that greeted Roosevelt at every stop reflected the fact that, unlike the previous week's Troy fiasco, this week's schedule had been well publicized. Thus, by the time the candidate arrived in Glens Falls, the 3000-seat opera house where he was to speak was filled to overflowing. The local Republican organization had to open up another large meeting room in the basement, but even this was not enough to accommodate everyone who wanted to hear Roosevelt. He was forced to make a third speech to the crowd that had patiently waited in the street outside. In his first address, he stressed the importance of what he called "the interests of labor," but when a group of hecklers in the balcony started a disturbance, he won his loudest cheers by contrasting their disorderly conduct with the behavior of his Rough Riders under fire in Cuba.

By the time Roosevelt retired at 10:30, he could look back on a day of unqualified success, during which he had spoken to more than 25,000 people. He could now be confident that, as he had predicted to Odell and as the next morning's *Herald* confirmed, "the people . . . wanted to see him, hear him and cheer him." His fellow campaigners agreed, and even before his train reached Glens Falls, Youngs telegraphed State Chairman Odell:

"The trip has been one continued ovation. The Colonel's speeches splendid, the crowds immense, and enthusiasm unsurpassed."

In his talks that day and the next two, Roosevelt set the tone for the balance of his campaign. His speeches were short, with next to nothing of political or economic theory. His themes were support for the McKinley Administration's policy regarding the former Spanish colonies, attacks on the Democrats for not renominating Judge Daly, and an emphasis on political honesty and reform that he hoped would overcome popular discontent over the Erie Canal scandals. It was by stressing these points over and over that he hoped to convince the voters that he was the man they should send to Albany.[4]

❧ ❧ ❧

By 9:00 the next morning, Roosevelt was on the go again as his train, which he suggested be called "The Flying Squadron," continued its

Roosevelt Speaking from his Campaign Train
(Courtesy of the Theodore Roosevelt Collection,
Harvard College Library)

Roosevelt Greeting the Voters - (Bugler Cassi is on the
Right of the Train Platform)
(Courtesy of the Theodore Roosevelt Collection,
Harvard College Library)

northern course east of Lake George and then up the western shore of
Lake Champlain. The first part of his journey took him through a State
Senate district which the Republicans hoped to recapture in their effort to replace U.S. Senator Murphy with one of their own. During his
talks there, Roosevelt especially emphasized national issues. At Port
Henry, immediately after bugler Cassi sounded the cavalry charge, he
began his remarks with:

"You have heard the trumpet that sounded to bring you here.
I have heard it tear the tropic dawn when it summoned us to
fight at Santiago."

Then, equating the Republican campaign with national honor, he
referred to the "debate" at the Paris peace conference in which the
United States was seeking to annex Puerto Rico and the Philippines by
treaty, and argued:

"If you wish to vote for America, if you wish to vote for the flag
for which we fought this summer, . . . then you will vote to sustain the Administration of President McKinley and vote to sustain
the Peace Commissioners who are representing our side in the
conference at Paris. If this fall it appears by the record of the votes
of the people of this country that a blow has been administered to
the President; that his policy is condemned; that the Peace Commission is not sustained, then you may rest certain that you have
put the most powerful weapon into the hands of the Spaniards,
from whom we have just taken weapons; that you have strength-
ened every power that wishes us ill in continental Europe."

After stopping at Rouses Point, just south of the Canadian border,
the train turned west and made its way to Ogdensburg, a small city on
the southeastern banks of the St. Lawrence River. En route, the party
received an especially enthusiastic reception at the southern Adiron-
dack village of Malone from a crowd of 3000 that had come out on a
sunny afternoon to greet him. According to Clarke, as the train was

about to leave following Roosevelt's talk, Rough Rider Sherman Bell

"... [w]ith his tremendous voice had just started to make a talk when someone in the crowd made a disparaging remark about the Colonel. As Bell started to reply the bell cord was pulled and the train started and Bell's voice rose above the clatter of the train swelling into a grand crescendo as we moved off, 'I want to tell that blankety-blank-blank son of a blankety-blank-blank that if he will come out to the State of Colorado and make any remark like that we will give him a decent burial before sun-down.'"

Roosevelt's train did not reach Ogdensburg until 7 o'clock. As at Glens Falls, the meeting hall was filled to overflowing, and hundreds of disappointed citizens had to satisfy themselves with a glimpse of the candidate and an enjoyment of the fireworks, illuminations and band music that the St. Lawrence County Republican Committee had arranged to stir up interest in his visit. These special efforts were probably unnecessary, for seldom, if ever, had the residents of this remote corner of the state seen a public figure of such eminence, let alone a nationally renowned war hero. To most of those who heard or even saw him, his appearance was an event they would never forget.

In his Ogdensburg speech, Roosevelt stressed state taxation issues, and accused his opponents of trying to replace an excise tax that bore on "the liquor traffic" with new imposts that would fall most heavily on the "the farmer, the working man, the mechanic." Among the speakers was Mason Mitchell, an actor who as a Rough Rider had been wounded in Cuba. He had been dramatizing the regiment's story for $500 a week in Chicago and had now come to New York to try out his act there. He won loud applause as he closed his presentation with "and then out of the woods darted the Colonel with a revolver in each hand, and waving his sword in the air he shouted, 'Come on Boys' and led the charge up the hill." To say the least, he was miffed when, as he sat down after completing his bravura performance, his neighbor on the platform whispered, "Mason, if the Colonel had a revolver in each hand how did he wave his sword, with his teeth?"

The long day finally ended, but not before two of the Rough Riders nearly came to blows in a hotel bar, where with other members of Roosevelt's party they had been invited by a local politician who wanted to treat his visitors to glasses of champagne. According to a *Herald* reporter, they and their comrades "saw all that Ogdensburg had to show before being hustled to bed."[5]

❦ ❦ ❦

Although Tuesday's speaking had lasted well into the night, on Wednesday there was no rest for the weary, for Roosevelt had to be back in New York in time for a major Brooklyn evening rally. Thus, the train left Ogdensburg at 8:00 a.m., steaming south along the Adirondacks' western fringe. Before it reached Boonville, about 20 miles north of Utica, it had made five scheduled stops. At two other places, the size of the crowds standing in a drenching rain caused a brief halt so that the candidate could greet them. At Potsdam and Canton, Roosevelt alluded to that morning's newspaper reports of a "hitch" in the peace negotiations with Spain, and urged his listeners to support the Republican ticket and thus "sustain the Administration of President McKinley in insisting that we shall reap the benefits of our triumphs."

To anyone who was on the train that raw and rainy day, the experience was exhilarating. As William O'Neil, an ally of Roosevelt when they had served together in the Assembly who had joined him on Tuesday, wrote a friend several days later:

"As you say, Teddy is a wonder. On Wednesday, it rained all day and in spite of it there were immense gatherings of people standing in the mud and rain. He spoke about ten minutes – the speech was nothing, but the man's presence was everything. It was electrical, magnetic. I looked in the faces of hundreds and saw only pleasure and satisfaction. When the train started away, scores of

man and women ran after the train, waving hats and handkerchiefs and cheering, trying to keep him in sight as long as possible.

"Some Democrats say it was only the idle curiosity of the
crowd that always attends the entrance of a circus with a country
town. I thought it something else, perhaps my own love and admiration for the man blinded me to the real facts. Perhaps I measured others by my own feelings, for as the train faded away and I
saw him smiling and waving his hat at the people, they in turn
giving abundant evidence of their enthusiastic affection, my eyes
filled with tears, I couldn't help it, though I am ordinarily a cold-
blooded fish not easily stirred like that."

Before leaving home to spend two days with Roosevelt, O'Neil had
received a letter from an Albany friend, saying "For God's sake, tell
Roosevelt to stop his self adulation and talking about himself so
much." After his personal campaign experience, however, O'Neil was
moved to write the candidate on October 21 with very different advice:

"Continue to follow your own inspirations – You will shock
old fossils like the ex-minister to Spain – You will startle the machine politicians but will win the confidence of the voters. . . .

For the most part men are as nearly alike as peas – once in a
while Nature produces a new type which she never duplicates –
an original which sets at naught all previous standards – These
are the fellows who win the world, who can say and do things
when and how they please. You belong to this order. Don't attempt to change to suit the notions of others."[6]

❈ ❈ ❈

As soon as the Roosevelt party left Boonville, the engineer pulled out
the throttle and the train sped to New York, reaching Grand Central
Station shortly after 7:00 p.m. From there the candidate was rushed by
carriage to Brooklyn, where in the space of three hours he addressed
four meetings. The final event, at the Academy of Music, had drawn a

capacity crowd of several thousand well before its scheduled 8 o'clock opening. By the time Roosevelt arrived at 9:51, a combination of martial music and warmup speeches by Seth Low and other luminaries had roused the audience to a fever pitch, which reached its climax when the noise from outside the hall told the crowd within that their candidate was about to appear. After a ten-minute ovation, he finally was able to get their attention, but as soon as they heard him say "I hope you fellows will enjoy hearing me talk half as much as I enjoy your cheers," they erupted with another roar. The next morning's *Herald* reported that "[t]hose who thought the Carnegie Hall meeting was enthusiastic would have been dazed" by the Brooklyn reception, and

"His utterances were as different from those in Carnegie Hall as his reception had been. He challenged the democracy . . . and spurred into their camp with the newest war cry, the judiciary, daring them to combat. National issues he emphasized, but State issues he made the note of his loudest blasts."

The Brooklyn rally was also notable for the large number of women attendees, who were especially evident in the boxes and on the stage. Several of them repeatedly interrupted the speakers by calling out, "You are all right, Teddy," "Hooray for Teddy," or "Teddy, you're a peach." One of the women in the gallery became so excited during Roosevelt's speech that in leaning over to get a better view, she blocked the view of several men, who unkindly yelled at her, "Whom are you going to vote for?" Reflecting the state of affairs in this pre-women's suffrage era, the *Times* reported: "This brought her to a consciousness of her position, and sent her down with a blush into her seat."

The next day was filled with more of the same, as Roosevelt delivered three more speeches, all in Quigg's Manhattan Congressional District. He also found time to squeeze in a brief surprise appearance at an anti-Tammany German-American rally at a hall on East 56th Street, where the announcement that "Herr Roosevelt is here" brought the otherwise unemotional burghers to their feet, cheering, jumping up and down, and waving hats and coats. At one of the West Side meetings, he argued that "the most important issue before us . . . is the independence and honesty of the judiciary." He tried his best to make Judge Daly's cause his own by reminding his audience that it could "rebuke the men who have tried to imperil the independence of the bench . . . in but one way, and that is overwhelming defeat for the organization that is responsible for it." At the East Side rally, Clarke delivered what the *Times* called "the hit of the evening" as he ridiculed Croker's claim that it would be unwise to send a "mere soldier" to Albany: "They want to put it in the hands of a businessman, and they've got the firm all ready – Van Wyck, Van Wyck & Co. They ask us to give the administration to people who will clean up the canals, but who can't keep the streets of New York clean."

During that day and the next, Roosevelt spent several hours at party headquarters reviewing his upstate tour and finalizing the rest of the campaign. As Youngs recalled several years later, it was "the consensus of opinion" that Roosevelt's election "was at best very debatable":

"Probably in no other campaign in the history of the state of New York did the success of one or the other party fluctuate more frequently. Probably there has never been and never will be another occasion in the history of the state, where the parties were so evenly divided and where the popular pulse was so keenly and so thoroughly felt. There were days that were Roosevelt days, and other days when it appeared that the Democrats would win. Nor was this confined to special localities. The same feeling prevailed in all parts of the state, as was shown by telegrams which arrived from the different sections, showing the fluctuation of the popular pulse."

The major bright spot was the obvious success of Roosevelt's recent tour. The obvious course, therefore, was more of the same.[7]

❧ ❧ ❧

While Roosevelt was making his case to voters around the state, the just as essential "nuts and bolts" of the Republican campaign were being put together by State Committee Chairman Odell and his aides from a suite in the Fifth Avenue Hotel. Odell was assisted by William Barnes of Albany, who chaired the organization's Executive Committee, and by a treasurer and a secretary. "Besides these," explained a *Tribune* article headed RUNNING A CAMPAIGN, "there were many clerks, messengers, stenographers and the usual office retinue in the seven rooms through which for weeks there was a constant stream of office-seeking, office-making, information-giving and question-asking humanity."

One of the Committee's full-time employees chaired its "Literary Bureau," which was responsible for dispensing all kinds of campaign literature, including copies of speeches by the candidates, to locations throughout the state where it would do the most good. Even more important was the manager of the Speaking Department, which had on file lists of men who had been effective on the stump in previous campaigns. They were classified as to whether they were "humorous," "serious," or "all-around" speakers. Other categories included men fluent in foreign languages such as German, Italian, Polish and Hebrew who could to speak to immigrants in their native tongues. One separate listing was of orators whose use of the brogue would persuade voters that the men addressing them were "real Irish."

One of Treasurer Edwin A. McAlpin's tasks was to orchestrate what the *Tribune* called a "continuous battle" against "strikers" and "sawdusters." These were men who, for their own personal gain, "under various disguises and by all kinds of schemes, try to secure some of the money with which the campaign should be run." Some would claim to be able to "influence thousands" through a lodge, association or political organization, and a few would be brazen enough to suggest that they be provided an office from which they could "manage the work."

Masterminding this complex organization was Benjamin Odell. The *Tribune* described his duties as combining

> "...the politician, diplomat and organizer. He must have the courage to depart from beaten paths if circumstances demand it, and he must possess the faculty of inspiring those who work with him with courage and enthusiasm and to maintain a bold front under depressing circumstances."

As he weighed the stream of reports and requests for help that came in daily from all over the state and decided which were worth pursuing, the Chairman also had to "possess all the points of a first-class poker player." With an encyclopedic knowledge of political detail relating to almost every county, and with his background as a three-term Congressman, Odell fit these requirements as well as anyone could. Although he initially had erred in judgement as to Roosevelt's effectiveness on the stump, in retrospect the delay in doing so may have been helpful, since otherwise the campaign might have peaked too soon.[8]

❀ ❀ ❀

One of the voting groups that was especially important to the Republicans was the Afro-Americans. Only 33 years had elapsed since the Civil War's close, and many of them had spent their youths in slavery. To the majority of these voters, the Republicans were the party of Abraham Lincoln, and the Democrats, relying heavily in national campaigns on the "Solid South," were the party that practiced rigid segregation, which many black Americans had moved north to escape. It was not surprising, therefore, that the October 23 *Tribune* quoted the chairman of the Colored National Republican Committee as stating that the Democrats would not get more than 5000 out of the 35,000 to 40,000 votes that "colored men" would cast in the New York campaign. Nothing would be left to chance, however, and "numerous meetings" would be

Roosevelt's Forty League Boots
(*New York Herald*)

Judge Van Wyck Speaking in Buffalo
(*New York Herald*)

scheduled "in which the colored preachers will take an active part almost without exception." They would be held for Queens voters in Flushing and Jamaica, for Manhattan residents in the West Twenties and in Harlem, and even on Staten Island. Campaign headquarters had been established in Manhattan's Crystal Hall at 352 West 35th Street, "where nightly meetings will be held until Election Day."[9]

❀ ❀ ❀

While Roosevelt had been busy speaking upstate, Van Wyck had been relatively inactive. On October 18, due to "unannounced circumstances," he failed to appear at a large meeting at Tammany Hall, which "ratified" his nomination. Finally, on Friday, October 21, he left New York City for his first upstate tour, which he opened at Buffalo's Music Hall the following evening. His supporters wanted to give him a rousing send-off and provide him with a special car, but he would have none of it, preferring to travel with his secretary, Patrick Nolan, like any other passenger. In his Buffalo speech, which he delivered before an audience of 5000, he devoted most of his time to the canal question, accusing the Republicans of dodging the issue and "occupying the valuable time of the public in the discussion of questions which can never, by any possibility, require the official action of the Governor of this State."

Meanwhile, on October 20, in a show of Party unity, former Governor and Senator Hill spoke at the Brooklyn Academy of Music, where he attacked Roosevelt for implying that "the late war was a Republican war," and delivered a strongly felt definition of "Democracy: the people's cause." He got into trouble, however, when he commented on a letter that State Inspector of Elections John McCullagh had sent to the New York City police, reminding them that a recent judicial decision should not be construed as meaning that "one night's residence at a lodging house" is sufficient "to entitle him to register and vote from such lodging house," and that anyone acting under such a misconception "will be amenable to the law." The Inspector had gone on to furnish a list of "houses and places," mostly on Manhattan's East Side, "in which I am reliably informed colonization had been practiced, and from which there is every reason to believe a horde of floaters and repeaters will be sent forth to the polling places of this city to register as voters." "Among these places," he added, "are disorderly houses and cafes conducted for immoral purposes." Departing from his prepared text, Hill responded:

"If, on election day, one of these hireling Republican spies attempts to interfere with you in the exercise of the privileges of your citizenship, knock him down on the spot."

The *Herald* reported that "on hearing this fiery advice to resist the law, if misapplied, with force, the crowd took a sudden breath and leapt to its feet with a roar, . . . and men could be seen slapping each other on the back in enthusiastic approval." In his hotel room the next morning, Hill stood by his advice, and was supported by City Police Chief Devery. The Republican leaders, delighted that their opponents had apparently handed them another issue, adopted a "holier than thou" attitude, with Odell piously expressing surprise that Hill should make such a statement and emphasizing that "the law must be obeyed." Platt's sarcastic response was that Hill's advice "compares favorably with some things that Mr. Croker has been saying," and "there seems to be a competition between them as to which can say the worse thing."[10]

❋ ❋ ❋

On Friday October 21, Roosevelt, accompanied by Mason Mitchell, left Grand Central Station on the 6 o'clock train for a second upstate tour, this time for only a day and a half. Before he left, he busied himself attending to a seemingly never-ending series of campaign details, including writing a series of instructions to Quigg:

"I am told that in both the 4th and 8th Assembly districts, very little is being done. Jacob Riis of the *Sun* wants to give them all the help he can. He can help us with the Scandinavians and can help us with all the East Side people. Some financial aid should be given to the Blaine Club and possibly Dr. Wolbarst can do good service. Both of them in the 4th District. They were for Low last year and they are, I think, sincerely for me, but they are very poor and they have to have a little aid to hold meetings or get out banners.

"In the 8th District Commissioner Murray, or Reynolds of the University Settlement, should be consulted. Can't you see Riis?" There followed a handwritten addendum:

"In the 8th, can't Meyer Isaacs be asked to speak? And Von Brisen? Why isn't it possible to boom things, with speeches, etc., in the 8th? Do send for Riis – 301 Mulberry St."[11]

✿ ✿ ✿

That evening, Roosevelt spoke at Poughkeepsie's Collingwood Opera House before an audience of 3000 that included the Vassar College President and some of his students, as well as John Jacob Astor, who joined the group on the stage. In one box, the *Tribune* reported, sat the candidate's distant cousin James Roosevelt of Hyde Park "and his family," whom the Colonel noticed "and waved his hand to them." * They presumably did not include James' 16-year-old son Franklin, who was pursuing his studies as a "fifth former" (junior) at Groton.

In his address, Roosevelt first addressed tax and other fiscal matters, but soon turned to Justice Daly, arguing to this crowd of upstate voters who would have no chance to vote for or against the Judge that it was "not enough" to reelect him, "The men who are responsible for the attempt to discredit the whole bench must be buried in overwhelming defeat." He then drove his point home by linking that issue to Hill's suggestion that, as Roosevelt characterized it, voters who were

---

* Although he was a Democrat, family ties were even more important to James Roosevelt, and he was backing and planned to vote for Cousin Theodore.

challenged at the polls "should break the heads of certain election officers if those election officers acted in a way that would be repugnant to
the hearers:"

> "Incitement to lawlessness and riot at the polls is an entirely
> fitting corollary of the proposition that judges must be punished
> if they do not show a proper sense of their obligation to a political
> organization."[12]

❦ ❦ ❦

The next morning, the Roosevelt train left Poughkeepsie at the civilized hour of 10:30 and traveled up the Hudson and then west to the
small Mohawk Valley city of Little Falls. Well into the next century, factory employees normally worked a six-day week, but this Saturday afternoon the mills closed early so that everyone could see and hear
Roosevelt. Despite a heavy downpour that ended only a few minutes
before his arrival, the opera house was filled to overflowing, and the
candidate was forced to deliver a second talk to the people standing
outside. His train then reversed course and sped east to Johnstown,
where the factory whistles blew for more than a half hour and forced
the candidate to delay his speech. Later, when he arrived by trolley in
nearby Gloversville, he was greeted by fireworks and a mass of humanity that filled the streets for blocks and was reportedly the largest crowd
he had yet encountered. After speaking in the local opera house and to
an overflow throng in a nearby square, he finally boarded his train
shortly before midnight and started back to New York.

At his three Mohawk Valley stops, Roosevelt stressed state issues. At
Little Falls, he pressed his support of judicial independence for all it was
worth, reminding his audience that "my party . . . possessed the wisdom to renominate Judge Daly for the bench." He then scornfully
turned on Croker and the Democrats:

> "But his own party — and when I speak of the Democratic Par-
> ty in the State of New York, I never know whether to speak of him

or it — but his own party, speaking on this occasion in the singular, failed to nominate him, as Mr. Croker said that Judge Daly could not be nominated because while on the bench he had failed to show a proper sense of his obligations to Tammany Hall."

He then explained how the election of a New York City Tammany judge could affect this audience of upstate voters:

"Remember that Mr. Croker's Governor could send Mr. Croker's Judge to sit in judgment anywhere from Buffalo up to Plattsburg and down to New York."

Only by electing Roosevelt could the voters avoid such a dire result.[13]

14

"I Do Wish You Would Get That Medal Of Honor For Me"

As soon as he had finished speaking in Gloversville, Roosevelt and his party took a waiting trolley car for the ten-mile trip to Fonda, where a train was waiting at the station to take them to New York. It was nearly midnight before he was able to retire for the night, but he was one of the first to alight when the train reached Grand Central Station at 6:30 the next morning. He took a trolley to his sister Bamie's home at 689 Madison Avenue, between 61st and 62nd Streets, where Edith was waiting to welcome him.[1]

The previous week had been an exciting one for the Roosevelt family. Three years earlier, Bamie had surprised her family by marrying William Sheffield Cowles, then serving as an American naval attaché in London. They had returned to New York, and on October 18, Bamie, who had been crippled with a spine defect from birth and now at age 43 was increasingly crippled by arthritis, had given birth to a healthy ten-and-a-half pound boy. As soon as she received word that Bamie was in labor, Edith temporarily abandoned her Sagamore Hill campaign secretarial duties to be with her sister-in-law. When Roosevelt had returned from his first upstate swing, his campaign duties had permitted him to look in only briefly on his new nephew. This Sunday, he had more time to enjoy with his sister what must have been an especially "blessed" event.[2]

❀ ❀ ❀

As Roosevelt prepared for the next few days and also tried to get some much-needed rest, two potential problems were causing trouble. The first was that many New York voters, including some Republicans, did not share Roosevelt's strong endorsement of imperialism in general and the annexation of the Philippines in particular. Their opposition was part of a nationwide movement. At a June 14 meeting at Boston's Faneuil Hall, an Anti-Imperialist League had been formed. Its president was 80-year-old George Boutwell, who had been a Republican Senator and Secretary of the Treasury in the Grant Administration. Boutwell's major concern was that American expansion in the Pacific would lead to war with Japan, or, more likely, Russia. Others feared that the acquisition of overseas possessions would distract the public from facing political and social needs at home, and might increase the power of the central government at the expense of states' rights and personal liberties.[3]

Many prominent persons either joined the League or supported its goals. They included Presidents Eliot of Harvard, Angell of Michigan and Jordan of Stanford, Mark Twain and novelist William Dean Howells. In a June address at Lawrenceville School, former President Cleveland condemned "temptations so dangerous as those which now whisper in our ears alluring words of conquest and expansion and point out to us fields bright with glory of war." The anti-imperialism movement received strong financial support from Andrew Carnegie, who believed that expansion abroad would divert American energy from industrial development at home and would make it more difficult for the United States to gain respect in the world on the basis that it was different from the other major powers.[4]

Many of the most prominent anti-imperialists were political independents who had never returned to the Republican fold after working as Mugwumps to assure James G. Blaine's defeat 14 years earlier.

One of the most prominent, and especially influential in New York, was Roosevelt's old friend Carl Schurz. When he was only 19, Schurz's activities in the unsuccessful German Revolution of 1848 forced him to flee arrest for treason and emigrate to the United States. His marriage the same year to a wealthy heiress permitted him the freedom of devoting much of his time to politics, and as a strong anti-slavery advocate, he became active in the young Republican Party. His efforts with German voters were especially helpful in Lincoln's 1860 election. He was a strong supporter of the new President, and helped recruit and then commanded German forces in the Army of the Potomac, where he became a major general but did not distinguish himself as a military commander. He later served a single term as U.S. Senator from Missouri, was Secretary of the Interior in the Hayes Administration, and then moved to New York, where he joined Godkin in editing the *Evening Post*. Always in the forefront of such public-spirited causes as conservation and civil service reform, the tall, red-bearded Schurz was the most prominent German-American of the 19th century, and his influence with that block of voters was considerable.[5]

As might be expected, in New York political matters Schurz was strongly opposed to bossism, whether it existed in the person of Richard Croker or of Thomas Collier Platt. Although he and Roosevelt had differed on political issues such as the Blaine-Cleveland election, they remained personal friends. On October 14, Roosevelt had written to ask for his support, suggesting that "on State issues we are now as one, and the war is now over and I am as anxious for peace and quiet as you possibly can be."[6]

Roosevelt's effort was to no avail. On October 22, in a letter that the *Evening Post* printed in two columns at the top of its first page, Schurz announced that although when Roosevelt "was first spoken of as a candidate for the governorship, I greatly wished and hoped to be able to support him, . . . it is no empty figure of speech when I say that with painful reluctance I have come to an adverse conclusion." In his initial hope, he would have accepted the Republican nominee even "in his concession to the Republican party machine." "But," he continued,

".... we can hardly do the same with respect to certain utterances put forth at his speech at the Carnegie Hall meeting in which he sounded the keynote of the campaign. There he told us that the question is not whether he or his competitor will make the better Governor of New York but that by electing him we are to declare to the whole world that the State of New York stands behind the national administration in its annexation policy, how far that policy may ever go. And even more than that. He virtually asks us to endorse, by electing him, his kind of militant imperialism, which has no bounds."

Schurz admitted that "as Governor of New York" Roosevelt "would not have the power to carry such ideas into effect." Then, however, with an acute prophetic sense, he set forth what was probably the real reason that he could not support the Republican candidate:

".... we cannot elect him without seemingly countenancing this sort of imperialism ... Moreover, it is by no means improper to point out that an election to the governorship of New York, as it frequently has been, may again become, in Col. Roosevelt's case, the stepping-stone to the nomination for the presidency. Indeed, it is in everybody's mouth that if Col. Roosevelt succeeds, it will be so. I am not, therefore, dealing with a vague and remote contingency, but with a question of immediate interest which will come for actual decision in less than twenty months, when I say that we have considered the probable effect of Col. Roosevelt's election to the governorship from this point of view."

Finally,

".... as a veteran in the fight against unsound currency and against Tammany, whose sincerity and zeal nobody has a right to question, I do not hesitate to express the solemn conviction that there are worse things even than free silver and Tammany, and that one of them is the imperialism which in its effects upon the character and the durability of the republic I consider to be as pernicious as slavery itself was, and which we are now asked to countenance and encourage."

Therefore, Schurz would vote for the Independent ticket.

Not surprisingly, the *Post* echoed Schurz's sentiments. In an obviously synchronized editorial of the same day, it argued that his letter

". . . will command wide attention and exert a profound influence upon that large body of voters who are still hesitant as to their duty on election day. . . . Col. Roosevelt cannot find fault with it, since he himself invited it, and is daily adding to its force. When he declared that his election would mean approval of his 'militant' imperialism and his defeat its rebuke, he made it very hard for any independent voter who did not believe in that policy to vote for him, as we have warned him repeatedly."[7]

❊ ❊ ❊

A second problem area for the Roosevelt campaign involved Spanish-American war veterans and their friends. The repeated emphasis in his campaign on the Rough Riders was bad enough, since the vast majority of New York veterans had served in other regiments that they believed were equally deserving of praise. His well-publicized shoving aside of the 71st New York Volunteers so that the Rough Riders would be sure to get on a ship to Cuba had made matters even worse. Under the heading "SOLDIERS HISS ROOSEVELT," the October 22 *Times* reported that two days previously at a meeting in Brooklyn of 800 or more members of the 14th Regiment, Roosevelt was hissed when the men saw a campaign picture of the Colonel hanging in their mess hall. At the same time, they applauded a portrait of Judge Van Wyck, with one man offering "three cheers for the men who will down the only

Carl Schurz
(Courtesy of the Corbis-Bettman Archives)

Henry Cabot Lodge
(Courtesy of the Corbis-Bettman Archives)

hero of the war." When an intrepid private in the regiment attempted to display another picture of Roosevelt, there were shouts of "Tear it down" and "He slandered the infantry."[8]

This last reference was to a foolish mistake that Roosevelt had made in late July, when he was lobbying the War Department to let the Rough Riders participate in the invasion of Puerto Rico. In a letter to Secretary Alger, he had suggested that his soldiers were "three times as good as any State troops" and that the 4000 men of a calvary division that included his regiment "would be worth, easily any ten thousand National Guards armed with black powder, Springfields or other archaic weapon." During the last few days, the Democrats had obtained a copy of the letter, which they gleefully publicized, together with Alger's reply, which would have put anyone less intrepid than Roosevelt in his place:

"The regular army, the volunteer army and the Rough Riders have done well, but I suggest that unless you want to spoil the effects and glory of your victory you make no invidious comparisons. The Rough Riders are no better than other volunteers. They had an advantage in their arms, for which they ought to be very grateful."[9]

To blunt these attacks, and also to combat rumors that he had never charged up the San Juan Heights, Roosevelt mounted a campaign to have himself awarded the Congressional Medal of Honor before Election Day. This was not a new idea. On July 7, less than a week after that victory, he wrote to Lodge: "Gen. Wheeler says he intends to recommend me for the medal of honor; naturally I should like to have it." Three and a half weeks later, in a letter in which he discussed the possibility that he and many other soldiers would die from yellow fever unless they were promptly evacuated from Cuba, he told Lodge that "if I do go, I do wish you would get that medal of honor for me anyhow, as I should awfully like the children to have it, and I think I earned it."[10]

Probably because Roosevelt returned to the United States in perfect health, Lodge did not pursue the matter until he received a frantic request from his friend to see if he could get McKinley to expedite the award. On October 24, in New York making a speech for Roosevelt, the Senator rushed to the *Sun* office, from which he "telephoned the White House about the medal . . . and gave the message to Mr. Montgomery, one of the clerks whom I know, and put it in the strongest possible terms." The next day he followed up with a letter to the President:

"I took the liberty of telephoning yesterday from New York in regard to giving Colonel Roosevelt at this time the medal for distinguished gallantry for which he was recommended by General Wheeler. I assume that there is no doubt that the medal will be conferred on him sooner or later. Just now it would have a very important meaning and value and would put at rest many stories which are being circulated by the Democrats. In view of the immense importance of the New York election I felt justified in bringing the matter to your attention and desire to express my most earnest hope that this medal may be awarded to Colonel Roosevelt in the course of the next few days. I would not be so urgent were I not thoroughly assured of the importance of the action at this time."

McKinley, however, was not prepared to bypass the Washington bureaucracy even to help win an important election for the Republicans. Soon after Lodge had left the *Sun* office, one of its editors received a message from the White House: "President says he is appointing Board to award those medals and will be glad to comply with your wishes in seeing to it that there is no delay in T.R.'s case." Well versed in the ways of Washington, Lodge wrote Roosevelt that "I do not feel myself that this is very satisfactory, because I do not believe that a board can be appointed in time to do it." The Senator was right, and Roosevelt never received the medal during his lifetime. He later wrote to a friend that the authorities had "taken exactly the right position." [11]*

❧ ❧ ❧

If Roosevelt had found time during that generally restful October 23 to read the current newspapers, he might also have been concerned by a report in the previous day's *Evening Post* that Tammany was making "a great effort" to register every possible Democrat and that "if the total registration in the Boroughs of Manhattan and the Bronx shows a falling off from last year's figures, Tammany will not be the sufferers on election day." "The almost perfect organization of the Tammany forces," the *Post* explained:

> "makes the work of bringing out their voters comparatively easy. Every election district has its captain, who knows every Tammany man in the district, and every man who is likely to vote the Democratic ticket. When the order comes from the district leader, the captain sends out his men to find out who have not registered and to bring the laggards to the registry places."

It was not just a case of reminding the party faithful of the need to renew their registration. As the *Post* described a time-honored Tammany tradition:

> "In some of the down-town districts where many voters must receive 'inducements' to register, it is said that the Tammany leaders put in their requisitions for funds, and it is said everyone of them received all he asked, together with the assurance that he could have more if he found it necessary to make an additional requisition. The importance of this condition of affairs is recognized by all local politicians. It means that in the lodging-house districts, the Tammany registration will be all that is desired by the leaders, and that the purchasable vote will figure largely on the last day of registration."

---

* In 1998 Congress posthumously voted Roosevelt the medal.

As for the Republicans, the article echoed Roosevelt's comment to Lodge several days earlier that their organization was performing "a little rustily:"

> "The captains seldom work together, . . . and in many election districts it is impossible for a Republican to find out the name of his captain. The result is that in most districts the campaign is conducted in a haphazard way . . . In fact, the Republican leaders generally seem to put their trust in luck and brass bands."[12]

Thus, if Roosevelt was to prevail, it would be only with the help of the much stronger organizations outside the City.

15

"He Kept Ev'ry Promise He Made To Us, And So He Will To You"

ON MONDAY, OCTOBER 24, ROOSEVELT WAS UP WELL BEFORE DAWN. At 6.30 he was driven from his sister's house to the Erie Railroad ferry on West 23rd Street. From there he crossed the Hudson to Jersey City, where his special train, made up of a Pullman sleeper and the "private car 'Mascotte,'" was waiting. To augment its oratorical powers, on this week's swing the party included Chauncey Depew, whose many years of New York politics had provided him with acquaintanceships in almost all of the places to be visited. Presumably to counter criticism that the previous week's tours had been too much a series of Rough Riders rallies, Bugler Cassi had been left behind with the excuse that he was needed to cultivate French and Italian voters in the city. The only two Rough Riders aboard, Buck Taylor and Sherman Bell, were now clad in civilian attire, since, as the *Sun* correspondent wrote, "they were going, . . . not as soldiers (for the regiment had been mustered out and scattered), but as friends and well wishers, who felt thoroughly and altogether competent to speak of him [Roosevelt] as a teller of truth and an undaunted leader."[1]

The "truth" came out in an unexpected way when at 11 o'clock the train made its fifth stop of the morning at the city of Port Jervis on the upper reaches of the Delaware, where the New Jersey and Pennsylvania borders meet the New York line. Ever since they had left Jersey City, Buck Taylor had been pressuring Youngs and Clarke to let him finish his talk and explain why he was experiencing his life's "proudest moment." They finally relented, and they and the audience of 2000 heard the following:

> "I want to talk to you about mah Colonel. I want you to know him as we knew him and if you do you will love him and follow him as we done. He kept ev'ry promise he made to us, and so he will to you. When he took us to Cuba he told us we would have to bury dead horses and we done it. He told us we would have to lie out in the trenches with the rifle bullets climbing over us and we done it. He told us we would have to drink dirty water and we done it. He told us we might have to go with mighty little food, sometimes only hard-tack and dirty water, and we done it, but he had it just the same. He told us we might meet wounds and death and we done it, but he was thar in the midst of us, and when it came to the great day he led us up San Juan Hill like sheep to the slaughter and so he will lead you."

As Roosevelt later wrote: "This hardly seemed a tribute to my military skill, but it delighted the crowd and as far as I could tell did nothing but good." Nevertheless, Buck never was given a chance to make another speech.[2]

The crowds that greeted the Roosevelt party were large and just as enthusiastic as those that had cheered him the week before. At Middletown, two bands, one made up of Afro-Americans and the other of white men, competed with each other's rendition of "A Hot Time in the Old Town Tonight" to the background accompaniment of exploding "track torpedoes." In the village of Hankins, the candidate was greeted by a semicircle of horsemen, one of whom was carrying a banner on which was roughly inscribed:

> "We are rough and tough, but all ready

On the eighth of November to vote for Teddy."

Another held aloft a linen placard reading:

"They all do say at Oyster Bay, that Teddy did his taxes pay,

And, to protect his Riders true, his income awfully overdrew."

Not everyone felt that way about the candidate's taxes. In the afternoon, after its stop at Binghamton, the train made a 30-mile side trip north to Cortland, where his speech in the opera house was interrupted by a heckler who called out: "How about that Oyster Bay incident?" To loud cheers, Roosevelt replied that,

> ". . . when I was working night and day to get ready the fleets with which Dewey fought at Manila and Sampson at Santiago, when I was raising my regiment, one-fourth of whom were wounded or killed on Spanish soil, and one-half of the remainder brought to death's door, or beyond, by fever, I took the pains to write, both to my lawyer and to the man who had charge of my business while I was at war, that they were to see that my taxes were paid, either in New York or in Oyster Bay. Owing to the death of my uncle, they were not paid in Oyster Bay, where they should have been, and as soon as I found this out, on getting home, I directed that,...they should be paid at once, in New York, and they were paid there on the first day when it was legally possible to pay them."

Although not entirely accurate, this account would be the Republican "party line" throughout the campaign, and it contained enough of the truth that Roosevelt's opponents were unable to make much out of the issue.

It was after 8:00 p.m. when the Roosevelt Special, 50 minutes late, reached Elmira. There was no rest for the weary, however, as with apparently unflagging stamina Roosevelt addressed three meetings in the normally Democratic city. As he had throughout the day, he stressed tax relief and economy and honesty in government. His remarks were reasonably restrained, unlike his earlier rear platform talks where, the *Herald* reported, in "aggressive and vehement" tones "more like the Roosevelt of his Police Board days than at any previous time during the campaign," he "denounced 'Tammanyized democracy'" and accused New York City Democrats of raising a "corruption fund" from local dens of iniquity to finance their upstate campaign.[3]

❧ ❧ ❧

The next morning and early afternoon saw more of the same as the Roosevelt Special made its way from Elmira through the small towns and villages of west central New York. Although there was no letup in effort at the day's eleven stops, the candidate and his party were clearly focusing on their reception in Buffalo, the state's second largest city, where they arrived a little before 5 o'clock. They need not have worried for, as the next morning's *Sun* described it, while Van Wyck's welcome three days before "was a visit from a candidate; this has been a triumph to a conquering hero." From the station, where he was met by a corps of buglers and a group of uniformed mounted men calling themselves the Buffalo Rough Riders, to his hotel, where according to the *Sun*, the scene in the corridors "can only be compared to those seen in a college after an athletic victory" and "gray headed men acted like boys of twenty," his arrival was a continuous hurrah.

That evening, Roosevelt's pursuit of ethnic voters would have done proud any late 20th century politician. At one meeting on Buffalo's East Side, he addressed an audience of Germans. He then invaded a Polish neighborhood, where he made three speeches. One of them was chaired by a Father Pitass, who was dean of the local Roman Catholic clergy. Although he was known for Democratic leanings, he invited Roosevelt into his house for a glass of wine before accompanying him to the meeting hall. Finally, it was on to the last event of the evening at the Music Hall, which was presided over by a man described as the most influential German in western New York. The stage was occupied

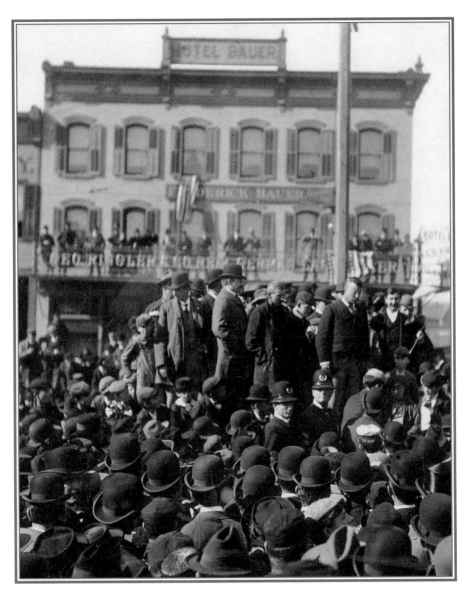

Roosevelt Speaking in an Upstate Town
(Courtesy of the Theodore Roosevelt Collection,
Harvard College Library)

by many German Democrats, including a prominent brewer. A Jewish leader also occupied a prominent seat on the dais. In his address, Roosevelt promised that if any person involved with the work on the canal system "has been guilty of corruption, he shall be punished wholly without regard to any question of personal or party consideration to the utmost of my power." As he had throughout his tour, he argued that even more important than Judge Daly's reelection by New York City voters "is . . . to crush in overwhelming defeat the party which has tried . . . to establish the principle that hereafter the attitude of the judge must be one of cringing subserviency to the political dictates of the moment."

It was obvious that Roosevelt was relishing what another candidate would have found an exhausting experience. Between his arrival in Buffalo and his departure from his hotel for his evening speeches, his suite was filled by a stream of politicians, other local dignitaries and ordinary citizens. At about 7 p.m., the *Sun* reported, "the committee felt that it was time to rescue the candidate from his friends . . . and told him that they thought he had better rest for a while and they would close the doors." Roosevelt strongly demurred, saying "with characteristic energy, 'I am in this fight to the finish.'" Not to be denied, his hosts "went down and told the police to close the doors and then they went back and told their candidate that the people had stopped coming in, when as a matter of fact the police were having a rough time of it because they would not let them."[4]

❦ ❦ ❦

Wednesday, October 26, dawned cloudy. By 9:15, when the train was scheduled to depart, a fine steady rain had begun to fall. The weather did little, however, to dampen the spirits of the passengers, who since breakfast had been regaling each other with tales of the events of what by all accounts had been an evening of unqualified success. A story that demonstrated one of their candidate's previously unrecognized political skills involved a young man who was waiting in line to shake his hand at the late afternoon hotel reception. Out of the corner of his eye, Roosevelt spotted him, leapt by the three men ahead of him in line, and grabbing him by the shoulder, shouted with pleasure, "Why, Fitch, what are you doing here?" Afterwards, the teary-eyed Fitch, who had been a Rough Rider in the regiment's Troop G, exclaimed to an inquiring reporter:

> "The idea of his remembering me! He never saw me until I enlisted in the regiment. He saw no more of me after that than he did of a thousand other men. It only shows the way he looked out for all of us."

That day's tour took the Roosevelt Special north to Tonawanda and Niagara Falls, and then east, paralleling the Erie Canal, to Rochester. The train soon fell behind schedule. By early afternoon the engineer was concerned that before it could reach a siding near Rochester, it might be overtaken by and hold up the Empire State Express. He apparently had not been notified that the train's schedule included a stop at Holley, about 25 miles west of Rochester. Thus, when he responded to a signal to stop there, unaware that Roosevelt had started to speak from the rear platform, he concluded that there had been a mistake and sent the train forward while the candidate was in mid-sentence. An hour or so earlier, just as the train was leaving Medina, an inebriated local resident had tried to follow it down the tracks, at the same time shouting, "Hurrah for Bryan!" At the next stop, a highly amused Roosevelt used the incident to remind his audience of the continuing Democratic split on the free silver issue by remarking that "the candidate for whom my amiable friend probably intends to vote, Mr. Van Wyck — I say Van Wyck, but there is no use in paraphrasing — I mean Mr. Croker — Mr. Croker, then — does not dare say whether he is for Bryan or not except in the presence of his sworn friends, for fear somebody will raise a cheer and thus hurt the feelings of somebody else."

Not surprisingly, as his party made its way east with the Erie Canal no more than a few miles to its left, Roosevelt carefully avoided a discussion of the scandals that had so upset the local citizenry, and emphasized far safer topics like Judge Daly and Boss Croker. That evening, however, the canal issue came to the fore. Lieutenant Governor Woodruff had joined the Roosevelt party in Buffalo and asked to speak there. Fearing that he would talk about the canal, Depew and Youngs told him that there was no room on the program. By the time the Roosevelt Special reached Rochester, however, they had to concede that as a candidate for reelection, Woodruff was entitled to say a few words. The result was a disaster. Faced with a crowd impatient to hear Roosevelt, and according to the *Herald*, suffering from tonsillitis, he had spoken for ten minutes, when the audience had had enough of hearing him defend "those who were connected with what is known as the canal scandals" and "broke out in such wild disorder that the Lieutenant Governor was forced to give up his labor after one-sixth of the speech had been delivered." He had no course but to announce that he would "impose on the good nature of my newspaper friends here and obtain your leave to have my speech printed."

By this point, the uproar was so great that even Depew was unable to bring the crowd to order. It only quieted when Roosevelt was introduced, and, having received advance word as to what Woodruff planned to say, received "prolonged applause" when at once he announced:

"If there be trouble in the system on which the canal is administered I will change it if elected Governor, or present suggestions to the Legislature for a change. If there is dishonesty or inefficiency, I will punish it. More than that no man can say, and I leave it to you to judge whether our opponents or I can do it best."

The next day, Depew minimized the incident, claiming that the Lieutenant Governor's difficulty with the crowd was only the result of a bad voice, and that "the interruptions, if they could be called so, were no greater or no different than those that always occur.' It was announced, however, that Woodruff's tonsillitis would probably put an end to his speaking.[5]

❧ ❧ ❧

While Roosevelt apparently was trying to be seen and heard by every voter in the state, his opponent was continuing to operate on a relaxed schedule. On October 24, after spending a quiet Sunday in Buffalo, Van Wyck took the train to Rochester. That evening he addressed what the *Times* described as that city's "largest and most enthusiastic Democratic demonstration . . . in years." He charged that "beyond any sort of question" large amounts of money appropriated for canal improvement "have been squandered upon political favorites and political contractors," and added that "no one who troubles himself to look into the matter of canals will experience any difficulty in understanding why our opponents are so profoundly concerned with foreign problems and so markedly indifferent to the actual Government of the State of New York."

The next day, while Roosevelt was barnstorming from Elmira to Buffalo, Van Wyck remained in Rochester, conferring with local Democrats and preparing the speech he was to give in Syracuse the following evening. It was a cogent explanation of why "[n]o vote cast for me will have any other than a State significance." Although his careful explanation based on the division of power between "State and Federal affairs" sounded more like one of his judicial opinions than a campaign speech, the large crowd that had assembled in the Alhambra Rink, where he had been nominated less than a month before, responded enthusiastically.[6]

❧ ❧ ❧

While Van Wyck was on his upstate tour, back in New York City he again was being upstaged by Croker. On October 24, as described in the

Herald under a banner three-column headline "CROKER'S SAVAGE ATTACK ON ROOT AND DALY," from his Tammany Hall head-quarters he charged that Daly "is not an upright Judge and that he is a man who does not attend to his duty properly." He then accused the Bar Association, "composed of a lot of corporation and trust lawyers," of permitting itself to be used by the Republicans. He reserved his strongest attack for Elihu Root, who as a 26-year-old fledgling lawyer had been part of a distinguished legal team that unsuccessfully defended Boss Tweed after he had been indicted for forgery and grand larceny. After reciting the "facts" of Root's involvement in that 25-year-old proceeding, he explained that he was doing so

> " . . . only to remind you that this eminent reformer, who is now so solicitous about the purity of the Bench, and incidentally for the success of the Republican Party in the State, was not so scrupulous in 1873, at which time he served William M. Tweed to the extent of insulting the distinguished Justice who presided at the trial, and escaped punishment only on account of his inexperience." [*]

The next day, the Tammany boss continued his rampage, telling a reporter that in his previous attack he had failed to mention that "Judge Daly put thousands of dollars in the way of" Docks Commissioner Richard P. Henry "who got office with him from Tweed for stopping their fight against Tweed." [7]

❧ ❧ ❧

The fact that there may have been some truth in Croker's accusations did not improve his position. As *The Nation* commented in its October 27 issue, by his continuing utterances,

---

[*] The incident to which Croker referred involved the judge's displeasure over a motion filed by Tweed's group of counsel that he disqualify himself as the trier of fact because of "prejudice" against Tweed he had allegedly shown at a previous trial.

"[H]e is calling public attention to himself and to his system of government in a way which leaves no doubt in anybody's mind as to what he represents in politics. He is thus bringing it home to the minds of the people what bossism really is."

Even more important:

"Croker is by all odds the most active campaigner for Col. Roosevelt that there is in the field ... When he admits, as he did in his first deliverance upon the subject, that he would not allow Judge Daly to be renominated because he (Daly) had not given 'proper consideration' to Croker's demands since Tammany had a right to expect 'proper consideration' from a judge whom it had put upon the bench, he gives everybody to understand that what he expects of his nominees for the bench he expects also of his nominees for other positions, including the governorship."

As *The Nation* observed, Republican orators were taking full advantage of Croker's outbursts. On October 24, Henry Cabot Lodge spoke in support of Roosevelt at a Cooper Union rally. Although as a United States Senator from another state he not surprisingly stressed national issues, he pointed out that "the protection of the bench and the integrity of the judges of this great city are of interest and importance to me, as they are to every American." He stressed to his audience:

"You do not want to merely make a victim of the man selected by Croker to serve his purposes. You want to strike down the whole ticket."

When Roosevelt read a report of Lodge's speech, he telegraphed him on October 26 that "it was the best delivered in my entire campaign." It was soon forgotten, however, for at a rally that night Joseph Choate delivered to more than 1200 persons who had braved pouring rain what the *Tribune* called "a masterpiece of incisive logic and epigrammatic brilliance" in which some of his "sayings about the Tammany boss and his satellites will live as long as the men referred to continue in public life." He began by thanking Croker for attacking him, for "I regard it as the highest compliment for any respectful citizen of New York to be abused by him." Then, the *Herald* reported, the "enthusiastic Republicans who crowded the hall shouted with uproarious delight" as he compared Croker to a Biblical ass:

"He never speaks when things are going in the way to suit him. I ask you why this shrewd and calculating politician at his hour has found it necessary to open his lips."

"His conduct, his speech, why he spoke, recall to my mind the familiar story of Balaam's ass, and in two or three points Mr. Croker reminds me of that celebrated beast of burden."

"In the first place, till the ass spoke, nobody in the world imagined what a perfect ass he was. If he hadn't spoken, he would have passed into destiny as an ordinary, silent ass. But when he spoke he was distinguished from all the other assess in the land."

"Why did the ass speak? Do you remember the story?"

"Because he was frightened. Because, as the Bible says, he got into a tight place where he could neither turn to the right nor left. When he saw the one bearing the flaming sword confronting him, at last he spoke. You can tell me who the young man was who bore the sword." *

Choate concluded by praising Roosevelt, whom "I've known . . . man and boy for 25 years," and who, regarding the canal scandal, would "take greater pride in carrying a Republican scalp at his belt if a Republican had been wicked in this matter than that of one of his political enemies." It was not these words, however, but his ridicule of Croker as "Balaam's ass" that had the audience still chortling as it left the hall and brought laughter to the whole City when its residents read the next day's newspapers.[8]

---

* The story of Balaam and his ass appears in Numbers, Chapter 22. In the biblical text, Choate's "young man who bore the sword" is an angel with "his sword drawn in his hand." In Choate's story, the angel of course was Theodore Roosevelt.

❊ ❊ ❊

The intensifying campaign was not being waged only in public forums and the press. By late October it had spread to the streets as well. The October 26 *Times* front page, under the headline "BATTLE OF STERE-OPTICONS," described how a Tammany worker had sabotaged a "magic lantern" show that had been casting Republican slogans on a screen at the northeast corner of Broadway and West 37th Street by secretly setting up a competing machine. When the unsuspecting Republican operator withdrew his first slide and was about to insert the second, on the screen suddenly appeared, "Platt & Sons are doing business at the same old stand." The Republican "Roosevelt's round robin saved sick soldiers," was quickly followed by "Teddy's rough riding was done in Mulberry Street." [*] After a few more exchanges, "following with his eye the hostile rays," the Republican operator

"... got a good notion of the whereabouts of the Democratic stereopticon, and tried to stare it out of the countenance, so to speak, by turning his light upon it. After concentrating his fire on the belligerent instrument for a reasonably long time, the Roosevelt illuminator, satisfied with his reproof, turned back to his duties, and tried again, with –

"Roosevelt keeps all his promises – Croker keeps all he can get.'

"The Democratic retort that serenely followed was 'Platt has broken every promise he ever made.'"

At this point, the frustrated Republican operator suspended operations. By now, a good-sized crowd had gathered, so that when several of the Republicans "resorted to the use of small stones, such as they found on the roof," to hit the Democratic machine, "this resulted disastrously to some of the spectators in the street below, as the attacking

---

[*] The reference was to Roosevelt's tour as Police Commissioner.

Davids flung not wisely but too well." Eventually, the stone throwing was stopped by a policeman, but only "after the pattering upon his helmet had continued for a season."[9]

🌼 🌼 🌼

It is less than one hundred miles from Rochester to Syracuse, where the Roosevelt party was to spend Thursday night, but en route on that clear and bracing October 27 the train made eight stops, at each of which the candidate was greeted by enthusiastic crowds. As soon as the train had left Rochester, Depew led Roosevelt forward to a dining car that had been attached in Buffalo to satisfy the appetites of this hardworking group. After the candidate was persuaded to take a seat, Depew announced that he had "ascertained that this is the fortieth birthday of our candidate for Governor." Observing that each man "on this remarkable political trip has come closer to the Colonel than in an ordinary life of acquaintance would have been possible" and praising his "honesty, fairmindedness, ability and courage," to the applause and cheers of the entire party, Depew presented Roosevelt with a solid ebony gold-headed cane that several of the group had purchased in Rochester.

In Syracuse, Roosevelt made three speeches, one of them a nonpolitical talk at a fair that was raising money for veterans who had become ill in the recent war and for their widows and orphans. He delivered his major address in the same hall where Van Wyck had spoken the day before. The pro-Roosevelt *Sun*, with more than a grain of truth, observed that, as the Republican candidate had followed his Democratic opponent across Central New York, "the contrast between the way the two men are received becomes more and more noticeable." For the two days Van Wyck had spent at Syracuse's Yates House, "a great many of his fellow guests in the hotel did not know that he was under the same roof with them." On Roosevelt's arrival, however, "[t]he hotel lobby was jammed so that no business could be done over the counter for an hour."[10]

Friday's schedule involved a swing north to Oswego and Watertown, and then a late day return south to the Mohawk Valley cities of Rome and Utica. Although the Roosevelt Special was not scheduled to leave Syracuse until 11:30 a.m., for the balance of the day the Republican managers had scheduled fifteen speeches at eleven stops. The first was at the small town of Phoenix, where the crowd consisted largely of farmers whom the *Sun* reporter wrote "had not the look of men who would be easily stirred to applause or laughter," and to whom "[i]t was perfectly apparent that life was a very serious hard fight . . . and they took politics for a duty." After contending that his opponent's fiscal policy would increase their taxes, Roosevelt, referring to an existing surplus in the state treasury, suggested that "Tammany say it wants to get hold of the state to administer it honestly." Then, the *Sun* reported:

"Col. Roosevelt leaned over the brake handle and looked at one face after another quizzically. The first man he looked at laughed and the next and the one afterwards and so on. The Colonel and everyone in the crowd was laughing. The Colonel held up his hand for silence.

"'Why should you think,' he said, 'that Tammany would break its record?'

"The farmers didn't wait for him to look at them this time; they slapped one another on the back and laughed until one man said so loud that the people on the back platform could hear him; 'Jiminy, but he's a good one.'"

More than 3500 people showed up at Fulton, where the station was some distance out of town and an audience of only a few hundred had been expected. As Roosevelt was praising the efforts of Civil War and Spanish-American War veterans, a railroad worker at the back of the crowd interrupted him: "What about us being represented on the Railroad Commission?" Roosevelt's response was prompt: "On every commission in the State that has to do with the interest of labor there

The Betting is Now Even
(*New York Herald*)

Amusing Himself
(*New York World*)

should be a labor representative, and, if elected, I shall see that there is one." As the crowd applauded loudly, the questioner shouted back, "Then I'll vote for you."

As Billy O'Neil had observed several days earlier, one need not listen to Roosevelt to be won over by him. At Oswego, a *Sun* reporter "who had gone down into the town . . . to do some shopping during the thirty-five minutes that the trains stopped there met on his return a group of six or seven men in working clothes coming away from the meeting.

"'Is the meeting over,' he asked them."

"'No,' said one of them."

"'Why did you come away?'"

"'We only got ten minutes off,' said the one who had spoken before, 'to go up and see what he looked like. We wanted to see if he looked as square as he talked.'"

"'And he did?' asked the reporter."

"'You bet he did," said two or three of them at once, 'He's all right,' and they went on."

After another busy day, the Roosevelt party arrived at Utica at 7:00 p.m., and after a quick dinner, went to two more meetings. At both Roosevelt discussed tax issues, emphasizing how the Republicans had been "making all pay in equal proportion, when before thousands were permitted to escape taxation altogether."[11]

❋ ❋ ❋

In presenting Roosevelt with his birthday cane the day before, Depew had spoken of the "camaraderie" that had grown among the men on the campaign train. Buoyed by their candidate's high spirits, at least one of them was willing to have a little fun at another's expense if the occasion arose. At stops where Roosevelt was making more than one speech, his associates, including Depew, Billy Youngs and John Procter Clarke, also would address the crowds in both places. Clarke was especially proud of his remarks, which became known as the "Only a

Soldier" speech, and he persuaded the press not to publish it so that he could deliver it on almost every occasion. Youngs had heard it so many times that, as he later told Clarke, he had committed it to memory. Accordingly, he recalled, at one town late on the current tour he delivered Clarke's speech at one hall while Clarke was addressing the crowd at another. Thus, when they exchanged places, and Clarke made his speech at the meeting where Youngs had just given it, he was surprised that it drew no audience response. That night, he said to Youngs, "Billy, I cannot understand it. I have roused the whole State with that speech of mine and I did not get a handclap." Youngs' response was noncommittal.[12]

❋ ❋ ❋

At 9:30 Saturday morning, the train was off again, going 80 miles east along the Mohawk Valley to Schenectady. En route, the party made five stops. Roosevelt's voice was becoming hoarse, but he had no trouble making his scheduled talks. At Palatine Bridge, when he heard that the train's engineer wanted to shake his hand but could not leave his post, the Colonel, according to the *Times*,

"... said in his emphatic way, 'Well, I'll go and see him if he can't come to me.' He walked forward to the engine, and, after shaking hands, said, 'I'd like to ride to the next station with you,' and up he climbed and sat in the cab until Fonda was reached, expressing great interest in all the mechanical arrangements."

At Schenectady, the crowd included thousands of men from the Edison electrical plant and the city's locomotive works, who had been given the day off by their pro-Roosevelt employers. Union College President Raymond presided at one of the meetings, and shedding any academic reserve he may otherwise have possessed, announced that every patriotic or honest man in the state should vote for Roosevelt.

By 3:30, the party was back on board the Roosevelt Special and en route non-stop to New York. The journey provided the only rest that the candidate was to have all day. As soon as the train pulled into Grand Central Station four hours later, he was hustled into a cab, which sped to the Battery. From there a tug and chartered trolley car took him to Staten Island's Prohibition Park. He was more than an hour late, but this did not dull the enthusiasm of the large crowd that awaited him and listened quietly as with a rapidly failing voice he spoke for 12 minutes. Then, it was back to Manhattan via the same trolley and tug that had taken him to Staten Island, and by cab to Cooper Union, where a rally sponsored by the Irish-American Union had been listening to diverse speakers and band music for more than two hours. The *Times* reporter called Roosevelt's reception "one of the most deafening demonstrations vouchsafed a candidate in this city," and wrote that some of the audience "flung things in the air for five minutes, one old woman waving American bunting before the candidate's eyes." In his brief speech, he emphasized: "If there has been any one thing for which I have stood, in deed as well as in word, it is that all Americans should be treated as Americans, without regard to creed, birth or nationality." Then, in what must have been a relief even to a man of his energy, it was off to bed at his sister's Madison Avenue home, and on to Sagamore Hill the next morning.[13]

❊ ❊ ❊

Compared to Roosevelt's strenuous efforts, Van Wyck seemed to be trying to make a virtue of lassitude. With no more speeches scheduled following Wednesday's Syracuse address, he returned to New York and immediately conferred with Croker, Senator Murphy and others. According to the October 29 *Herald*, they "decided that when he starts on his next tour he will go through the State at a more lively rate than that which characterized the three speech tour he had just finished." Lest anyone think, however, that there would be a major change in strategy, the Judge would not make his next speech until he visited Utica on Monday, only eight days before Election Day.

Unlike Roosevelt, who was taking every opportunity to make himself available to the increasingly appreciative group of newsmen who were riding on his campaign trains, the interview that Van Wyck gave the press on his return from Syracuse was the first since his nomination. In it, he praised the "enthusiastic audiences" on his upstate tour, which showed "every evidence that the Democrats are a unit in their desire to rebuke the corrupt party that is now maladministering the affairs of the State."[14]

❦ ❦ ❦

Van Wyck may have been relatively inactive, but his supporters definitely were not. As one example, at 8:30 p.m. on October 28, local residents and passers-by along Eighth Avenue were treated to what the next morning's *Times* called "a curious spectacle." Along the still uncovered road bed of the Eighth Avenue subway, the local Tammany organization had engineered an "underground trolley political parade," in which "a long line of trolley cars, bunched as near one another as safety allowed, swirled by, to the accompaniment of wild yells, the sputtering of fireworks, and the baleful gleam of red fire." The train's cars bore cloth strips covered with slogans such as "Republican Rascality Has Increased Your Taxation." The music of a band in the first car added to the noise that announced the train's arrival.

Less innocent were reports from Republican storekeepers on the Lower East Side that they had been subjected to abuse by the police when they refused to remove pictures of Republican candidates from their windows. A leader of a Republican club with its headquarters at Grand and Forsyth Streets claimed that he had been threatened by the local Tammany boss to "gouge your eye out" if he continued to help other club members in filing complaints at police headquarters. Another man, a wholesale candy dealer, told the *Times* that he had been "dragged . . . to the station house without giving me time to put on my coat and hat."

Tammany also was trying to assure its candidate's success in more direct ways. A *Tribune* reporter who was crossing City Hall Park one night recalled that usually "the benches which line the walks of the park are, long before midnight, filled with vagrants, who, in default of a sleeping place, sit and doze all night on the hard boards of the seats, . . . as much a part of the park as the grass or the fountain." But, during this last week of October,

> "He who at present passes the park at night will find not a single soul to yawn and blink at him from the benches. The *Tribune* reporter who noticed this sought explanation from one of the park policemen.

> "'Why, that's easy,' he replied. 'What's the use of their sleeping here when they can get free beds in the lodging houses uptown? Why, Tammany has raked in every 'bum' in the city and given them free lodging for two weeks or more. You know what that's for. They'll all be good citizens and good voters on Election Day, with homes and families and everything else. Yes, they're all gone, even the charter members,' he soliloquized mournfully. 'But they'll be back by regiments on the 9th of November, – don't worry about that. And I'll tell you one thing right here,' he added, confidentially. 'That's the way to get votes in this city, and don't you forget it.'"[15]

❊ ❊ ❊

With only a week and a half to go before Election Day, spokesmen for both sides were making confident predictions. On October 28, although State Chairman Odell was forecasting only a "safe plurality," his associates were openly talking of a 35,000 vote Roosevelt victory. For their part, Croker and his aides were predicting a 50,000 to 75,000 vote plurality, but, according to the *Evening Post*, the Democrats always made "the bolder guesses."

As the *Post* also noted, these predictions were only "bald, general statements," and that the only difference between these guesses "and those of other people is that they are colored to suit party purposes." Gambling odds perhaps were more reliable, but even there some bets were offered purely for propaganda purposes, with nothing but bluff behind them. Thus, on October 27, according to the *Herald*, a gentleman named Carter "flourishing in his hand what looked like a large roll of greenbacks" appeared at the Fifth Avenue Hotel and announced: "I've got a thousand dollars here that I want to bet even on Van Wyck." Initially, he found no takers, but Odell suddenly appeared on his way back from dinner, announced that he would bet and said, "reaching for his pocketbook, 'Put up your money.'" When Carter replied, "weakly" and "edging away," that he would "have it here at ten o'clock tomorrow morning," Odell asked him what he had in his hand. As the *Herald* reported:

> "Investigation showed that it was a roll of paper, with a twenty dollar bill, a two, and a one wrapped around it. Mr. Carter beat a hasty retreat."

Serious bets that were actually made at week's end were mostly at even odds, and confirmed the general impression that the race was extremely tight. So also did a poll that the *Herald* had conducted and published in its Sunday, October 30, edition. Consisting of a county-by-county assessment from "republican, democratic and independent sources," it showed Van Wyck with a narrow statewide lead of 7,100 votes. His projected New York City majority of 81,000 (including 65,000 from Manhattan) was enough to edge out the small Roosevelt pluralities that were predicted in all but six of the State's other counties. The *Herald*'s commentary described the results as confirming "a great struggle between the cities and the rural locations." It also noted:

> "Republican apathy, which threatened Roosevelt with an overwhelming defeat two weeks ago, has very largely disappeared. Although political prophets shook their heads ominously when he

went on his tour through the State, it is conceded on all sides that only by making this tour did he instill any life in the republican campaign."

The poll's results came as a rude shock to the Republican leaders, especially those in the rural counties, who had been expecting that they would turn out much larger pluralities for Roosevelt than the *Herald* was predicting. Clearly, the race would go right down to the wire, and the efforts of both parties in its final week would be decisive.[16]

16

"My Real Opponent Is Not Mr. Van Wyck, But Is Mr. Croker"

Roosevelt spent Sunday, October 30, at Sagamore Hill, resting his voice. After two weeks away from his children, he devoted the entire day to family activities, and had no political visitors. He did, however, spend a few minutes with a *Herald* reporter who had "left his card" in the hope that the Colonel would come out to the porch and see him. Roosevelt used their short talk to disprove a rumor that had started to spread in New York City to the effect that he was coming down with yellow fever.

The Oyster Bay rest was brief, for the next morning Roosevelt returned to New York and conferred at the Fifth Avenue Hotel headquarters with party leaders and other visitors. Among them was Quigg, whose campaign for reelection to the House had run into trouble. Many reformers who had supported Seth Low for Mayor the preceding fall were still angry at Platt for not backing him. As the Easy Boss's henchman, Quigg was an easy target for their wrath, and Democrat William Astor Chanler's blue-blood credentials made him an easy alternative to support. Quigg was so worried that he had turned over his duties in the state campaign so that he could devote his full time to his reelection bid.[1]

Roosevelt had very little time to worry about Quigg's difficulties.

Surprisingly, the Republicans were facing money problems. At the campaign's outset, it had been assumed that they could replicate their successful efforts of 1896, when, under Mark Hanna's leadership, banks and other businesses were systematically assessed to provide funds to assure McKinley's election. But, as the *Herald's* October 26 issue reported under the headline "REPUBLICANS ARE SHORT OF CASH:"

"Wall Street, which supplied so much money in 1896 to elect McKinley, has not proved responsive to appeals this year. The financiers can not be convinced that they are in any immediate danger of free silver while the present administration lasts, and, feeling that they have paid for immunity once, they are reluctant to do so again."

Meanwhile, the Democrats seemed to be awash in funds. U.S. Senator Murphy's efforts to secure a legislative majority to assure his reelection had led to highly successful visits by his agents throughout the state to pry funds from his supporters. Republican efforts to enforce the excise tax laws were causing brewers and others in the liquor business to open their purses for the Democrats, and such traditional Wall Street Democratic loyalists as the Belmonts and Whitneys were providing their expected support.

Tammany's assessors had also moved into high gear. Office holders were regularly charged a "tax rate" of 1 percent on a $1000 salary, and, on a $1500 salary, 1 ½ percent. Each of the three Supreme Court candidates, who would expect to earn an annual salary of $17,500 (or a total of $245,000 for a full 14 year term) was expected to contribute $25,000 to Tammany for the privilege of serving on the bench. Legislative candidates were charged lesser amounts.

No doubt in the hope that, if elected, Roosevelt would keep Superintendent Payn in office, the Mutual, Equitable and New York Life insurance companies had already made generous gifts to his campaign. So also had New York City's Metropolitan Street Railway and several state railroads. With Election Day rapidly approaching, however, these and other funds would not be enough. As Platt later recalled, Roosevelt had learned on his upstate tour that Van Wyck's campaign manager, State Senator Patrick McCarran, Croker and others "had just made a raid on Wall Street and acquired what was reported to be the biggest bundle of cash" that had been raised in several years. Accordingly, as soon as he arrived at Republican headquarters this Monday morning, Roosevelt "burst in" on Odell and shouted "in tones of mixed indignation and fright, 'Croker and McCarran are trying to buy the State!' and asked the State Chairman what they 'were going to do about it.'" Odell's response was that "[w]e shall have to raise some more money ourselves, or we are licked." When Roosevelt admitted that he had no idea where it could be found, Odell suggested, "Well, let's go see the old man. Perhaps he does." They immediately walked around to Platt's nearby apartment and apprised him of the situation. Then, according to the Easy Boss's autobiography, the following exchange ensued:

"'How much money do you need, Ben?' asked Senator Platt of Odell."

"'We require $60,000 at once, or we are whipped,' was the response."

"'You shall have the $60,000,' quietly observed the 'old man.'

'Why, where are you going to get it?' queried Roosevelt in amazement."

"Platt took pencil and paper and put down six names, headed by J. Pierpont Morgan."

"'Each of these gentlemen will give $10,000. That will make up the $60,000,' remarked Platt as he read off the names."

"'But I cannot accept contributions from the men you mention. Really, I must decline,' protested Roosevelt."

"'Who is running this campaign?' demanded Platt impatiently."

"'Why, you and Odell are,' was the answer."

"'Then, I'll go downtown, and get the $60,000,' said Senator Platt, as he called a cab and hurried to the money center."

"He brought back the money." [2][*]

❧ ❧ ❧

That evening, Roosevelt's speaking tour took him from Manhattan's lower East Side to Brooklyn, and then to Harlem and back to Manhattan. According to the next morning's *Sun*, "In all his campaigning trips through the State, Col. Roosevelt never had to undergo a more trying ordeal." After driving a *Sun* reporter trying to keep up with the candidate's breakneck speed through Brooklyn for an agreed upon dollar an hour for three hours, an exhausted cabman, standing in front of his sweating horse, announced: "The next time a man says 'Col. Roosevelt for three hours' to me he puts down seven dollars before we start, and no drawback in case of a breakdown." The *Times* called the "furious ride" through the "the boulder-paved highways of Brooklyn" by Roosevelt and the several cabs of reporters "a nerve racking experience to every one except the candidate. He unblushingly said he liked it."

Equally unique, according to the *Times*, were "the private entrances to Brooklyn halls" with their "devious ways and labyrinthian passages to each of the various stages. . . ." At Knickerbocker Hall, "the Roosevelt party, unable to get into the hall in the orthodox way, was conducted by mysterious guides through a stable yard reached by a long lane, up a winding outside iron stairway leading to a fire-escape in the rear of the stage, finally to crawl through a window before it could

---

[*] In an obviously self-serving statement, Platt wrote in his autobiography that Croker and McCarran asserted that if he had not obtained these funds, "Van Wyck would have defeated Roosevelt handily," that "[t]hat would, of course, have made Roosevelt an impossibility for Vice President and President," and "Is it any wonder that 'Old Guardsmen' to this day maintain 'Platt saved Roosevelt.'?"

reach its destination." Roosevelt said that the climb reminded him of San Juan Hill. In his short speeches at each of his six Brooklyn meetings, he stressed "sound money and honest government and a good judiciary." Everywhere he was greeted by enthusiastic audiences, except for a disappointed looking small girl sitting in the front row of the Palm Garden on Hamburg Avenue. When her father asked what was the matter, with a lisp she replied: "Why, why, I thought he was a great big man an' had a sword and a pistol. He ain't big a'-tall."

From Brooklyn, Roosevelt sped by tugboat up the East River to a pier at the east end of Manhattan's 125th Street, and then on to the casino in Sulzer's Harlem River Park, where an audience of 3000 was jammed into a casino built to hold only half that number. His last stop was at the Lenox Lyceum, at Madison Avenue and 59th Street. The meeting had been billed in advance as a unity rally, with Governor Black scheduled to give his first speech of the campaign. It was a disappointing performance, and the audience responded with only polite applause as he defended his administration's policy on the canals and referred only once to Roosevelt, who had not yet arrived. When at 11:05 he finally did so, the two men shook hands and smiled at each other without any great show of cordiality. Despite the late hour, the combination of Roosevelt's presence and his speech aroused the crowd, and when the rally adjourned shortly before midnight, he was almost carried on to his carriage through a throng yelling "Our next Governor! Our next Governor!"[3]

❀ ❀ ❀

No less enthusiastic was the crowd of 3000 that heard Van Wyck that evening in a Utica opera house filled far beyond its announced capacity. Not surprisingly in this Erie Canal city, he argued that it was time to "turn the rascals out to the end that new accountants may examine the books and correct the evils, that the ill gotten gains may be recovered for the state treasury, and punishment meted out to the offenders" so that "an honest and efficient administration of the business affairs of the State may soon be restored." Van Wyck shared the platform with former Senator Hill, who drew even greater applause as he followed the candidate to the rostrum and strongly supported his election. Hill, who had not met Van Wyck before, later praised the Judge's speaking style, which was quite different from his own:

> "I discovered that at first the audience paid silent attention, then became deeply interested, and at the conclusion broke out into applause. Judge Van Wyck had delivered a scholarly, conservative and dignified address . . . You may claim that a political audience pays no attention to the quality of an address, but I tell you that they do."

The canal issue was influencing many voters who otherwise might have leaned to Roosevelt. The November 1 *Times* summed up the Democratic case when it wrote that "every consideration, personal and political, will urge on Gov. Van Wyck to be swift and stern in dealing with the Republican Canal thieves." Roosevelt, on the other hand,

> "[is] making his campaign in strange companionship – Platt, Aldridge, Woodruff. If he can be on such good terms with the Republican maladministration in the campaign, what reason have we to expect him after election to turn upon his present associates with sudden asperity . . . If any voter wants the canal frauds punished he will veto his intent if he votes for Roosevelt."[4]

❧ ❧ ❧

With many voters reaching the same conclusion and with Tammany putting forth a maximum effort, it was not surprising that the betting odds on October 31 were five to four in Van Wyck's favor. Despite all his efforts, Roosevelt needed one last piece of luck to turn the tide. Fortunately, Richard Croker again stepped forward to provide it.

The current episode had its roots in an article titled "Wide-Open

New York," that appeared in the October 22 issue of *Harper's Weekly* [*]. It opened by asserting that "Richard Croker and his assistants have set in full operation a system of Tammany government under which vice flourishes openly for a price." Among many examples that it then gave to support its author's claim was this picture of "the Tenderloin station house in West Thirtieth Street about eleven o'clock some evening:"

"From ten to twenty creatures of the street are brought in, and, within an hour or two, are released under bail furnished by a professional bondsman, a Tammany Hall leader, William R. Nelson, proprietor of the famous 'black and tan' saloon on Seventh Avenue. The next day these creatures are fined in the police court. According to newspaper accounts, Nelson gets at least $5 for every bond that he signs. No other man is permitted to have the actual privilege he enjoys. The street sinner probably pays another $5 for her fine, and to make up for what has been taken from her under due process of law and with the co-operation of the police for Nelson's profit, she must prowl the streets again, only to fall into the clutches of Nelson's pull again. . . . In other words, a distinct part of the earnings of the creatures of the Tenderloin are diverted every night – a sum amounting from $50 to $100 – to the coffers of "Bob" Nelson, Tammany leader."

On October 26, more fuel to the fire was added in a Lower East Side speech delivered by Frank Moss, who had succeeded Roosevelt as President of the Police Board in Mayor Strong's reform administration. At a Republican rally at which the former Mayor presided, Moss charged, according to the *Herald's* account, that "vice under Tammany protection flaunts itself even more brazenly" than in the days when public outrage had led to Strong's election. He described what he saw on a trip along nearby Allen Street the previous evening:

---

[*] A publication that advertised itself as a "Journal of Civilization."

"Women lolled out of windows and sat in the doorways and nodded and winked and invited passersby to enter their vile dens. This was all done very openly in the presence of the police, who had their orders not to interfere. Your little girls, swarming in the tenement houses and in the crowded streets, look on these sights with wonder and are in danger of being corrupted. In one instance I actually had a card of one of these vile places thrust into my hand by a little girl who could not have been more than twelve years old. Vagabonds hang about in gangs, contriving mischief and making life unsafe and miserable for decent people."

All this was too much for Croker to take lying down. On October 29, he fiercely turned on his attackers. He first claimed that one of the members of the Harper firm not only had "attended a dinner he described as " – one of the most infamous exhibitions ever given in this country," but also "took a prominent part in that affair, and from the statements made by some of the guests he provided some entertainment for the diners," along with the 'notorious' dancer 'Little Egypt.'" He then charged that, as Police Board President, Roosevelt "tried to stifle the investigation of this notorious affair and protect his high-toned friends." "No longer," he boasted, "is . . . the disgusting work done by police spies under Colonel Roosevelt . . . permitted to disgrace the city and shock the world."

Croker was doing his best to fit Choate's description of him as an ass that could not stop braying. Three days later on November 1, apparently stung by Moss's speech, he made an all-out attack on Roosevelt:

" . . . when the Roosevelt Police Board was hunting women with the aid of policemen in hired dress suits, when children of tender age were being used to induce saloon keepers to violate the law by selling cans of beer, murder after murder was being committed, and in the hurly-burly of Roosevelt's fanatical policy nearly every murderer escaped."

By now, Croker was caught up in his own rhetoric, as he continued:

"Flats were robbed while the demoralized police force in the disguise of men about town were trying to entrap women to commit crimes. Safes were blown open while an almost useless Police Department was watching side doors. . . . Thieves went through scuttles undisturbed, while Mr. Roosevelt himself in his sensational night trips through the city was trying to sneak upon a policeman who stopped walking for a minute."[5]

❧ ❧ ❧

As yet unaware of Croker's most recent outburst, Roosevelt was preparing for the appearances that had been scheduled for him that evening. Although to the *Herald* reporter who saw him at the end of his prior day's speeches "his voice was in excellent condition," the *Evening Post* described it as "weak and hoarse" and said that "he must rest it or lose it altogether." Fortunately, he had no engagements that afternoon and what for him was a light schedule of only four appearances that night.

Again, much of the evening was spent going from one location to another, as Roosevelt spoke first in Upper Manhattan at 170th Street and Amsterdam Avenue, then across town by carriage to 170th Street and Third Avenue in the Bronx, from there to Cooper Union at Astor Place and 7th Street with the help of a train provided by Depew, and finally by the same train north to Yonkers. At all four meetings, Roosevelt was wildly cheered by large crowds, but at Cooper Union the audience came as an especially pleasant surprise. The gathering had been organized as a German-American rally, and an anticipated defection of large numbers of German voters who were still unhappy over Police Commissioner Roosevelt's Sunday beer garden closings had led some Republican leaders initially to oppose holding it. They could not have been more mistaken, for, according to the *Herald's* account, "[s]uch a wild burst of enthusiasm has not before greeted Colonel Roosevelt in this campaign." Clearly, the German vote was not to be written off.

While the German-Americans were cheering Roosevelt, Van Wyck was receiving help from two widely diverse sources. A group of almost all New York City's theater managers announced that on Sunday evening they would put on a "first night" show for the Democratic candidate, complete with a 75 man orchestra. Although the managers claimed to be acting entirely on their own without any prior "hints" from Tammany, the State Democratic headquarters quickly announced that it would reserve a number of boxes for its "delegation," including one for Richard Croker.

From the other end of the political spectrum came an attack on Roosevelt from Dr. Parkhurst. In a letter to the *Evening Post*, that crusading clergyman castigated the Republican organization for making possible Tammany's mayorality victory the prior year by running its own candidate instead of backing Seth Low. Perhaps especially frustrated because his sermons had had no effect on Platt when he sat in his pew every Sunday morning, Parkhurst charged that the Easy Boss "would rather see New York converted into Sodom than to have even as magnificent a man as Low made Mayor independent of the machine and of the boss who works the machine." Because "punishment is good for the soul," he took "a kind of grim satisfaction" from the fact that the city "will have to stew in its own juice, and three years remain at least in which this uncomfortable process of broiling will have to be continued." In sorrow, he then attacked Roosevelt, who "turned his back on the superb opportunity" of running independently and instead 'went to see the old man,' and in that way and to that degree made public confession of Platt's righteous authority . . ." Without saying how he would vote, he concluded his letter by saying that any ballot that he might cast for Roosevelt "means admiration for the man at the same time it means abhorrence of the candidate."[6]

❦ ❦ ❦

With pre-election political news filling the day's press, November 1 saw the actual start of the vote. Under a special election law, soldiers and sailors were permitted to cast their ballots in advance. Each regiment would vote on a date chosen by it up to and including Election Day. Although the Astor Battery in Manila was too far away for ballots to reach it in time, troops from as far distant as Honolulu would be able to vote on ballots that were on their way from San Francisco by steamer. If the election were extremely close, these absentee ballots could determine its outcome. The victor's identity therefore might not be known until they had been received in Albany, well after Election Day.

Both sides were hoping that the soldiers' vote would lean their way. At Pennsylvania's Camp Meade, however, only the Republicans had put up posters and made other efforts, and, according to the *Herald*, "Democratic candidates lost many votes." One straw in the wind may have encouraged the Republicans. While the 22nd Regiment was voting at its New Rochelle camp, its officers took an informal count of how the canvas was going. On November 1, as soon as the balloting was completed, several of them visited Republican headquarters at the Fifth Avenue Hotel with the good news that they had counted 302 votes for Roosevelt and 290 for Van Wyck. Perhaps the veterans were not as annoyed with Roosevelt as his advisers had feared. Nevertheless, at day's end, the betting odds remained five to four in Van Wyck's favor. [7]

❦ ❦ ❦

Looking back on a number of elections, a single defining event sometimes emerges in which a candidate has turned the tide of battle or otherwise assured his victory. Examples include Harry Truman's 1948 announcement that he would call the "do nothing" Republican Eightieth Congress into special session on "Turnip Day," and Dwight Eisenhower's 1952 pledge that if elected President, "I will go to Korea." Theodore Roosevelt's November 2 Long Island campaign swing fell into that category.

A Tenderloin Broil
(*New York Herald*)

The Two Orphans
(New York Herald)

Until then, the Republican candidate's attacks on Richard Croker had been those of any good government candidate supporting judicial independence and battling corruption. No longer was this the case. Now that Croker had accused Roosevelt of softness on crime during his term as Police Commissioner, the issue had become personal. Such charges would have had a powerful effect on any candidate, but to a proud man like Roosevelt, who considered his personal integrity to be above reproach, the effect was, as Billy Youngs later recalled, "almost magical."

"It was as if a general, holding in control the army under his command, had made a sudden dash and onslaught against a weak point, turned the center and caused a retreat."

A first-term Republican Congressman from Buffalo, writing twenty-five years later, described how Roosevelt

"... for the first time, perhaps, came into full consciousness of his peculiar power. Speaking straight to the people, often with the downward stroke of a clenched fist, with teeth disclosed, and with a squinting eye that seemed to vision the cloud of a great misfortune hanging over the State, he told them things already familiar, but in words and tones that vibrated in the very center of their being."[8]

The reporters who were covering Roosevelt that early November day also sensed an even greater intensity in his efforts. The account in the next morning's *Tribune* began: "If the people who still believe Van Wyck will be elected had swung around Long Island with Colonel Theodore Roosevelt yesterday, they would have had a different opinion." In each of his 22 talks at the 300 mile trip's eighteen stops, the major subject was Croker. As the *Sun* described the day, Roosevelt treated him as "a personal issue, a city issue and a State issue." His audiences

"... chuckled when Col. Roosevelt indicated what was to be

the tenor of his remarks about Mr. Croker, and then, before the candidate was through with him, they were cheering, first with cheers of commendation and sympathy, and then with shouts of righteous anger and yells of derision for the object of his merciless scorn."

Roosevelt had not been aware of Croker's personal attack on him until he read the morning newspapers. Thus, his response was spontaneous, but no less effective, when at the day's 8:30 first stop at Valley Stream he shouted, "My real opponent is not Mr. Van Wyck, but is Mr. Croker, who has put the soiled hand of a dictator on the white ermine of the Judge." He closed his Bayshore speech with, "Burly Mr. Croker has brushed nice Mr. Van Wyck out of the way." At Freeport, the *Herald* reporter wrote, "with all his force, leaning over the platform railing, he said:

'Mr. Croker, I am glad to say, has put himself forward as the chief issue of the campaign. The shadowy figure of Mr. Van Wyck has faded, and through it we see the burly figure of Mr. Croker. Every debaucher of virtue, every purveyor of vice, all of that class who were put out of business by me are back in business again, and will willingly pay blackmail to continue their nefarious trade. If Mr. Croker wants to make himself an issue, he may. I'll welcome him gladly."

Despite his anger at Croker, Roosevelt was enjoying himself. He also continued to demonstrate an uncanny ability to reach out to young and old. Jacob Riis recalled that when a group of public school children turned out at one stop to see "Teddy" and try to shake his hand, he noticed "a pale, freckled little girl, in a worn garment" whom the "stronger children" had pushed back as she "was struggling eagerly but hopelessly to get near him." At once,

" . . . [g]oing down the steps even as the train started, he made a quick dash, clearing a path through the surging tide to the little girl and taking her hand, gave it the heartiest shake of all, then sprinted for the departing car and caught it."[9]

❀ ❀ ❀

The day's events were fully reported in newspapers throughout the state, and from the popular reaction that was reported to Odell and his associates, "it was felt," Youngs wrote six years later, "that the battle was won." This was by no means the general opinion at the time, however, when most observers believed that the race was neck and neck. Thus, in Cooper Union, where German-Americans had cheered Roosevelt the evening before, a pro-Van Wyck audience of Germans hissed when the Republican candidate's name was mentioned.

The major Democratic event that November 2 evening was at Carnegie Hall, where a large crowd had assembled under the auspices of the Businessmen's Democratic Association. Former Senator Hill was the principal speaker, and the audience responded with enthusiasm as he ridiculed "the exaggerated exploits of the Rough Riders under Colonel Wood." As for the charges that New York was a "wide open city," he asked:

> "What do these people want? Would they prefer to have this city 'shut up' and 'closed' like a deserted village, or a Chinese town with a wall around it, or like Senator's Black's National Bank in Oswego."

Croker did not arrive at the Carnegie Hall meeting until Hill was well into his speech, and his longtime foe looked distinctly unhappy as the Tammany boss took his seat to wild cheers. Van Wyck was noticeably absent. Although it had been announced that he would speak at the meeting, following his return from Utica the previous evening he remained all day at his Brooklyn residence. His excuse was that he was too busy preparing the speeches he would deliver during an upstate tour he would commence the next morning. It seems more likely, however, that he believed an appearance on the same platform with

Croker would damage his position as an independent candidate who, if elected, would refuse to do Tammany's bidding.[10]

Elsewhere on this last Wednesday before the election, Platt found it necessary to issue a statement denying rumors being spread, he said, by "our . . . demoralized Democratic opponents" that "I am lukewarm to the candidates of the Republican State ticket, headed by Col. Theodore Roosevelt." The campaign was also being fought in the streets, as a group of about 200 Republicans, known as the Bidwell Rough Riders, was stoned from roofs and windows as it tried to parade east on Manhattan's West 62nd Street from West End Avenue to Amsterdam Avenue.[11]

❈ ❈ ❈

The next day, November 3, Roosevelt spent the morning at his sister's Madison Avenue home before leaving at 1 o'clock for speeches in Troy and Albany. His friends had told him that it was imperative that he rest his failing voice, and not stop by the Fifth Avenue Hotel headquarters, where he would be accosted by politicians and reporters. In his absence, State Chairman Odell spent much of the day promising victory but refusing to provide any prediction of its margin. By evening he finally relented, and told the press: "I claim the State of New York for Colonel Roosevelt by at least 40,000." When reporters raced this news a block up Broadway to Democratic State Headquarters at the Hoffman House, State Chairman Frank Campbell called Odell's statement "a dream." "New York State," he announced, "is going to give 50,000 to Van Wyck."[12]

On his arrival in Troy, Roosevelt's greeting was far different from his tepid reception four weeks before. More than a thousand people greeted him at the railroad station, and flags decorated the buildings along his route. An hour before the candidate reached the opera house where he was to speak, it was filled by an audience of 3000, with more than double that number being turned away. Governor Black introduced Roosevelt to his neighbors, and his cordiality was intended to make up for the lukewarm attitude that he had displayed in New York earlier in the week. In Albany, although Roosevelt's train from Troy did not arrive until after 9:30 p.m., crowds lined the streets from the station to the hall, which was crammed by nearly 5000 partisans. Others held an overflow meeting outside. On his entrance the crush was so great that he was literally dragged to the platform. At both Troy and Albany, he continued to press his case that Croker rather than Van Wyck was his real opponent. By the time he had spoken briefly to the overflow meeting, it was after midnight, and his train back to New York did not leave until 1:50 a.m.[13]

❦ ❦ ❦

Van Wyck had followed Roosevelt upstate, addressing a mass meeting of 2000 at Poughkeepsie's opera house. He was welcomed at the railroad station by a band and an enthusiastic crowd of adherents. He spent most of his speech on the canal issue, deriding his "opponent's traveling band of speakers, driving through the State on a special train, reeling off hundreds of speeches,

> " . . . accompanied and ministered to by Mr. Chauncey Depew, the President of the New York Central and Hudson Valley Railroad Company, the interest of which is greater than that of any other natural or artificial person in the decline of our canal waterways."

The most excitement on the Democratic side was generated not in Poughkeepsie, but in New York. This Thursday evening was the occasion of a big campaign-end Tammany rally, and its Wigwam on the north side of 14th Street between Third Avenue and Irving Place was packed to overflowing. Several minutes after the meeting had begun, the oratory inside the hall was brought to a halt as, with brass bands blaring, a ø15,000 man parade headed by the members of the Timothy D. Sullivan Association and led by State Senator Sullivan, squeezed its way through the crowds on 14th Street. Croker and other notables were summoned from within the building to reviewing stands that had been set up outside, where they received a series of ovations by the marchers.

Croker also found time to respond to Roosevelt's speeches written from Long Island. As reported under a headline penned by the editors of the pro-Roosevelt *Sun*, "CROKER WON'T KEEP STILL," he issued a statement in which he charged that the Republican candidate "must be ashamed" of his record as Police Commissioner,

> "or he would not get so angry and go galloping up and down the State, telling falsehoods about the Democratic Party, the Democratic issues and myself. Col. Roosevelt dodged his taxes in 1897. He is dodging State issues and now in his Wild West style he is prancing around dodging his record as Police Commissioner. Every time he says a word on any question he shows his true character. He is erratic, untruthful and untrustworthy."

This same day, the 71st Regiment held what the *Times* called "a most remarkable election" at the armory at Park Avenue and 34th Street. To the *Times* correspondent,

> " . . . it was easy to observe that the old palmy days of voting had returned and that there was no such thing as a secret ballot law ever enacted by the Legislature of the State of New York. As an election under the safeguards that are nowadays cast around the ballot it was a failure; as a huge and continuous case of skylarking it was an immense success."

The *Times* reported that although "the men have not been paid . . . and a few days ago were stating that they were 'broke,' many of them were supplied with money yesterday, and frequent pilgrimages were made to the corner saloon, where the man who set up the drinks usually had a Democratic argument to give to his guests." Since the soldiers were helping each other fill out their ballots, it was public knowledge how each of them had voted. Not surprisingly, when the votes were counted, Van Wyck had won by a two-to-one margin.[14]

❀ ❀ ❀

All the excitement of the Roosevelt-Van Wyck race did not keep the press from covering a "mass meeting" that had been called to support the Independent ticket. Confirming the "lost cause" nature of the efforts of the Citizens Union and its adherents, Chickering Hall on Fifth Avenue at 18th Street was only half filled by an audience that John Jay Chapman described in his opening remarks as "small but intelligent." Carl Schurz was the principal speaker, and he spent most of his time arguing why the United States should not annex the Philippines. Referring to Roosevelt and Van Wyck as "two evils," and announcing that between them "I choose to vote for neither," he won enthusiastic rounds of applause from the otherwise unresponsive audience only when he attacked the Republican candidate:

> "Roosevelt tells us that we must 'dare to be great.' I tell him that in order to be truly great we must first dare to be honest."[15]

❧ ❧ ❧

Perhaps Thursday's most revealing development was a shift in the betting odds. In the morning, Tammany men continued to bet on a ten to seven basis, in part in the belief that it was necessary to encourage the faithful by keeping up the appearance that nothing had changed.* By noon, however, reported the *Herald*, "Tammany's bankroll, bet through the medium of certain Stock Exchange brokers and book-makers, . . . became exhausted, owing to the persistent manner in which it was covered by admirers of Colonel Roosevelt." By the end of the day, to the extent that an observer could determine with any precision, the prevailing odds appeared to have gone to even.[16]

❧ ❧ ❧

Friday brought no letup in the feverish activity that was making this campaign one of the most exciting in New York political annals. On his return to Manhattan from Albany, while Roosevelt spent the morning

---

* Croker reportedly had set aside $70,000 for this purpose.

and afternoon resting his voice for the eight speeches he was to deliver that evening, he wrote to Lodge:

"I have no idea how this fight is going. It is evident that the National Guard will give a majority against me, partly on account of my letter to Alger, but more on account of the fact that they were really not very good soldiers and are sore and angry and mortified about the hardships they have encountered. I have had a very hard campaign, but at any rate I have made the best fight I could, and if Blifil and Black George win, why, win they must."[17] *

Six of the evening's eight meetings were in Brooklyn. The distances between them were not great, and the *Times* reporter who accompanied Roosevelt was undoubtedly pleased to write that the carriage rides were "leisurely," and that the preceding visit's "wild rush . . . over boulder paved streets was lacking." The evening's largest crowd jammed the Clermont Avenue Rink to its 7000 person capacity. The *Times* correspondent was especially struck by the "well-dressed women" in the audience, who "are politicians to the core" and who "don't hesitate to shout and to stand up in their chairs, wave handkerchiefs, and howl at the candidate – at least when that candidate is Roosevelt . . . ."

From Brooklyn, the Roosevelt party returned to Manhattan, where the candidate spoke first at a hall on East 11th Street, and finally at a Chickering Hall mass meeting, where the overflow crowd blocked Fifth Avenue and 18th Street on two sides of the building. As he had in his seven previous appearances, he repeated his Long Island refrain that the "burly" Croker had "shoved the nice Mr. Van Wyck aside." Fortunately, his voice, which had been hoarse earlier in the day, seemed to improve as he spoke, so that he was able to articulate his message to his enthusiastic audiences.

---

*The reference was to two evil characters in Henry Fielding's 18th century novel *Tom Jones*.

After the Chickering Hall meeting ended, Roosevelt returned to the Fifth Avenue Hotel, where, to the sound of firecrackers set off in Madison Square, and joined by Platt and Odell, he stood on a balcony to review a parade of Italian-American supporters. The show was also visual, as, opposite the hotel, a local Republican club set off what the *Times* called "a set piece of pyrotechnics" promoting "Theodore Roosevelt for Governor' . . . in a myriad of colors." Further excitement was provided when there appeared on a stereopticon screen atop a nearby truck that the Democrats had parked earlier in the day the words "Roosevelt now spells his name P-L-A-T-T."

Odell's appearance marked the end of a busy Friday spent assuring that no stone would be left unturned to protect Republican interests on Election Day. As reported in the next morning's *Times*:

> "Extra telephones will be put in at the Fifth Avenue headquarters, and the local leaders in every town, city and county in the State will be instructed to report to the chairman at noon the condition of affairs at that hour, several lawyers of high standing will be at headquarters during the day to pass upon legal questions that my arise, and special attention will be bestowed on cases of attempted illegal voting."

Odell's aides also were taking steps to combat rumored offers of bribes to vote the straight Democratic ticket or at least stay away from the polls. Republican organizations in many counties were posting placards in prominent locations pointing out that such a crime was subject to three to twelve months' imprisonment and offering a $500 reward for information leading to its detection.[18]

�֍ ✖ ✖

Both parties considered the Albany area an important and closely contested battleground. Thus, it was not surprising that it was the next to last stop of Van Wyck's campaign. The decision to send him there was confirmed by his reception by what the *Times* called "in every way as

large and enthusiastic a crowd as welcomed Col. Roosevelt here yesterday." His route to the same hall where his opponent had spoken the
night before was lined by cheering people, and when he was formally
introduced by the Mayor he received several minutes of sustained applause. Like Roosevelt with Croker and the judiciary, Van Wyck's efforts were now concentrating on a single issue – the canal scandals –
and in his Albany speech he pushed it for all it was worth.

Back in New York, at Tammany Hall, Friday was the first "dough"
day when, according to the *Evening Post*, "each district leader will get all
the money he wants", so that "there will be no lack of Tammany workers near the polls next Tuesday." The going rate per worker was $5, and
it was understood that the payment would also obligate the recipient
to vote the Democratic ticket.[19]

❦ ❦ ❦

Saturday saw Van Wyck wind up his formal campaign with a mass
meeting in Troy. The difference in style between the two candidates
was apparent when he told the committee in charge of the arrangements not to plan a demonstration for his early afternoon arrival, and
not even to make public the hour that his train from Albany would
reach the city. Except for a reception attended by a number of prominent local Democrats, he spent the afternoon quietly at his hotel. By
shortly after 8:00 p.m., however, when he reached the meeting hall, it
was packed by more than 3000 seated supporters and another 2000
standees. Particularly in its discussion of the canal scandals and analy-
sis of the report of the Canal Investigation Committee, Van Wyck's
speech sounded more like one of his judicial opinions than a piece of
political oratory. It nevertheless was enthusiastically received.[20]

Roosevelt's busy day, of course, was the exact opposite of his opponent's. It was spent entirely south of 34th Street in Manhattan, and
opened with a noon speech to a crowd of 2500 at the corner of Broome
and Sheriff Streets. This was followed by an appearance, which accord-

ing to the *Times* he made only "after much persuasion," before a large audience that had waited for several hours in front of the Sub-Treasury, across Wall Street from J.P. Morgan's banking house. These were only warmups, however, for the main event, when he would reportedly be the first candidate in state history to make a complete tour of the Bowery. He had been warned what awaited him, for, according to the *Times*:

> "Early in the afternoon men began pouring into his headquarters . . . – men with long faces and scared looks – to tell the Colonel that the Sullivans and the Engels and the 'Marion Street crowd' and other political organizations had prepared a reception for him that would be little short of a riot. They said all the Democrats had conspired to "do him up," and that if he reached Marion and Spring Streets, it would be lucky for him if he got any further."

Despite these warnings, Odell decided that Roosevelt could go, but suggested that he keep his head inside the carriage or, better yet, keep the windows closed. Roosevelt's only response was a laugh.

After having his ailing throat sprayed at a physician's house on Madison Avenue and 30th Street, Roosevelt took off for his first meeting, at a hall at Hudson and Bank Streets. During his ten minute stop he drew the loudest applause when he announced, "My voice is going back on me, but I don't care so long as Croker's is in good order." From there, it was on to a meeting at an Afro-American church and to a large rally at Cooper Union. All was relatively peaceful until his phalanx of carriages entered the Bowery, when bricks began to fly but fell wide of the mark. By the time he reached Bayard Street, the crowd was so thick that even with a flying wedge with the press carriage at its center, he could not get to the wagon from which he was to speak. His only recourse was to stand on his carriage seat, but the din was so loud and his voice so hoarse that for the first time in the campaign he could not make himself heard.

As his carriage turned into Grand Street, Roosevelt busied himself trying to shake off boys who had climbed over the back of his carriage and perched on the lowered top. It was here, the *Times* correspondent wrote,

" . . . that the worst of the tour was encountered. At points along the line men and boys were stationed in small crowds, who hurled bricks and stones at the carriages. One of these struck the driver of Col. Roosevelt's carriage square in the face. Another hit one of the horses, and others came so close to the occupants of the carriages that it was considered best to close them and this was done as the horses dashed along amid hoots and cries. In Mott Street came the volley of feline remains. It was not dangerous, but it did not have the odor of Araby. None of the flying cats came within twenty feet of the carriages. But as they drove along an occasional thump on the back of one or another of the vehicles told that a well-aimed stone had struck home."

Fortunately, just as the Roosevelt party galloped toward the hostile throng at Marion Street, "a dozen husky policemen, clubs in hand," came to the rescue. Surrounding the carriages, they managed to direct the group to safety behind a 20-foot fence. The rioters, "clearly outwitted by the police, . . . contented themselves with banging on the gates and yelling, 'Afraid to come out!'" Roosevelt was escorted to a balcony, from which he addressed "a crowd whose noise was not all friendly cheering." Eventually, his carriages were able to extricate themselves, and, escorted by a group of horsemen in Rough Riders costumes, made their way north to the hospitable surroundings of Stuyvesant Square, where cheering men and women leaned over rooftops and out of second and third story windows. By now Roosevelt's voice had shrunk to a barely audible whisper, but he was clearly reveling in his escapade, which must have reminded him of his charge up San Juan Hill.[21]

❋ ❋ ❋

Now that the formal campaigning had practically ended, what remained before Election Day was, as the *Herald* headlined, "a game of bet and boast." On Saturday, Odell, who continued to predict a Roosevelt plurality of more than 40,000, on behalf of a pool, wagered $20,000 "even" on his candidate through a Lower Manhattan broker. A Tammany operative named "Smiling Johnny" Kelly delivered the offsetting money. For his part, Democratic campaign manager McCarren predicted a Van Wyck victory of 33,500.

As contrasted with its poll of a week earlier, this Sunday morning's *Herald* survey did not predict a winner. Instead, what it called a "conservative" estimate for each of the upstate counties indicated "that Colonel Roosevelt would come down to Harlem River with a plurality in the neighborhood of 80,000, and that Judge Van Wyck's plurality in New York, Kings and Richmond counties must overcome it, or Roosevelt will be elected." In New York County (Manhattan) the Democrats were predicting victory by 65,000 to 75,000, in Kings (Brooklyn) by 12,000 to 15,000, and in Richmond (Staten Island) by 1600 to 2000. For their part, the Republicans were conceding Van Wyck a Manhattan majority of slightly more than 50,000, in Brooklyn of 5,000, and on Staten Island of 900. Queens, said the *Herald*, was "debatable ground."[22]

For all the speculation as to how the city would vote, it was obvious to both sides that the larger the Republican upstate plurality, the harder it would be for Van Wyck to overcome it. The state's western end was heavily Republican, and Odell had scheduled a last minute Roosevelt visit there on Monday to secure the largest possible turnout and perhaps provide extra votes for victory.

"I Have Played It In Bull Luck"

AFTER HIS SATURDAY NIGHT BOWERY FORAY, ROOSEVELT SPENT MOST of Sunday quietly at his sister's home, trying with some success to restore his voice for the next day's Southwestern New York campaign windup. * There was no rest, however, for the political leaders responsible for getting out the vote. The immediate concern of the Manhattan Republican district leaders was illegal voting on the Lower East Side. To that end, they asked State Superintendent of Elections McCullagh to join them at county headquarters at 1 Madison Avenue. When the Sunday evening meeting adjourned, the Superintendent released a letter addressed to the Board of Police Commissioners, in which he stated that it had come to his "official knowledge" that attempts would be made to intimidate Republican voters in the 6th Assembly District, and that "it is proposed to import into that district thugs, crooks, and panhandlers from New Jersey, Connecticut and the City of Troy, prominent among those of the latter city being some of the men identified with what has generally become known as the 'Bat Shea' gang."

This was by no means all. The Superintendent also had received a report that the Democratic leader of the 8th Assembly District had boasted that "he absolutely owns" the district's top police officer, and had warned the election inspector for the district "that he will 'run

---

* This is the one-day trip described in the Prologue.

things' to suit himself on the day of election, and . . . to either resign his position, or to remain away from his post of duty within that district in order to save himself from possible harm." He had also been told that "floaters" from a number of "hotels" and "cafes" had "surrendered their registration certificates for a consideration to certain persons in such districts, and that other 'floaters' and imported crooks and ex-convicts will be given these certificates of registration upon which to vote on the day of election." Since their "faces . . . are well known to the members of the detective force under your command, . . . many of these persons can be apprehended and incarcerated . . ." Finally, the Superintendent warned the police of a "colonization of crooks" from Chicago, Philadelphia and Pittsburgh who had settled within the boundaries of what has become known as the "Tenderloin District," and of evidence of "widespread frauds in the procurement of naturalization papers" by men seeking work in New York and neighboring counties, whom Tammany presumably would like to take to the polls.

McCullagh's letter prompted a quick response from the Police Commissioners, who promised "a strict and rigid enforcement of the laws with respect to the elective franchise." "[U]nder the circumstances," wrote the *Herald* correspondent, "they could hardly do less." Meanwhile, the Election Superintendent provided proof of his warnings by obtaining a confession from a man who had been providing illegal naturalization papers. This led to the arrest of three of State Senator Timothy Sullivan's followers, one of them an election district captain. They were turned over to the Federal authorities, who had jurisdiction over immigration matters and to whom, the *Herald* noted, "political influence does not extend."

McCullagh spent Monday morning at his office giving instructions to several hundred election inspectors. At the same time, Tammany was handing out the final installments of "dough" to its district leaders. The largess was plentiful, and one of the smiling recipients was heard to

announce, "I have more money than I know what to do with." To anyone who seemed interested, Croker was predicting "a great victory tomorrow." When asked about Roosevelt's last minute tour, he scoffed:
"Why, this fellow will still be talking next Saturday night."[1]

❀ ❀ ❀

As is its wont, except for the voters, the press insisted on having the last
word. The *Tribune* displayed its strong Republican bias not only on the
editorial page, but also in its news columns, in which were interspersed
occasional short bold-face plugs for that party's nominees. Although
the *Sun's* coverage was more balanced, editorially there was no doubt
that it also backed Roosevelt. The *World* was equally ardent in its praise
of the Democrats in general, and Van Wyck in particular. So, also, was
Hearst's *Evening Journal*, The *Times*, whose news reports if anything
seemed to lean toward Roosevelt, editorially accused him of "wearying
the voters" with "claptrap about the war, all crude and tawdry stuff
about keeping the flag where it has been planted, and the cheap theatrical trick of parading a few Rough Riders through the State . . ." "A
good many" men "who had previously resolved to vote for him," the
Times predicted, would now choose Van Wyck.

Neither the *Evening Post* nor the *Herald* formally endorsed a candidate.
In a "plague on both your houses" position, the *Post* could only wring
its hands:

> "Is there any more deadly foe of popular government than the
> boss system as it is administered by Croker, and Platt and Aldridge
> and Payn? How can honest men fight these common foes and at
> the same time join hands with some of them and extol them as
> upholders of good government?"

Although the *Herald's* coverage seemed to lean slightly toward
Roosevelt, editorially it prided itself on the "absolute impartiality" with
which it had "gathered" and "presented . . . all the facts – the news – of
the campaign." It would take no position, for to do so would be to set

itself up "like an old fashioned pedagogue with a rod," treating its readers "like a lot of schoolboys, who could be lectured and coerced into
voting as they were told." Its subscribers, the editors concluded, "are intelligent persons who do their own thinking and are quite competent
to make their own deductions from facts placed before them."[2]

❋ ❋ ❋

Election Day dawned fair throughout most of the state. The good
weather continued all day as a storm over Lake Superior moved east-
ward more slowly than some had predicted. With nothing to deter upstate farmers from traveling to the polls, it was generally regarded as
"Republican weather." Particularly in New York City, lines had already
begun to form before the polling places opened at 6:00 a.m., and the
heavy voting continued all day.

Despite, or perhaps because of the dire predictions of trouble, the
day passed remarkably peacefully. As reported by the *Herald*:

> "There was not a riot, not a man followed Senator Hill's advice
> to 'knock 'em down,' and one couldn't find bloodshed with a
> search warrant. . . . Of course, there were arrests – many of them
> – but the dragging of men to court by wholesale, a horrid vision
> that had oppressed the imagination of campaign spellbinders,
> faded and was gone."

Contrary to the expectations of some, policemen and election inspectors "worked side by side in amity almost perfect" and in some cases "chatted cheerily" with each other.[3]

❋ ❋ ❋

Unlike the last part of the twentieth century, when New York voters
could cast their ballots as late as 9:00 p.m., in 1898 the polls closed at 5
o'clock. Thus, even though in this pre-voting-machine era ballots were
counted by hand, by 10 o'clock the outcome had become clear. It was a
Roosevelt victory, and many Manhattanites were among the first to
get the news by watching as a powerful light that the *Herald* had set up

atop Madison Square Garden's tower beamed eastwards toward Long Island and Oyster Bay. *

Roosevelt received the news of his victory at Sagamore Hill at about 10:45 from reporters who had heard the returns at the telephone office at Oyster Bay. He had arrived there by train at 3:09, and immediately went to the upstairs polling place in Fisher's Hall. After being signed in as "Theodore Roosevelt, 284," he entered the voting booth at 3:52. He emerged a minute and five seconds later, and, dropping his ballot in the box, laughingly remarked, "It was a fake." To a reporter who asked what he meant, he replied: "Why, I was told that the Democratic Committee had sent word to challenge my vote here. They don't seem to have done it, though."

After voting, Roosevelt was driven to his home, where he had dinner with his family. Then, dressed in evening clothes, he went to his "den," where he and his 14 year old daughter Alice read and Edith knitted. After assuring himself that the initial reports of his triumph were correct, he issued a statement that he appreciated the "honor" of being chosen by the voters, and "even more deeply the responsibility involved in the honor." Confirming his Republican allegiance, he then asserted his belief that "I can serve the Republican party by doing everything I can to help it serve the State." He promised to try "to administer the office of Governor in the interest of the whole people," for it was "by so doing that I can best show my appreciation of the support given me by the independents and Democrats who have themselves put the welfare of the State first, declining to follow those of their leaders who in this crisis either ranged themselves outright on the side of the forces of dishonesty, or else supported them in effect by standing aside from the real contest."[4]

---

* If Van Wyck had won, the light would have been directed south in the direction of his Brooklyn home.

❉ ❉ ❉

The first reports that Roosevelt received that election night were that his plurality might exceed 30,000 votes. His final margin however, was only 17,794 out of a total vote of some 1.3 million. As expected, the size of his upstate majority was crucial. Van Wyck carried New York City by more than 80,000, with more than two-thirds of his majority coming from Manhattan. This was almost exactly the same as the *Herald* had predicted a week earlier, when it forecast a statewide 7000 vote Democratic victory. Van Wyck also took Albany and Erie (Buffalo) Counties, which the *Herald* had predicted Roosevelt would win by small margins.

In none of the many counties that Roosevelt carried was his plurality greater than 8000 votes. It was the cumulative effect of his small majorities that determined the outcome. Especially interesting were the results from the State's three westernmost counties that Roosevelt had visited only the day before. Compared to the total plurality of 10,300 that the *Herald*'s weekend poll had predicted, his actual margin exceeded 12,800 votes. Obviously, his last-minute tour had paid dividends.[5]

❉ ❉ ❉

In their post-mortems, both sides recognized that the election's outcome easily could have swung the other way. To an acquaintance who congratulated him at an encounter at the Fifth Avenue Hotel a few days later, Roosevelt conceded, "If this campaign had lasted ten days more, I am afraid I should have been defeated because this Spanish War issue was being worn to a frazzle." When Roosevelt's friend relayed this comment to Croker later that day, the Tammany boss agreed, blurting out, "You fellows think you had an easy victory, don't you? Well, I want to tell you that if this campaign had lasted ten days more, we would have thrashed you to pieces."

Croker's suggestion that Roosevelt's victory was a case of lucky timing could not disguise the fact that the Tammany boss was generally credited with losing the election for Van Wyck. In its November 9 issue, the *Times* wasted no time in affixing blame, arguing that the Judge's majority in Manhattan "was 30,000 less than the figure that would have been reached in this Democratic year if the ugly menace of Crokerism had not risen to . . . send thousands of Democrats to the ballot box with Republican votes in their hands." It was "[t]o Richard Croker and him alone" that belonged "the responsibility of the Democratic defeat . . . . He enforced his brutal and selfish will in the judiciary nominations at a time when the tide was visibly carrying his party to certain victory."

All this was true, and in his *Autobiography* Roosevelt admitted, "This gave me my chance." But it was only his unique combination of energy and ability to dramatize an issue that enabled him, as he later put it, "to fix the contest in the public mind as between himself and myself . . ." As Platt conceded, ". . . no man besides Roosevelt could have accomplished that feat in 1898."[6]

In the days following the election, the Governor-elect took time to reflect on his victory. On November 25, in response to a congratulatory cable from his good friend, British diplomat Cecil Spring-Rice, he spoke of his good fortune:

"I have played it in bull luck this summer. First, to get into the war; then to get out of it; then to get elected. I have worked hard all my life, and have never been particularly lucky, and I am enjoying it to the full. I know that this luck will not continue, and it is not necessary that it should. I am more than contented to be Governor of New York, and shall not care if I never hold another office . . . ."

In a letter he wrote the same day to British historian and diplomat James Bryce, Roosevelt was more specific. The Republican machine, he said,

". . . would not have nominated me if I had not been a straight Republican, one who while always acting on his own best judgment and according to his own beliefs in right and wrong, was yet

anxious to consult with and if possible come to an agreement
with the party leaders. In other words I had what the Mugwump
conspicuously lacks, and what the Frenchman, * and in fact all
people who are unfitted for self-government, likewise lack,
namely the power of coming to a consensus with my fellows.
But, of course, the Machine never dreamt of asking a promise of
any kind or sort. I had a big burden of scandals, both of the National and State administration, to carry, and I was opposed by
the professional Independents, like Carl Schurz, Godkin, and
Parkhurst and the idiot variety of 'Goo-Goos,' partly because they
objected to my being for the war with Spain, and partly because
they feared lest somebody they did not like might vote for me.
However, we took the aggressive, and got a great many not only
of the Independents proper but of the Independent Democrats,
away from them; and, after a very close, uphill fight, we won."[7]

❉ ❉ ❉

In predicting to Spring-Rice that his luck would not continue, Roosevelt was mistaken. The chance to become a war hero and the opportunity that Croker handed him were to be just the first of several
unexpected pieces of good fortune that would place him in the White
House in less than three years.

Although at heart Roosevelt's interests lay more in national rather
than in state matters, he enjoyed being Governor. It was his first government job in which he could exercise authority as "top dog," and the
diversity of issues it presented provided ample grist for his active and
energetic mind. He did his best to cultivate friendly relations with Platt,
meeting with him at the Amen Corner almost weekly. He also went

---

* Roosevelt probably was referring to the controversy over the guilt or innocence of
French Army Captain Alfred Dreyfus, which seemed about to plunge France into
civil war.

out of his way to praise the Senator for his assistance to the McKin-
ley Administration in securing ratification of the peace treaty with
Spain, under which the United States acquired Puerto Rico and the
Philippines.

By the end of March 1899, however, the two men parted company
when Roosevelt announced his support for the imposition of a franchise tax on public utility corporations. The legislation, which was
sponsored by a New York City Democratic senator, had been bogged
down in committee, but when the Governor announced that he liked
the idea, it quickly gained momentum. An angry Platt tried to defer action until the next legislative session so that the issue could be thoroughly studied, but Roosevelt defied him, and with broad popular
support secured the bill's passage.

Early in 1900, the break between the two men widened over the con-
tinuation in office of Insurance Superintendent Louis Payn. Entirely
apart from a lingering animosity toward Payn caused by his efforts to
derail Roosevelt's gubernatorial nomination, the Governor regarded
the Superintendent as the epitome of an old-time spoils politician,
whom Elihu Root had less charitably described as "a stench in the nos-
trils of the people of the State of New York." Thus, in mid-January,
when an investigation ordered by Roosevelt confirmed that Payn had
borrowed several hundred thousand dollars on shaky collateral from a
bank controlled by several of his friends, the Governor, at a "bloody
breakfast" with Platt, announced that the Superintendent had to be replaced. Although Payn's support of Governor Black for renomination
had angered the Easy Boss, by now their long-standing friendship had
reasserted itself. When Roosevelt threatened to make a public issue of
the matter, however, Platt reluctantly decided not to oppose him, and
Payn was replaced. Jubilantly, Roosevelt wrote to a friend: "I have always been fond of the West African proverb: "Speak softly and carry a
big stick; you will go far."

From then on, the troublesome Governor became *persona non grata* to Platt, who resolved that he had to go. The question was where and how. One possibility would be to find another candidate to run for Governor that fall. The Easy Boss knew, however, that this man whom he had picked for the job less than two years earlier would not take this sitting down. Moreover, even if Platt was able to find a viable alternative nominee to replace Roosevelt, a blatant ouster of the popular Governor would so cripple the Republicans that the Democrats would coast to victory in November.

Another and likely more productive alternative was the Vice-Presidential nomination. Vice President Garret Hobart had died in November 1899, and Platt argued that Roosevelt was an obvious replacement: he could stump the country for McKinley while the President again conducted a dignified "front porch" campaign. The large and enthusiastic crowds that had greeted Roosevelt on a June, 1899, cross-country trip to a Rough Riders' reunion at Las Vegas attested to his nationwide appeal.

Lodge supported this course, arguing that the Vice Presidency would provide his friend a better launching pad for the Presidency in 1904 than the New York governorship. Roosevelt initially disagreed. The job's only prescribed duty of presiding over the Senate was far from attractive to a man with Roosevelt's energy. Much more appealing would have been the post of Secretary of War or the Philippine Governor Generalship, but McKinley had already filled them with, respectively, Elihu Root and Judge William Howard Taft. A further obstacle was that the President was lukewarm to the idea, and Mark Hanna, recalling numerous altercations with Roosevelt when he had been Assistant Secretary of the Navy, was violently opposed.

These difficulties did not stop Platt, who enlisted the aid of Matthew Quay, the Pennsylvania Republican boss , who was no friend of Hanna's, to help organize a groundswell for Roosevelt among the prospective convention delegates. Their efforts, made easy by Roosevelt's continued popularity, were so successful that the Easy Boss was able to boast that "Roosevelt might just as well stand under Niagara Falls and try to spit water as to stop his nomination." Roosevelt's friends advised him that the only way to avoid being nominated was to stay away from the convention when it opened in Philadelphia. Instead, although he was still protesting that he did not want the Vice Presidency, after most of the delegates and audience had been seated at the June 19 opening session, with a broad-brimmed Rough Rider style hat atop his head, he strode down the aisle to the chant of "We want Teddy! We want Teddy!" An observer accurately predicted that he was wearing "an acceptance hat." The pressure from Platt and others who told Roosevelt it was his duty to the party to run was too great, and he bowed to the inevitable. Hanna was apoplectic, exploding: "Don't any of you realize there's only one life between this madman and the Presidency?" By now, however, the Ohio senator had lost much of his influence over McKinley. Thus, when the President left the nomination entirely to the convention, it chose Roosevelt with only one dissenting vote – his own.

Once again, William Jennings Bryan was McKinley's opponent, running on a platform that stipulated "imperialism" as the campaign's paramount issue. While the President remained at his Canton, Ohio, residence receiving groups of visitors, Roosevelt took the Republican cause all over the country. By Election Day he had made 673 speeches in 567 different locations. Although he strongly defended the United States's recent colonial acquisitions, the voters were more impressed by the fact that the country was prosperous and had no desire to abandon the gold standard that had won the Republicans the White House four years before. The result was that Bryan was defeated by even larger electoral college and popular majorities. The next March, a highly satisfied Platt joked as he left New York to attend the inaugural ceremonies, "We're all off to Washington to see Teddy take the veil."[8]

Roosevelt's cloistered Vice Presidency lasted only six months. On September 6, 1901, at a public reception at a Pan-American Exposition at Buffalo, McKinley was shot by an anarchist. He died eight days later. By another stroke of "bull luck," Theodore Roosevelt had become President of the United States.

❀ ❀ ❀

Other major figures in the 1898 contest were less fortunate. Even Platt's triumph in seeing Roosevelt leave New York was short-lived. Odell was nominated to take Roosevelt's place in Albany, and, in the McKinley-Roosevelt sweep, carried the State by a large majority. He was reelected by a smaller margin two years later. Once in office, he ignored Platt on appointments and other matters, and soon wrested Party leadership from the Easy Boss. Platt managed to secure reelection to the Senate in 1902, but his power was gone. When, a broken old man, he died in 1910, his obituaries painted him as the epitome of the corrupt boss of the Gilded Age.[9]

Quigg's fall from political power was even faster. In 1898, he lost his Congressional seat, as independent voters punished him for his participation as Platt's loyal lieutenant in the rejection of Seth Low as the prior year's Republican mayoral candidate. In 1900, when Odell was seizing the Republican reins from Platt, he also ousted Quigg from his Manhattan leadership post. The balance of Quigg's career was spent as a lobbyist on behalf of New York City traction mogul Thomas Fortune Ryan.

❀ ❀ ❀

After the Independent ticket's crushing 1898 defeat, a discouraged John Jay Chapman never returned to politics. He spent his remaining 35 years first authoring generally undistinguished plays for both children and adults and later, with better critical success, writing a variety of essays as well as studies on Shakespeare, Dante and Greek literature.

At his death, even though his eulogists could point to no significant victories in his efforts to improve American public and private life, he was widely praised as a brilliant and honest man of letters and an enthusiastic reformer.

❦ ❦ ❦

Croker's political sway was even shorter than Platt's. In 1899, a Republican-controlled Assembly investigating committee found that both "honest" and "dishonest" graft had increased in proportions that exceeded even the corruption whose revelation had led to Mayor Strong's 1894 election. In 1901, the Republicans joined the reformers in backing Seth Low for Mayor as a fusion candidate. The Democrats tried to distance themselves from the increasingly unpopular Croker by naming as their candidate an anti-Tammany Brooklyn lawyer, but it was to no avail. Under the slogan "Down with Croker," Low won an easy victory.

After this defeat, Croker abandoned politics and spend most of his time in England and Ireland, breeding horses that won a number of Irish races and, in 1907, at ten-to-one odds, the Epsom Derby. For the rest of his life he boasted that he was prouder of this victory than any election, and tried to forget that King Edward VII had snubbed him by not inviting him to the traditional Derby Dinner that honored his horse's triumph. After his wife's death in 1914, Croker married a 23-year-old Cherokee Indian from Oklahoma, who inherited $5,000,000 on his death in 1922, only to lose most of it in court battles with his children.[10]

❦ ❦ ❦

In all the excitement over Roosevelt's victory, little attention was paid to the man whose rejection by Croker had helped make it possible. Perhaps this was because, notwithstanding the efforts of the Bar Association and other like-minded citizens, Judge Daly was defeated by more than 40,000 votes. Apart from his appointment in 1900 as a commissioner to revise the laws of Puerto Rico, he spent the remainder of his life as a Manhattan lawyer. When he died in 1916 in his 77th year, a *New York Times* editorial described him as "an authority on theatrical literature and history, a just and appreciative critic of actors and acting, and a man of broad and varied sympathies." "It is natural," the editors concluded, "that the obituaries should lay most stress on the fact that he was 'turned down,' but he leaves a host of friends in various walks of life who feel that such a mishap was of comparatively small importance in a career so rich in achievement and endeavor."[11]

Epilogue
What If?

ON READING OF DALY'S DEATH, BOTH HISTORIANS AND LAYMEN might have pondered what the course of American life would have been if Richard Croker had not blocked his renomination and Roosevelt had been denied the issue that most observers believed was vital to his narrow victory. Today, as scholars are becoming increasingly intrigued by the "what ifs" of history, the significance of Roosevelt's election becomes especially clear when one considers what his future would have been had he been defeated. [1]

With Roosevelt's paramount interest in national affairs, and with the aid of Lodge and other well-placed friends, he almost certainly would have sought an important federal position. His strong support of the McKinley Administration's colonial policy would have earned him such an appointment. At first impression, the most obvious, especially in view of Roosevelt's service in Cuba and his prior Navy Department experience, would have been to replace the widely unpopular Russell Alger as Secretary of War. McKinley's thoughts, however, likely would have run along other lines. In mid-1899, when Quigg, acting as the President's emissary, told Elihu Root that McKinley had chosen him for the job and Root objected on the basis that "I know nothing about war" and "nothing about the army," Quigg replied that the President was not looking for anyone with those qualifications. Instead, "he has got to have a lawyer to direct the government of these Spanish islands." Particularly given the reputation for impetuous action that Roosevelt had gained as Assistant Navy Secretary, one is entitled to doubt strongly that he would have been McKinley's choice. [2]

A second possibility would have been appointment to head the government of the newly acquired Philippines. This would have appealed to Roosevelt, especially since he would have been operating thousands of miles from any supervisory authority and thus could have acted with a relatively free hand. Here, however, in appointing Federal Judge William Howard Taft to the position, McKinley, according to his biographer, wanted "someone as sincere and disinterested as Solomon, yet possessing the extraordinary tact and patience that would be required to bridge an interim period of control with the military government." Also, when Taft suggested to the President that he was not the man for the job because he had been opposed to acquiring the islands, McKinley's response was that Taft didn't "want them any less than I do," but since we had them, "in dealing with them I think I can trust the man who didn't want them better than I can the man who did." Roosevelt obviously would have satisfied neither of these criteria.[3]

The only other Washington job that was available was the seat of Democratic Senator Murphy, who would be replaced in early 1899 by the Republican-controlled legislature. That possibility would have been only theoretical, however, for Boss Platt would never have agreed to have the troublesome Roosevelt as his Senate colleague, as opposed to his friend and actual choice, the politically safe Chauncey Depew. Thus, there is a good chance that, at least for the immediate future, Roosevelt would have been confined to pursuing his literary career, with occasional speeches to keep his name before the public.

Under none of these possibilities would he have been nominated for Vice President in 1900. Platt would have had no reason to push his candidacy, and with Hanna's opposition, the convention delegates would have looked elsewhere. Moreover, if Roosevelt had been given either the War Secretaryship or the Philippine post, he would have had no interest in surrendering a position in which he could demonstrate qualities of executive leadership for a job whose only defined task was presiding over the Senate. McKinley's health was excellent, and no Vice President had been elected to succeed a sitting President since Martin Van Buren had followed Andrew Jackson to the White House in 1837.

The goal of Lodge and other Roosevelt supporters was to obtain the Presidency for him in 1904. McKinley's assassination secured this result three years earlier. But if Roosevelt had not been nominated and elected Vice President, the Presidential office would have devolved on another. One can only speculate who that would have been, but the two men whom Hanna was most seriously considering in 1900 as alternatives to Roosevelt were Roosevelt's old boss, Secretary of the Navy John Long, and Jonathan Dolliver, like Roosevelt only 42 years old but already in his sixth term as a Congressman for Iowa. Since the perceived need was an active running mate who would stump for the ticket while McKinley remained at home, as between the two the choice would likely have been Dolliver, who was 20 years younger than Long and a man whom later historian described as "a natural orator of great power." It is inconceivable that if Dolliver had been President in 1904 he would have surrendered his presumed right to run for reelection in favor of Roosevelt or anyone else.[4]

Fortunately for the nation, these "what ifs" never occurred. Roosevelt thus was able to lead the United States to meet the dramatic challenge he made to the delegates at the 1900 Republican Convention: whether in the twentieth century's "opening years . . . we shall march forward to fresh triumphs or whether at the outset we shall cripple ourselves for that contest." The result, as the *New York Times* editorialized at the century's close, was that, as President, Roosevelt "would enshrine progress and economic justice as national ideals," and "created the powerful modern presidency as an institution capable of shaping both this nation's goals and world events." His election as Governor, no less than his charge up the San Juan Heights, was essential to obtaining that result.[5]

Author's Note & Acknowledgements

WHEN I WAS A BOY GROWING UP IN OHIO, I AQUIRED FROM MY FATHER his strong interest in American history and politics. During college vacations I worked locally on Republican Senatorial and Presidential campaigns, and my Princeton senior thesis explored the highly successful financing of Dwight Eisenhower's White House bid. After moving to New York I was one of many young people who helped in John Lindsay's Congressional campaigns and also became active in an Upper East Side Republican organization, through which I met the woman to whom I have been happily married for thirty-seven years.

Thus, when I discovered, in writing a previous book, *1898: Prelude To A Century,* that no author had ever thoroughly described Theodore Roosevelt's exciting gubernatorial campaign, I became intrigued with the possibility that I might do so. My appetite for the project grew as I came to realize that if TR had been defeated he probably would never have made it to the White House and that his effort to balance a commitment to reform with loyalty to a political party whose leadership had different priorities provides lessons that are just as relevant today as they were more than one hundred years ago.

❦ ❦ ❦

Although the responsibility for this book is entirely my own, I would be remiss if I did not acknowledge the important help that I have received from others. First, I want to thank G. Wallace Chessman for his thorough review of a draft of my manuscript and for his many suggestions, most of which I have incorporated. I have also especially appreciated the assistance I received from Wallace Dailey, Curator of the Theodore Roosevelt Collection at the Harvard College Library; John A. Gable, Executive Director of the Theodore Roosevelt Association; and Charles Marcus at the Theodore Roosevelt Birthplace in New York City.

As he did with my book on the year 1898, Charles Davey skillfully provided invaluable service in this book's design and production. I also want to thank Patricia Quinn for her careful word-processing of the manuscript and Lena Giardina for taking time from her busy work schedule to help with correspondence and other details. Others whose help I gratefully acknowledge include Vincent Duffy, Joe Florio and Theodore Roosevelt Kupferman.

This book could not have been written without access to the collections of the New York Public Library, especially its microfilms of New York City newspapers. I also made use of the libraries of Harvard and Sarah Lawrence Colleges, and of Columbia and Princeton Universities, the New York Society Library, and the following other public libraries: Bronxville, Chautauqua and Jamestown, New York, and Denver, Colorado.

Last, but far from least, I want to thank my wife Emily for her many helpful suggestions and her never-failing encouragement, understanding and love.

Endnotes

Prologue

1 *Times*, November 8, 1898; *Tribune*, November 7, 1898; *Herald*, November 8, 1898.

2 *Tribune*, November 8, 1898; *Herald*, November 8, 1898; *Times*, November 8, 1898; Jamestown *Evening Journal*, November 7, 1898.

3 Jamestown *Evening Journal*, November 7, 1898; *Times*, November 8, 1898; *Tribune*, November 8, 1898.

4 Chessman, 66; Riis, *Roosevelt*, 203-204.

5 Riis, *Roosevelt*, 206-207; William J. Youngs, "A Short Resume of the Administration of Theodore Roosevelt as Governor (1904)" unpublished memorandum in TRC.

1

1 Morris, 136-143; Pringle, 57-58.

2 Pringle, 57; *Autobiography*, 56.

3 *Autobiography*, 54-55; Pringle, 55-57; Morris, 93-94, 143-144; Putnam, 238-239.

4 Morris, 144-145; Pringle, 58-59.

5 Morison, 735; Morris, 147, 150.

6 Morris, 149-150; *Autobiography*, 59.

7 Morris, 150-151.

8 *Ibid.*, 152-153; *Autobiography*, 61-62.

9 Morison, 55; Morris, 160-171; Pringle 65-67; Burrows & Wallace, 1102.

10 *Autobiography*, 77; Putnam, 261-263; Morris, 172-174.

11 Putnam, 264-267; Morris, 175-178.

12 Putnam, 267-272; Morris, 180-181; *Times*, June 3, 1882.

13 Putnam, 273-275.

14 *Ibid.*, 276-279; Morris, 184.

15 Morris, 190-191.

16 *Ibid.*, 191-192; Nevins, *Cleveland*, 115-117.

17 Morris, 193-194; *World*, March 10, 1883.

18 Putnam, 280-282.Morris, 187-188, 195.

19 *Times*, March 26, 1883; *Harper's Weekly*, April 21, 1883; Morris, 227-228; Morison, 634.

2

1 Putnam, 368-369.

2 Ibid., 371-373; Morris, 229.

3 Putnam, 375.

4 Ibid., 374-375, 380-382; Morris, 230-234; *Times*, February 6, 1884.

5 Putnam, 376-380; Morris, 236-237; McCullough, 275.

6 Morris, 237, 240; Chanler, 195.

7 Morris, 240-241; McCullough, 282-284.

8 Morris, 242, 247-248; Morison, 66.

9 Morris, 248-251.

10 McCullough, 153.

11 Morris, 251-252; Putnam, 413-416.

12 Putnam, 415-418; *Times*, April 23 and 24, 1884; *Sun*, April 24, 1884.

13 *Evening Post*, April 29, 1884.

14 *Herald* June 1, 1884; *Times*, June 2, 1884.

15 *Times*, June 2, 1884; Morison, 69.
16 Morris, 258-260.
17 Putnam, 430-432; *Evening Post*, May 31 and June 4, 1884.
18 *Times*, June 4, 1884.
19 *Ibid.*
20 *Herald*, June 5, 1884.
21 *Ibid.*, June 7, 1884.; Morison,72.
22 *Times*, June 7, 1884.
23 *Ibid.*; World, June 7, 1884.
24 Putnam, 446-448.
25 Morison, 66-67.
26 Morris, 280.
27 Morison, 75-76; *Evening Post*, July 21, 1884.
28 Morris, 280, 288-290.
29 Morison, 88; Morris, 292; Busch, 54.

3

1 Busch, 54; Morris, 303.
2 Morris, Chapters 12 and 13.
3 Miller, 173; Morris, 342-344; Burrows & Wallace, 1098-1100; Alexander, 74-77.
4 Alexander, 78-79; Morison, 111-112; Morris, 345.
5 Morison, 111-113.
6 *Times*, October 20, 1886.
7 *Ibid.*, October 28, 1886.
8 *Ibid.*, October 25, 29 and 30, 1886; *Sun*, October 30, 186; Morris, 357
9 *Times*, October 30, 1886.
10 *Ibid*, October 31, 1886.
11 *Ibid*; Morison, 115; Nevins, *Hewitt*, 468.
12 Nevins, *Hewitt*, 468; Morris, 354-355.
13 Burrows & Wallace, 1105-1106.
14 Nevins, *Hewitt*, 468; Alexander, 82-83.
15 *Sun*, October 21, 1886.

4

1 Morris, 364-373; Morison, 134-136.
2 Morris, 379-381, 386-389, 462.
3 Morison, 141-142, 149.
4 *Ibid*, 157-158; Morris, 391-393.
5 The discussion of Roosevelt's years in Washington is largely drawn from Morris, 395 -427, 433-437 and 446-457; Harbaugh, 79-80; and Brands, 221-258.
6 Morison, 135-136.
7 *Ibid*, 328-329.
8 *Ibid*, 340.
9 Burrows & Wallace, 1108-1110; Stoddard, 89-91.
10 Burrows & Wallace, 1167-1169; Mitgang, 48.
11 Burrows & Wallace, 1108-1109, 1192; Stoddard, 146.
12 Burrows & Wallace, 1192; Morison, 352; Morris, 473-475.
13 Morison, Vol. 8: 1433; Burrows & Wallace, 1193-1194.
14 Morris, 477-478; Morison, 437-439.
15 Steffens, 257-258.
16 Morris, 484-491; Burrows & Wallace, 988-989.
17 Steffens, 263; Burrows & Wallace, 1201.
18 Riis, *Making*, 212.
19 *Ibid*, 213-214.
20 *Ibid*, 214; Burrows & Wallace, 1201.
21 Chanler, 195-196; Morison, 462-463.
22 Morison, 464; Morris, 496-500; Burrows & Wallace, 1202-1203.
23 Burrows & Wallace, 1203.
24 Morris, 512-513, 519-522; Stoddard, 99-102.

25 Gosnell, 319; Morison, 156; Stoddard, 103-104.
26 *Autobiography*, 298-299.
27 Undated note of Mr. Riggs, TRC; Morison, *Turmoil*, 80.
28 Gosnell, 57-58; Sullivan, 77.
29 Burrows & Wallace, 1230-1235; Morris, 518-519.
30 Morris, 518-519; Morison, 498-500, 509.
31 Morris, 520-521; *Times*, January 24 and 25, 1896.
32 Morison, 510; Morris, 511-526.

5

1 Leech, 17-35.
2 Morison, 542-543; Rhodes, 57.
3 Morison, 544.
4 *Ibid*, 550.
5 Quoted in Beer, 523.
6 Morris, 424-425; 555.
7 Morison, 55.
8 *Ibid*, 572; *Times*, December 17, 1896.
9 Lodge, 252-254; 260-261; Mott, 74; Morison, 588.
10 Lodge, 261-262; 266; Mott, 74.
11 Morison, 601-603; Iriye, 48-53.
12 London *Times*, May 5, 1898.
13 *Works, XIII*, 185-186.
14 O'Toole, 82.
15 Morison, 602-603; 637-638.
16 *Ibid*, 685-686, 695-697; *Sun*, August 23, 1897.
17 Morison, 626.
18 *Times*, June 19, 1897.
19 Morison, 692-694; Chessman, 24.
20 Morison, 697-698, 711; Chessman, 14-15; Burrows & Wallace, 1207-1208.
21 Morison, 774-775.

22 *Ibid*, 759-763; Morris, 595.
23 Morris, 602; Morison, 784-785; Beale, 63.
24 Foreign Relations, 750-759, 760; Millis, 138-140; Leech, 188, 190-191.
25 Morris, 594; Morison, 758.
26 Morris, 613-614.
27 Adams, *Letters*, 172; Chanler, 285; *Sun*, April 18, 1898.
28 Morison, 809-810; 816-818.
29 Morris, 614-615; 618-620; Brown, 205.
30 Morris, 624-625; *Works, XI*, 39-40.
31 Smith, 56-57.
32 Morris, 630-638.
33 *Ibid*, 638-645; Morison, 845-846.
34 Morris, 649-654.
35 Davis, 218-220.
36 O'Toole, 317-319; *Works, XI*, 131-135. There is some reason to believe that this exploit instead took place on Kettle Hill. Morris, Chapter 25, n. 112.
37 *Works, XI*, 96-97; Brown, 321-322.
38 Chanler, 196; Morison, 849-850.
39 O'Toole, 323-325, 345-351.
40 *Ibid*, 359-360.
41 Millis, 350-351.
42 *Ibid*; O'Toole, 360; Morison, 864-866.
43 Millis, 351-353.

6

1 *Times*, August 16, 1898.
2 *Ibid*; *Herald*, August 16, 1898.
3 Lodge, 325-329; Morison, 861-864.
4 Alexander, 256-259, 282.
5 Chessman, 12; Miller, 396; Pringle, 212-213; *Times*, February 2, 1897.
6 Alexander, 286; Chessman, 12-15.
7 Alexander, 287; Chessman, 14-15.

8 Chessman, 15; Alexander, 287, 291-292.

9 Chessman, 15-16.

10 Alexander, 302.

11 *Times*, August 2; Alexander, 302; Chessman, 16-17.

12 Alexander, 302-303.

13 *Times*, July 13 and 16, 1898.

14 *Ibid*, July 26 and August 10, 1898; Chessman, 19.

15 *Times*, August 19, 1898.

16 *Ibid*, August 8, 1898; White & Willensky, 484; Chessman, 7.

17 *Times*, August 8, 1898.

18 *Herald*, August 15, 1898.

19 *Ibid*; Chessman, 19-20; Alexander, 304-305; *Autobiography*, 270; Morison, 860.

20 Chessman, 21-23.

21 Chessman, 22-24; Platt to Roosevelt, May 9, 1899; in Barnes v. Roosevelt, p. 2369; Morison, 1474.

22 Chessman, 22-24 (quotation is from *New York Mail* and *Express*, August 22, 1898).

23 *Herald*, August 15, 1898.

7

1 Leech, 307-310.

2 *Autobiography*, 270-271; Morris, 667-668.

3 *Autobiography*, 270-271.

4 *Ibid*, 271.

5 *Ibid*, 271-272; *Herald*, August 20, 1898.

6 *Herald*, August 21, 1898.

7 *Ibid*.

8 *Ibid*, August 23, 1898; *Times*, August 24, 1898.

9 Howe, 1-9; Chessman, 26-28; Hovey, 81.

10 Howe, 142-143; Chessman, 28-29.

11 *Ibid*, Hovey, 81.

12 Morison, 869; Roosevelt "The Manly Virtues and Practical Politics," *Forum* (July, 1889) quated in Chessman, 31.

13 Chessman, 26; Morison, 869-871.

14 Howe, 143; Morison, 1476.

15 *Times*, September 10, 1898.

16 *Herald, Sun, Times* and *Tribune*, September 4, 1898; Leech, 310-312.

17 *Post*, September 1 and 4, 1898; *Times*, September 3, 1898.

18 Chessman, 17, 34.

19 *Dictionary of American Biography*, Russell, 356; Depew, 160-162.

20 *Tribune*, September 8, 1898; *Herald*, September 9 and 10, 1898.

21 *Barnes v. Roosevelt* (record on appeal), 2354 - 2361; Morison, 1009.

22 Morison, 874-875.

23 *Barnes v. Roosevelt*, 2364; Chessman, 41.

24 *Times*, September 11, 1898.

25 *Herald* and *Times*, September 11, 1898; Chessman, 38; Morison, 875; *Times*, September 14, 1898.

26 *Herald*, September 14, 1898.

27 *Ibid*.

28 *Times*, September 18, 1898.

8

1 *Times*, September 18, 1898.

2 *Ibid*; *Post*, September 19, 1898.

3 *Times*, October 1, 1898.

4 *Ibid*, September 18, 1898; Bennett, 107.

5 Morison, 876-877.

6 Chessman, 43-44; Howe, 469.

7 *Times*, September 20, 1898.

8 Howe, 468.

9 *Herald* and *Times*, September 22, 1898.

10 Chessman, 44.

11 *Times*, September 21 and 23, 1898.

12 *Ibid*, September 21 and 22, 1898.

13 Morison, 877.

14 Howe, 139-140.

15 *Ibid*, 141-143; Chanler, 248.

16 Howe, 141-143; Chanler, 248.

17 *Herald*, September 25, 1898.

18 Howe, 143; Hovey, 81; Sullivan et al, 1794.

19 Howe, 141, 420.

20 Bennett, 107-108.

21 Morris, 676; Brands, 365.

9

1 *Times*, September 24, 1898; *Herald*, September 23 and 24, 1898; *Tribune*, September 24, 1898; Jessup, 198.

2 Chessman, *Roosevelt's Tax Difficulty;* Morison, 807.

3 Platt, 370; *Herald*, September 24, 1898.

4 Platt, 370-371; *Herald*, September 24, 1898.

5 *Ibid*.

6 *Ibid*; Edward Martin, 188-189; Morison, Turmoil, 67-69.

7 Leech, 380; Jessup, 198-199.

8 Platt, 371-372; Jessup, 198-189.

9 *Tribune*, September 26, 1898; *Times*, September 25, 1898.

10 *Post*, September 25, 1898.

11 *Herald*, September 25, 1898.

12 *Sun*, September 24, 1898; *Herald*,

September 25, 1898.

13 *Sun*, September 27, 1898.

14 Barrett, 149-182; Beer, 108-109.

15 *Sun*, September 25, 1898.

16 *Herald*, September 26, 1898.

17 *Times*, September 26, 1898; Morison, 880.

18 *Times*, September 26, 1898; *Herald*, September 26, 1898.

19 Platt, 371-372; Jessup, 199.

20 *Tribune, Herald*, and *Times*, September 27, 1898.

21 *Herald* and *Sun*, September 28, 1898.

22 *Herald*, September 28, 1898.

23 *Herald* and *Times*, September 28, 1898.

24 *Ibid*; Depew, 162; Jessup, 200.

25 *Herald* and *Tribune*, September 28, 1898.

10

1 Chessman, 50-53, Sullivan *et al*, 1779-1790; Nevins, *Cleveland*, 99, 470 *et seq.*; Alexander, 310.

2 *Herald*, September 28, 1898; Alexander, 312-313.

3 *Herald*, September 29 and 30, October 1, 1898; Alexander, 313-315.

4 *Herald* and *Times*, September 30, 1898; Alexander, 314-315.

5 *Herald* and *Times*, September 30 and October 1, 1898; *Post*, October 1, 1898; Alexander, 314-315.

6 *Times*, September 30, 1898.

7 *Post*, October 1, 1898.

11

1 TRC; Low MSS; Morison, 881.

2 *Times*, September 30 and October 2, 1898.

3 *Tribune*, October 2, 1898; *Times*,
  October 9, 1898, Hagadorn, 71-72.
4 *Times*, October 1 and 4, 1898; Pringle,
  204; Chessman, *Roosevelt's Tax
  Difficulty*; Morison, 882.
5 *Times* and *Herald*, October 5, 1898;
  Hagadorn, 72-73.
6 *Times* and *Herald*, October 6, 1898.
7 *Times*, October 7, 8 and 9, 1898;
  Chessman, 79-80.
8 *Times*, October 7, 8 and 9, 1898.
9 *Times*, October 11, 1898; *Herald*,
  October 11, 13, 14 and 15, 1898; TRC;
  Clarke, 368-369; Alexander, 281.
10 O'Toole, 173, 195-196; Leech, 299-300.
11 Leech, 314-315.
12 *Times*, October 12, 1898.
13 *Tribune*, October 10, 1898; *Herald*,
  October 15, 1898.
14 *Times*, October 15 and 16, 1898; *Herald*
  and *Tribune*, October 15, 1898;
  Robinson, 183.
15 Odell to Quigg, October 12, 1898
  (Quigg MSS); Morison, 884-885.
16 Morison, 885-886.

12

1 The discussion of Croker's
  background is taken for the most
  part from Stoddard and from
  Conable and Silberfarb's chapter on
  Croker.
2 George Martin, 169-170.
3 *Times*, August 7 and 8, 1916 (obituary
  and editorial).
4 The history of the Bar Association is
  taken from George Martin. See also
  Times, October 16 and 17, 1898; Breen,
  178.

5 *Herald*, October 15, 1898.
6 *Times*, October 22, 1898.
7 *Dictionary of American Biography*;
  Manchester, 225-226; Churchill, 272-
  273.
8 *Herald*, *Times* and *Tribune*, October 22,
  1898.
9 McGurrin, 186.

13

1 *Post*, October 17, 1898.
2 *Ibid*; Clarke memo; Roosevelt MSS.
3 *Herald*, October 18, 1898; Clarke
  memo.
4 *Herald* and *Times*, October 18, 1898.
5 *Herald*, *Times*, and *Tribune*, October 19,
  1898; Clarke memo; *Herald*, October
  20, 1898.
6 *Times* and *Tribune*, October 20, 1898;
  Morison, 885-886; TR MSS (LC).
7 *Herald*, and *Sun*, October 20, 1898;
  Times, October 20, 21 and 22, 1898;
  Youngs memorandum.
8 *Tribune*, November 13, 1898.
9 *Ibid*, October 23, 1898.
10 *Herald*, October 19, 21 and 22, 1898;
  Sun, October 21 and 23, 1898.
11 *Sun*, October 22, 1898; Morison, 887.
12 *Times* and *Tribune*, October 22, 1898;
  Morgan, 62.
13 *Herald* and *Times*, October 23, 1898.

14

1 *Herald*, October 24, 1898.
2 S. Morris, 188.
3 Dulles, 167; Tuchman, 152.
4 Tuchman, 152-153; Millis, 253-254.
5 *Dictionary of American Biography*.
6 Morison, 884.

7 *Post*, October 22, 1898.
8 *Times*, October 22, 1898.
9 *Herald*, October 17, 1898.
10 Lodge, 321-322; 331-332.
11 *Ibid*, 359-360; Pringle, 207.
12 *Post*, October 22, 1898.

15

1 *Sun*, October 25, 1898.
2 Clarke memorandum; *Autobiography*, 128.
3 *Herald* and *Sun*, October 25, 1898.
4 *Sun*, October 26, 1898.
5 *Sun* and *Herald*, October 27, 1898; *Evening Post*, October 28, 1898.
6 *Times*, October 25 and 27, 1898; *Herald*, October 24 and 26, 1898.
7 *Herald* and *Times*, October 25, 1898; *Herald*, October 29, 1898; Martin, 110-114.
8 *The Nation*, October 27, 1898; *Times*, October 25, 1898; Lodge, 360; *Tribune* and *Herald*, October 27, 1898.
9 *Times*, October 26, 1898.
10 *Sun* and *Times*, October 28, 1898.
11 *Ibid*, October 29, 1898.
12 Clarke memorandum.
13 *Times*, October 30, 1898.
14 *Herald*, October 29, 1898.
15 *Times*, October 29 and 31, 1898; *Tribune*, October 28, 1898.
16 *Evening Post*, October 29, 1898; *Herald*, October 28 and 30, 1898.

16

1 *Herald*, October 30 and 31, 1898; *Evening Post*, October 31, 1898.
2 *Herald*, October 18 and 26, 1898; Croly, 219-220; *Barnes v. Roosevelt*, 1835-1838; Platt, 537-538.
3 *Sun*, *Herald* and *Times*, November 1, 1898.
4 *Herald* and *Times*, November 1, 1898; *Herald*, November 3, 1898.
5 *Harper's Weekly*, October 22, 1898; *Herald*, October 27 and 30, and November 1, 1898; *Times*, November 2, 1898.
6 *Herald*, *Evening Post*, *Times*, *Sun* and *Tribune*, November 2, 1898.
7 *Sun* and *Times*, November 2, 1898; *Herald*, November 3, 1898.
8 Youngs memorandum; Alexander, 321.
9 *Tribune*, *Sun* and *Herald*, November 3, 1898; Riis, *Making*, 383-384.
10 Youngs memorandum; *Herald*, November 3, 1898.
11 *Herald* and *Times*, November 3, 1898.
12 *Evening Post*, November 3, 1890; *Herald*, November 4, 1898.
13 *Herald* and *Times*, November 4, 1898.
14 *Ibid.*, *Sun*, November 4, 1898.
15 *Times*, November 4, 1898.
16 *Herald*, November 4, 1898; *Evening Post*, November 5, 1898.
17 *Times*, November 5, 1898; Lodge, 361-362.
18 *Times*, November 5, 1898.
19 *Ibid.*; *Evening Post*, November 5, 1898.
20 *Times*, November 6, 1898.
21 *Ibid.*
22 *Herald*, November 6, 1898.

17

1 *Herald* and *Times*, November 7 and 8, 1898; *Post*, November 7, 1898.
2 *Tribune*, *Sun*, and *World*, November 6,

1898; *Journal*, November 4 and 5, 1898, *Times*, November 7, 1898, *Post*, November 7, 1898; *Herald*, November 8, 1898.

3 *Post* and *Times*, November 8, 1898; *Herald*, November 9, 1898.

4 *Herald* and *Times*, November 9, 1898.

5 *Herald*, November 9, 1898.

6 *Times*, November 9, 1898; *Autobiography*, 272; Platt, 373.

7 Morison, 888-889.

8 The discussion of Roosevelt's Governorship and Vice-Presidential nomination and campaign is based primarily on Brands, 376-404; Miller, 321, 344; and Morris, Chapters 27 and 28. (which relied heavily on Chessman).

9 Much of the material in this and other biographical summaries that follow is taken from the *Dictionary of American Biography and American National Biography*.

10 Connable and Silberfarb, 221-230.

11 *Times*, August 8, 1916.

Epilogue

1 See, e.g., Ambrose *et al, What If?*, G.P. Putnam's Sons, 1999.

2 Leech, 379.

3 *Ibid*, 484.

4 *Ibid*, 531-537; Bowers, 328.

5 *Works, XIV*, 342-345; *Times*, December 31, 1999.

Bibliography

UNPUBLISHED MATERIALS

Theodore Roosevelt Collection ('TRC'), Harvard College Library, Cambridge, Massachusetts.

Theodore Roosevelt papers ('TRP'), Library of Congress, Washington, DC (reviewed at Princeton University Library, Princeton, NJ).

Seth Low Papers, Columbia University Library, New York, NY.

Lemuel Quigg Papers, New York Public Library, New York, NY.

BOOKS

Adams, Henry. *Letters*, 1892-1918, ed. Worthington Chambers Ford. Boston, 1938.

Alexander, DeAlva S. *A Political History of New York State. Vol. 4: 'Four Famous New Yorkers.'* New York, 1923.

Beale, Howard K. *Theodore Roosevelt and the Rise of America to World Power.* John Hopkins Press, 1956.

Barrett, Richard. *Good Old Summer Days*, D. Appelton-Century, 1941.

Beer, Thomas. *Hanna, Crane and the Mauve Decade.* Knopf, 1941.

Bennett, John W. *Roosevelt and the Republic.* New York, 1908.

Bowers, Claude G. *Beveridge and the Progressive Era.* The Riverside Press, 1932.

Brands, H.W. *T.R. The Last Romantic.* Basic Books, 1997.

Breen, Matthew, *Thirty Years of New York Politics, Up to Date.* New York, 1899.

Brown, Charles H. *The Correspondent's War.* Scribners, 1967.

Burrows, Edwin G, and Wallace, Mike. *Gothan: A History of New York City to 1898.* Oxford University Press, 1999.

Buach, Noel C. *T.R. ñ The Story of Theodore Roosevelt and His Influence on Our Times.* Reynal & Co., 1963.

Chanler, Mrs. Winthrop. *Roman Spring.* Little, Brown, 1934.

Chessman, G. Wallace. *Governor Theodore Roosevelt; The Albany Apprenticeship 1898-1900,.* Harvard University Press, 1965.

Clarke, Joseph I.C. *My Life and Memories.* New York, 1925.

Connable, Alfred and Silberfarb, Edward. *Tigers of Tamany: Nine Men Who Ran New York.* Holt, Rinehart & Winston, 1967.

Croly, Herbert. *Marcus Alonzo Hanna, His Life and Work.* Macmillan, 1912.

Davis, Richard Harding. *The Cuban and Puerto Rican Campaigns.* Scribners, 1899.

Depew, Chauncey M. *My Memories of Eighty Years.* New York, 1922.

Dulles, Foster Rhea. *The Imperial Years.* New York, Crowell, 1956.

Gosnell, Harold F, *Boss Platt and His New York Machine.* New York, AMS Press, 1969.

Hagadorn, Hermann. *The Roosevelt Family of Sagamore Hill.* Macmillan, 1954.

Harbaugh, William H,. *The Life and Times of Theodore Roosevelt.* Oxford University Press, 1975.

Hovey, Richard B. *John Jay Chapman, An American Mind.* Columbia University Press, 1959.

Howe, Mark A. DeWolfe. *John Jay Chapman and His Letters.* Houghton Mifflin, 1937.

Iriye, Akira. *Pacific Estrangement: Japan and American Expansion, 1879-1911.* Harvard University Press, 1973.

Jeffers, H. Paul. *Commissioner Roosevelt. The Story of Theodore Roosevelt and the New York City Police, 1895-1897.* John Wiley, 1994.

Jessup, Philip C. *Elihu Root.* Dodd, Mead, 1938.

Leech, Margaret. *In the Days of McKinley.* Harper & Row, 1959.

Lodge, Henry Cabot. *Selections from the Correspondence of Theodore Roosevelt and Henry Cabot Lodge.* Vol. 1, Scribners, 1925.

Manchester, William. *The Last Lion — Winston Spencer Churchill: Visions of Glory, 1874-1932.* Little Brown, 1983.

Martin, Edward Sanford. *The Life of Joseph Hodges Choate.* Vol. 2, Scribners, 1920.

Martin, George. *Causes and Conflicts: The Centennial History of the Bar Association of the City of New York, 1870-1970.* Houghton Mifflin, 1979.

McCullough, David. *Mornings on Horseback.* Simon & Schuster, 1981.

McGurrin, James. *Bourke Cockran, A Free Lance in American Politics.* Arno Press, New York, 1972.

Miller, Nathan. *Theodore Roosevelt, A Life.* Quill William Morrow, 1992.

Millis, Walter. *The Martial Spirit.* Dee, Elephant Paperbacks, 1989.

Mitgang, Herbert. *Once Upon a Time in New York.* The Free Press, 2000.

Morison, Elting. *Turmoil and Tradition: A Study of the Life and Times of Henry L. Stimson.* Houghton Mifflin, 1960. (Cited as E. Morison).

Morison, Elting E. and Blum, John, eds. *The Letters of Theodore Roosevelt.* Harvard University Press. Unless otherwise indicated, Vols. 1 and 2. 1951 (sequential paging). (Cited as Morison)

Morgan, Ted. *FDR, A Biography.* Simon & Schuster, 1985.

Morris, Edmund. *The Rise of Theodore Roosevelt.* Coward, McCann & Geoghegan, 1979. (Cited as 'Morris').

Morris, Sylvia J. *Edith Kermit Roosevelt: Portrait of a First Lady.* Coward, McCann & Geoghegan, 1980. (Cited as S. Morris).

Mott, T. Bentley. *Myron T. Herrick, Friend of France.* New York, 1924.

Nevins, Allan. *Grover Cleveland, A Study in Courage.* Dodd Mead, 1932.

———*Abram S. Hewitt and Some Account of Peter Cooper.* Octagon Books, 1969 edition.

O'Toole, G.J.A. *The Spanish War: An American Epic 1898.* Norton, 1984.

Platt, Thomas Collier. *The Autobiography of Thomas Collier Platt.* New York, 1910.

Pringle, Henry F. *Theodore Roosevelt, A Biography.* Harcourt, Brace, 1939.

Putnam, Carleton. *Theodore Roosevelt, The Formative Years.* Scribner's, 1958.

Rhodes, James Ford. *The McKinley and Roosevelt Administrations, 1897-1909.* Macmillan, 1932.

Riis, Jacob A. *The Making of an American.* Macmillan, 1922.

——*Theodore Roosevelt the Citizen.* Johnson, Wynne Co., 1904.

Robinson, Corinne Roosevelt. *My Brother Theodore Roosevelt.* Scribner's, 1921.

Roosevelt, Theodore. *Autobiography.* Scribner's, 1926.

——*The Works of Theodore Roosevelt,* Scribner's, 1926.

Russell, Francis. *The Shadow of Blooming Grove: Warren G. Harding in His Times.* McGraw Hill, 1968.

Smith, Albert E. *Two Reels and a Crank.* Doubleday, 1952.

Steffens, Lincoln. *Autobiography.* Harcourt Brace, 1931.

Stoddard, Lothrop. *Master of Manhattan, The Life of Richard Croker.* Longmans, Green, 1931.

Sullivan, Mark. *Our Times: The United States: 1900-1925 Vol. II, America Finding Herself.* New York, 1927.

Sullivan, James, ed. *History of New York State, 1523-1927.* New York, Lewis Historical Publishing Co., 1927.

Tuchman, Barbara. *The Proud Tower: A Portrayal of the World Before the War, 1890-1914.* Macmillan, 1966.

White, Norval and Willensky, Elliot. *AAA Guide to New York City.* Macmillan, 1978.

ARTICLES

Chessman, G. Wallace, 'Theodore Roosevelt's Personal Tax Difficulty.' *New York History*, January, 1953.

Matthews, Franklin, 'Wide-Open New York.' *Harper's Weekly*, October 22, 1898.

NEWSPAPERS AND PERIODICALS

Jamestown, NY *Evening Journal*

London *Times*

The Nation

New York *Daily Tribune*

New York *Evening Journal*

New York *Evening Post*

New York *Herald*

New York *Sun*

The New York Times

New York *World*

MISCELLANEOUS

In the Matter of Robert L. Meehan, Petitioner, v. James P. Lomenzo, Secretary of State of the State of New York, Adam Wilensky, et al, Respondents, 63 Misc. 2d 490 (May 24, 1970), *affirmed*, 34 App. Div. 2d 1034 (June 1, 1970), *affirmed* 27 N.Y. 2d 600 (June 4, 1970)

William Barnes v. Theodore Roosevelt, N.Y.S. Supreme Court, Record on Appeal.

Dictionary of American Biography. Scribner's, 1946.

American National Biography. Oxford University Press, 1999.

Index

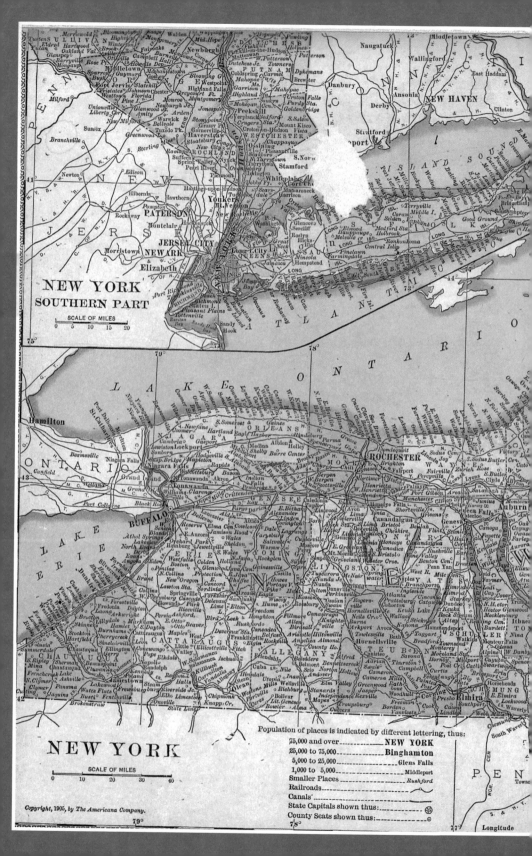

NEW YORK
SOUTHERN PART

SCALE OF MILES
0   5   10   15   20

NEW YORK

SCALE OF MILES
0   10   20   30   40

Population of places is indicated by different lettering, thus:

75,000 and over	NEW YORK
25,000 to 75,000	Binghamton
5,000 to 25,000	Glens Falls
1,000 to 5,000	Middleport
Smaller Places	Rushford
Railroads	
Canals	
State Capitals shown thus:	⊛
County Seats shown thus:	◉